The Principle of Changes:

Understanding the I Ching

The Principle of Changes:

Understanding the I Ching

by

Jung Young Lee

UNIVERSITY BOOKS   *New Hyde Park, New York*

To my father and mother

*who brought me into the world, raised me in their love
and taught me to appreciate all that God has created*

ACKNOWLEDGMENTS

In a book of this nature, it is almost impossible to make adequate acknowledgment of all the sources I have used. Anyone who is acquainted with this kind of work will immediately notice my indebtedness to numerous scholars in the field. While individual acknowledgment is not possible, I feel compelled to mention the names of James Legge, Richard and Hellmut Wilhelm, Carl Jung, Arthur Waley and others in the West as well as countless Chinese, Korean and Japanese scholars in the East. Since this book attempts to interpret the I Ching, one of Chinese classics, to the general readers in the West, extensive footnotes and technical treatments are avoided as much as possible.

A word of special gratitude is expressed to E. J. Brill for the permission to reprint the article "Some Reflections on the Authorship of the I Ching," which was written by me in Numen, International Review for the History of Religions, Vol. XVII, Fasc. 3 (December 1970). The article is reprinted here with a slight alternation under the subtitle "Concerning the Origin of the Main Texts of the I Ching" in the first chapter. The last chapter of this book contains the substance of both papers: "Issues and Problems in the Study of the I Ching," which was delivered to American Academy of Religion in New York in October 1970, and "The I Ching and Modern Science," which was presented to 28th International Congress of Orientalists in Canberra, Australia on January 8, 1971. At this time I would like to take the opportunity to send a word of my gratitude to Radio Australia for the special interviews of my paper and the I Ching, which were internationally broadcasted, during the session of 28th International Congress of Orientalists. I wish also to thank the Editors of University Books for their assistance and patience in the process of publishing this book.

Jung Young Lee

The Principle of Changes:

Understanding the I Ching

TABLE OF CONTENTS

INTRODUCTION

The book which was once pronounced as insane and heretical by Jesuit
missionaries in the seventeenth century has become one of the most popular
books in this century. The book, the I Ching or Book of Changes, is no
longer strange to the West. Many translations in English have appeared in
recent time. Among them James Legge's translation, which first appeared as
a part of The Sacred Books of the East, edited by Max Müller, and Richard
Wilhelm's translation into German, which is again translated by Cary F. Baynes
into English, are well accepted. Mao's little book is steadily declining but
the I Ching is steadily gaining its audience. Articles on the I Ching occupy
important columns of leading magazines in America. On most university cam-
puses and on the streets of most cities the I Ching is found in the hands of
the young and the old.

Why is this obscure and puzzling book popular to the highly cultured
people of the West? There must be in it something that attracts the Western
mind. I don't know exactly what attracts them. It is no doubt that this
book offers something that no other book can. The greatness and mystery of
this book are well expressed in one of its Appendixes: "Our use of the I
Ching is indeed wide and great. When we speak of what is far, it knows no
limits. When we speak of what is near, it is calm and correct. When we
speak of what is between heaven and earth, it embraces everything unto itself"
(Ta Chuan, Sec. I, Ch. 6).[1] It was not only the product of China but also the

---

[1]Unless otherwise indicated, the quotations of the I Ching are from
my own translation.

source of inspiration for the development of the Chinese, the Korean and the Japanese civilizations. However, this does not mean that the book belongs exclusively to the East. It belongs to all people. It shares the peculiar expressions of the East but contains the archetypes of natural phenomena. It is a microcosm of the universe. It is a key to the understanding of potentialities which are to be realized in all the walks of our life. Perhaps, that is why the book is popular in our time.

As Carl Jung said in his "Foreword" to Wilhelm's translation, the I Ching does not want to prove itself. It is like a part of nature, waiting until it is discovered. It is the textbook for the natural phenomena of the universe. We often forget that the real truth lies in what is natural. What is true is found in the phenomena of nature. Nature is our greatest teacher. We are so busy with building the Tower of Babel that we do not have time to observe and to hear the phenomena of nature. The I Ching is a description of nature in terms of lineal symbols. Since lines are the simplest symbols, they are closest to the realities which they represent. The I Ching contains all the possible phenomena of the universe. The life of our past, present and future is a part of this world phenomena. Thus the book correlates every possible situation of life in all strata, personal and collective, and in all dimensions. It can suggest the possible outcome of our future because future events are parts of the whole phenomenon of the universe. Just as the great teacher can guide our life in trouble, the I Ching can become our guide in time of uncertainty. It gives us access to all the potential situations we may confront in the future. Because it includes all possible human situations, it appeals to many people in the West.

The I Ching fulfills the emotional needs of people in our time. We live in a broken world. We sense the alienation of ourselves from reality. We seek our own identity. Gigantic machines overshadow human existence. We are insecure and afraid of growing dehumanization. We possess nuclear power to destroy the whole earth but we do not see the solution of the world's problems. The growing pressure of ecological problems and the increasing population of the world shatter our hope in the future. Perhaps the growing interest in the theology of hope in our time is an expression of uneasiness in life. Scientific technology has brought us comfort but robbed our souls. Western civilization has been one-sided. It has not taken mystical experiences seriously as essential aspects of human growth. Since man himself is mysterious, he cannot live without mystery. The greatness of the I Ching lies in its mystery, which is disclosed when it is consulted. It offers neither facts nor power by itself, but for the lovers of self-knowledge and mystery it seems to be the right book.[1]

The I Ching is not a religious book. Rather it is a wisdom book in a profound sense. As the first book of the Confucian classics, it has its root in the foundation of Chinese civilization. It grew out of ancient oracles, which must be understood as the primordial wisdom of China. Divination has nothing to do with the divine or with supernaturalism. It is a search for decisions in relation to action, which is the very purpose of Chinese wisdom. The I Ching is not simply a book of philosophy but a work of art as well. Chinese wisdom which includes both philosophy and art is practical and at

---

[1] Carl G. Jung, "Foreword "in The I Ching or Book of Changes, tr. by Richard Wilhelm and Cary F. Baynes (Princeton: Princeton University Press, 1967), Third Edition, p. xxxix.

the same time tends to be simple and penetrating.[1] It is dedicated to every-day life and ordinary action for all people. The I Ching does not draw rigid inferences from the social and political structures of early China. On the contrary, as Hellmut Wilhelm said, "the situations are always raised above temporal manifestations into a realm to illustrate the archetype but never to tie it to a particular manifestation. Thus the system of the texts appears timeless, or above time."[2] It transcends time and space but is not religious in nature. It is a wisdom book in the most inclusive and finest sense. That is why Confucius said, "If some years were added to my life, I would give fifty to the study of the I, and then I might come to be without great faults."[3] It is a hopeful sign that the I Ching is relevant to the searching minds of the youth of our time. However, I wish to express a word of caution on the study of the I Ching.

The Chinese people themselves have been repeatedly warned not to mis-use the I Ching. As Ta Chuan has indicated, we must approach it as we would approach our parents (Sec. II, Ch. 8). Much caution is required when we ap-proach the book. It must not be used lightly. According to an old saying, an improper approach to the I Ching is a road to insanity. The element of mystery cannot be taken away from the book. Before the mystery our analyti-cal and logical processes do not function. Our approach to the I Ching should

---

[1]Ch'u Chai and Winberg Chai ed., I Ching: Book of Changes tr. by James Legge (New Hyde Park, N. Y.: University Books, 1964), p. xl.

[2]Hellmut Wilhelm, "The Concept of Time in the Book of Changes" in Man and Time: Papers from the Eranos Yearbooks (N. Y.: Pantheon Books, 1957), p. 214.

[3]Analects, 7:16 (Unless otherwise indicated, the quotations of Chinese classics (except the I Ching) are from James Legge's translation).

be humble and committed to a search for reality. An arrogant attitude to it is self-defeating. Our attitude toward it must be sincere and genuine. Hsun Tzu said that anyone who knows the book well does not use it merely as divination. It has a deeper mystery than to give us a mere description of future events. We should not consult the I Ching for the satisfaction of our own curiosity. It cannot be manipulated. A right attitude is important in our understanding of real meaning. As Ta Chuan says, "if you are not a kind of person, the way does not reveal itself to you" (Sec. II, Ch. 8). The right approach to the I Ching requires both an innate capacity or an intuitive insight and the general comprehension of the book itself. It is, therefore, my intention to provide a general introduction to this book. What I hope to accomplish in the following chapters is to provide you some basis for your further enrichment and understanding of the I Ching. I hope they will assist you to appreciate more the world-honored book, the I Ching.

CHAPTER I.   THE I CHING, ITS ORIGIN AND DEVELOPMENT

1. About The Book of Changes.

At first glance we see the main texts which are separated from the Appendices. Within the main texts we find 64 hexagrams. Each hexagram consists of six lines which are divided or undivided. The hexagrams are the basis of the I Ching. Everything in the book can be nothing other than the interpretation of these hexagrams. Thus the I Ching is the book about the 64 hexagrams. Each hexagram is autonomous and self-sustaining in so far as it signifies the complete unit of a given situation. However, none of them can exist by itself. They are mutually interrelated one to another. Thus each hexagram is to be studied in relation to the others. No hexagram remains the same. It changes and is transformed into a new hexagram. Each hexagram is then seen in the light of constant change and transformation. Therefore, our study of the I Ching must be centered around the hexagrams in their relation to changes taking place within total situations.

Secondly, we observe that each hexagram has its own name. The name of each hexagram is the most concise form of its expression. The name has a single Chinese word, except in rare cases. Just as our names are merely symbols of our unique existence, the names of hexagrams also symbolize their unique characteristics. The names stand for those which they represent.

Thirdly, a brief text accompanies each hexagram. It is often called "t'uan," which is known in English as "decision" or "judgment." The judgment on the hexagram is different from the name of the hexagram. The former is the interpretation of the hexagram, while the latter the representation of it. The judgment on the hexagram can be compared with a decision of the judge at the court. The judge's decision on the case or situation, which is symbolized in the hexagram, reveals a definite value judgment of the court on the case. Like the decision of the court, the judgment on the hexagram conveys a value judgment on a given situation. Some of the common words used for the judgment are "correct," "success," "progress," "good fortune," "misfortune," and others.

Fourthly, a short text on the symbol of the hexagram is found in Wilhelm's translation, even though it is not true in Legge's translation. The text on the symbol of the hexagram belongs to the third and fourth wings of the Appendices to the I Ching. Wilhelm's interpolation of it in the main texts is to help clarify our understanding of the hexagram. The text on the image can be understood as the symbolization of the symbol, that is, the hexagram. Since the hexagram symbolizes a germinal situation, the text on the image is the re-symbolization of the situation. The judgment on the hexagram concerns itself with the actualization of the situation which the hexagram symbolizes, while the text on the image applies itself to human, social and cosmic situations. Some of the texts on the symbols convey a profound meaning. For example, the symbol on hexagram 23 says: "The mountain adheres to the earth: It is the symbol of Po (Breaking Apart). Thus the superior men increase their strength, and their people can secure peace." Here the expression is simple but beautiful.

Finally, each line of the hexagram has its own text, which is often called the judgment on the line. The judgment begins with the lowest line of the hexagram and ends with the upper line. It describes its predicament in relation to the other lines in the hexagram. Its expression is patterned after the judgment on the hexagram. Most frequently used words for it are "misfortune," "no blame," "no mistake," "good fortune," and others. The description on the line, like the image, is concerned with the application of that particular situation to human and social life. The judgment on the line cannot exist independent of the judgment on the hexagram, because the former is always relative to the latter.

The core of the I Ching has to do, not with the names and judgments which are expressed in words, but with the lines which form the simplest symbols of the situation in the hexagrams. Thus all the expressions in words are relative to the hexagrams, the hexagrams are relative to the lines, and the lines are relative to the reality of yin and yang forces. Here, the complexity of our understanding of the I Ching is an inevitable reality. Early attempts to explain the complex nature of the main texts have been the Appendices of the Ten Wings, which are attached to the last half portion of the I Ching.

Let us now briefly observe the Ten Wings or Shih I, which are supplementary commentaries to the basic texts of the I Ching. Since they are merely commentaries to the texts, they cannot be dealt with independently. They must be understood in the light of the basic texts of the I Ching. The first two wings are known as the T'uan Chuan, the commentary on the judgment.[1] This commentary intends to clarify and explain the meaning and significance of the judgment on the hexagram. Let us take several examples to illustrate how the judgments are commented on in the T'uan Chuan. The judgment on the hexagram

---

[1] Legge places the T'uan Chuan in Appendix I of his translation, while Wilhelm in Book III of his Third Edition.

15, Ch'ien or Modesty, reads: "Modesty brings success. The superior man who is modest can complete his works." Then the commentary on this judgment in the T'uan Chuan states as follows:

> Modesty brings success. It is the way of heaven to influence the below with radient light. It is the way of the earth, which is lowly, to go upward. It is the way of heaven to diminish the full and to increase the modest. It is the way of the earth to transform the full and to augment the modest. Spirits harm the full and bless the modest. It is the way of man to hate the full and to love the modest. Modesty that is honored produces radiance. Modesty that is lowly cannot be ignored. Thus the superior man will accomplish his task.

Here, the T'uan Chuan explains in detail why modesty creates success and the superior man carries out his works. Let us look at the hexagram 37, Chia Jen or the Family. The judgment on this hexagram is: "The Family. The correctness of the woman is advantageous." The commentary of this judgment in the T'uan Chuan reveals much extnesive analysis of various relationships in the family:

> The Family. The right place of the woman is inside, while the right place of the man is outside. The right place of both man and woman signifies the great righteousness shown in heaven and earth. In the family the parents are strict rulers. Let the father be a father and the son a son. Let the elder brother be an elder brother and the younger brother be a younger brother. Let the husband be a husband and the wife a wife. Then the house is on the right way. When the house is in order, everything under heaven will be firmly established.

The judgment on the hexagram speaks about the correctness of the woman only, but the commentary brings out the proper positions and roles of all members of the family. These places and roles of family members are relative to the location of individual lines in the hexagram. From these illustrations we notice some of the possible explanations of why the judgments are made. The T'uan Chuan is then one of the most helpful commentaries in our understanding of the hexagram as a whole.

The third and fourth wings belong to the Hsiang Chuan, the commentary on the images, which has already been treated in the main text of the I Ching.[1] The word "hsiang" literally means "images" or "symbols," and the word "chuan" signifies "treatise" or "commentary," which is differentiated from "ching," the classics. While the T'uan Chuan deals with the judgment on the hexagram, the Hsiang Chuan deals with the symbolic structures of the hexagram. The Hsiang Chuan attempts to interpret the hexagram in terms of the symbols of two constituting trigrams in particular.[2] For example, the hexagram 7, Shih or the Army, consists of the trigram K'un or the Earth

(☷) above and the trigram K'an or the Water (☵) below. Thus the commentary on the symbol says, "The water in the center of the earth is the Army. Thus the superior man strengthens his people through his generosity." Just as ground water is invisibly present with the earth, the military power of people is invisibly present in the masses. Thus the Hsiang Chuan approaches the hexagram through the analysis of the attributes of two constituting tri-grams.

The fifth and sixth wings deal with the most comprehensive and schol-

---

[1]See Appendix II in Legge's translation and in Book III of Wilhelm's.

[2]The Hsiang Chuan or the commentary on the images found in Appendix II in Legge's translation and in both Book I and III of Wilhelm's translation.

arly treatise on the basic texts of the I Ching. They are called Ta Chuan, the great commentary, which is also known by the name of Hsi Tz'u Chuan, the commentary on the appended judgments.[1] This commentary deals with the basic principles of both trigrams and hexagrams in detail. It offers the fundamental yet general introduction to the basic texts of the I Ching as a whole. It helps us enter into discussions on the metaphysical understanding of the hexagram, the development of civilization and the meaning of symbolism. Because the Ta Chuan discusses the profound philosophy of the I Ching, it attempts to answer many issues and problems related to the hexagrams. Some of them which the commentary tries to enter into discussion are:

> Why is it all like this? Why are these images, frequently so startling, coupled with the hexagrams and the lines? From what depths of consciousness do they come? Are they purely arbitrary creations or do they follow definite laws? Moreover, how does it happen that, in a given case, the images used are connected with the particular thought? Is it not mere caprice to seek a profound philosophy where, according to all appearances, only a grotesque fantasy is at play?[2]

An attempt has previously been made to answer some of these questions in the Ta Chuan. The Ta Chuan is certainly a philosophical masterpiece on the principles by which changes and transformations take place.

The seventh wing is known as the Wen Yen, the commentary on the words of the text.[3] This commentary contains important essays but is limited to the treatise of the first hexagram, Ch'ien or Creativity, and the second

---

[1] The Ta Chuan is in Appendix III of Legge's translation and in Book II of Wilhelm's translation of the I Ching.

[2] The I Ching or Book of Changes, tr. by Richard Wilhelm and Cary F. Baynes (Princeton: Princeton University Press, 1967), Third Ed., p. 255.

[3] See Appendix IV in Legge's translation and Book III in Wilhelm's.

hexagram, K'un or Responsivity,[1] only. It is believed to be the remnant of the commentary on the whole book. It is rather unfortunate that the rest of the commentary is not available. The Wen Yen deals not only with the hexagram as a whole but with each individual line, attempting to elucidate their meanings.

The eighth wing is called the Shuo Kua, the discussion of the trigrams. This is one of the important essays dealing with the symbolic correlations and the philosophic backgrounds of the trigrams. It is rather a short commentary or essay, consisting of eleven brief chapters.[2] In the last chapter of this essay, it attempts to summarize some of the symbolic implications of the eight trigrams in the I Ching. Let us observe how the symbolic meanings of the first two trigrams are expressed in the Shuo Kua:

> Creativity is heaven, round, the king, the father, jade,
> metal, cold, and ice. It is deep red, a good horse, an
> old horse, a lean horse, a wild horse, and tree fruit.

> Responsivity is the earth, the mother, cloth, a kettle,
> frugality, level, a cow with a calf, a large container,
> form, the mass, and a shaft. Among the different colors
> of soil, it is the black.

The ninth wing is known as Hsü Kua, the sequence of the hexagrams.[3] It traces the order of the hexagrams in the I Ching. Since the first and the second hexagrams, the heaven and earth, are the basis for the procreation of all other hexagrams in the I Ching, they are not included in the Hsü Kua. It is rather self-evident that some of the explanations in it are not really based on sound evidence. For example, the hexagram 6, Sung or Conflict, is

---

[1] The word "responsivity," the capacity of resonsiveness, is used here as the counterpart of "creativity." Responsivity is the power of creative reception. Thus it implies much more than a mere receptivity.

[2] See Appendix V in Legge's translation and Book II in Wilhelm's.

[3] See Appendix VI in Legge's translation and Book III in Wilhelm's.

followed by Hsü or Waiting. The reason for this is given in the Hsü Kua as follows: "Meat and drink necessiate the conflict. Therefore, it follows the hexagram of Conflict." The hexagram 22, Pi or Adornment, comes into being because of the following reason: "Things are not united irregularly. Thus there follows the hexagram of Pi. Pi means adornment." These examples show clearly that the justification of the order of hexagrams in the Hsü Kua is not only arbitrary but often lacks a sound reational basis.

The last wing is Tsa Kua, the miscellaneous notes on the hexagrams.[1] It has a brief description for each hexagram. For example, the first hexagram, Ch'ien or Creativity , is described in the Tsa Kua as follows: "The Ch'ien is firm." The second hexagram, K'un or Responsivity , has also a short description of the Tsa Kua: "The K'un is weak." As we have observed, descriptions on the hexagrams in the Tsa Kua are not helpful at all. They do not occupy an important place in the Ten Wings.

The Ten Wings as a whole are indispensable to the study of the I Ching. Especially, the Ta Chuan, the Great Treatise, and the Shou Kua, the Discussions of the Trigrams, are the most helpful essays, dealing with the philosophical foundations of the principle of changes. The rest of them are primarily commentaries on the hexagrams. There are some divergent views found in these commentaries as to the interpretation of certain issues. However, as a whole they are reliable supplementaries for our study. They render

---

[1]See Appendix VII in Legge's translation and Book III in Wilhelm's.

a great service by introducing some of the basic framework in which the I Ching is oriented.

2. Concerning the Origin of the Main Texts of the I Ching

Let us now consider the authorship of the I Ching. The origin of the I Ching is uncertain. Its authorship has been under debate throughout the centuries. In Shuo Kua, the Discussion of the Trigrams, the authors of the book are identified with the holy sages: "The holy sages formed the I Ching in ancient times" (Ch. 1). Much the same idea is also expressed in the Ta Chuan or the Great Treatise: "The holy sages formed the hexagrams in order to observe the images (or symbols). They wrote the judgments in order to define clearly good fortune and misfortune" (Sec. I, Ch. 2). According to the original version of Chinese texts, we do not know whether the term "sheng jen" (聖人) was intended to signify the "holy sage" or the "holy sages." Since there is not distinction between the singular and plural nouns in Chinese, it is difficult to say whether it meant plural or singular. However, the translation of "sheng jen" as the "holy sages" seems to be correct, because the multiple authorship of the I Ching has been accepted by Chinese tradition. According to the tradition, the I Ching originated from the practice of divination and was attributed to the legendary king, Fu Hsi (2953-2838 B. C.). Later King Wen, the founder of the Chou dynasty (1150-249 B. C.), re-arranged the sixty-four hexagrams and gave them the judgments, t'uan or kua tz'u. His son, Tan, who was Chou Kung or the Duke of Chou, composed the texts on the lines of hexagrams, hsiao tz'u, to supplement and to expound the kua tz'u, the judgments on the hexagrams. The Ten Wings, which are the commentaries to supplement the I Ching, were traditionally attributed to Confucius. The traditionally accepted author-ship of the Ten Wings has come under severe criticisms by recent scholars. Before discussing this controversial area, let us first examine the author-ship of the I Ching.

The I Ching went through four stages of formation in Chinese history. At first there was the stage of divination practice without reference to cosmology. The second stage was the creation of eight trigrams, which were meaningfully correlated with the primitive cosmology. The third stage was the formulation of sixty-four hexagrams and the judgments. Finally, the fourth stage was the elaboration and explanation of the lines of the hexagrams. We may take each stage of formation separately for a detailed examination.

The I Ching has its origin in the practice of divination. Thus it is most of all the book of divination. According to the Book of Rites or Li Chi, "The ancient kings made use of the stalks of the divining plant and the tortoise shell; arranged their sacrifices; burned their offerings of silk" (7:2). The sacrifices were offered to them, because they brought knowledge of the future. Again in the Book of Rites we read "In the various articles of tribute the tortoises were placed in front of all other offerings, because the shell gave knowledge of the future" (9:7). The use of both the stalks of the divining plant and the tortoise shells for divination was evident in early Chinese his-tory. Nevertheless, it seemed to suggest that divination by means of the tor-toise shell was much older than that by the stalks of the divining plant. As Legge has pointed out, "In the Shu King, in a document that purports to be of the twenty-third century B. C. (The Shu II, ii, 18), divination by means of the tortoise shell is mentioned; and somewhat later we find that method continuing, and also divination by the lineal figures, manipulated by means of the stalks of a plant (The Shu V, iv, 20, 31)."[1] It is uncertain why the tortoise shell was first used for divination. It presumes that the tortoise was thought to have the most mysterious and oracular powers of all living creatures. These mysterious and oracular powers were thought to derive from the tortoise, because it survived longer than any other living beings they knew. For the primitive mind the life of the tortoise was so long that it was recognized as the symbol of immortality. Because of its immortal life, it became the object of divination. In divination, the belly surface of the tortoise shell was incised with a red-hot stylus, so that the shell was cracked and lines of cracks also formed. The diviner then read the oracles from the cracks formed by the incision of the hot stylus. Since it became rather difficult to read and understand the cracks of the tortoise shell, a somewhat new process of divining was developed. The later development was the divination by means of the stalks of a divining plant. For sometime in Chinese history the divining method by both tortoise shell and plant stalks had continued. The use of both methods is well illustrated in the following account of a faithful wife who is waiting for her husband to come home: "The transport wagons did not come. Great was the distress of my sorrowing heart. For he did not arrive when the time was due, so that I am full of grief. Yet I have divined by tortoise shell and by the stalks; and they agree in saying

---

[1] See Legge's translation, p. 40. James Legge's translation of the I Ching was originally published by the Clarendon Press in 1899 as Volume XVI of "The Sacred Books of the East" and with the special designation of Part II of "The Texts of Confucianism." The unaltered republication is found in Ch'u Chai and WinbergChai, ed., I Ching: Book of Changes, tr. by James Legge (New Hyde Park: University Books, 1964).

that he is near. My soldier (husband) is at hand."[1]   The co-existence of
both methods of divination for a long time is evident. However, because of
the complexity of reading oracles from the cracks of the tortoise shell, divination by stalks seems to have become more popular and finally replaced
divination by the tortoise shell. It is not certain when the real transition
took place. However, it is clear that the I Ching has its origin in the use
of a fixed number of milfoil stalks. Because the use of the stalks for divination was easier than the use of tortoise shell, the name of the I Ching,
the Book of Easy (or easy divination), might be derived. Perhaps, this explains why the I Ching has been the alternative name of the Chou I. It was
named "Chou" from the fact that it was composed by the people of the Chou
dynasty, and "I" because its method of divination was an easy one.[2]

The second stage in the formation of the I Ching has to do with the
correlation of cosmic process with the oracles in terms of the trinity of
world principles. The three principles of the world include the subject
(man), object which has form (earth), and content (heaven). These three
principles constitute the eight trigrams which are the basic constituents
for everything that exists in the world. According to the tradition in China,
there was a map found from the Yellow River. This map, which is called Ho
T'u, the River Map, is described in the Ta Chuan. The accounts are as follows:

---

[1]D. Howard Smith, Chinese Religions (New York: Holt, Rinehart and
Winston, 1968), p. 26.

[2]Fung Yu-lan, A History of Chinese Philosophy, Vol. I (Princeton:
Princeton University Press, 1952), p. 380.

Therefore: Heaven produced spiritual things, which were perceived by the holy sages. The transformation of heaven and earth was imitated by them. They put images in heaven to indicate good fortune and misfortune. They reproduced these images. The Ho (Yellow River) brought forth the T'u (map), and the Lo (Lo River) brought forth a Shu (writing). The holy sages patterned after them (Sec. I, Ch. 11).

The River Map, the map which came from the Yellow River, was believed to be the basis for the formation of the I Ching. As indicated above, the map was believed to contain a certain scheme which gave a model to Fu Hsi, the legendary king, in making the eight trigrams. According to popular belief, this map was drawn on the back of a dragon-horse coming out of the Yellow River. Confucius himself seemed to believe in the map, for he mentioned it in his Analects.[1] Evidence for this belief is also recorded in the Book of Rites: "the map was borne by a horse" (8:4). There is no way either to prove or to disapprove the validity of this belief. However, the importance of this map cannot be denied. Furthermore, the real issue in relation to this map is not so much its existence but with the way in which it was acquired. As Chu Chün-sheng (1788-1858) pointed out in his Texts of the Sixty-four Hexagrams Explained, there were three persons who were thought to possess the map. According to the people of the Hsia Dynasty (2205-1766 B. C.), Lien Shan secured the map, so that it was named Lien Shan. According to the people of Shang Dynasty (1766-1150 B.C.), Kuei Ts'ang possessed the map, and it was therefore called Kuei Ts'ang. According to the people of the Chou Dynasty, Fu Hsi secured the map and called it Chou I, which is the present book of the I Ching.[2]

---

[1]Analects 9:8.

[2]Chu Chün-sheng, Liu-shih-ssu Kua ching chieh (朱駿聲 六十四卦經解) Peking, 1958, p. 2.

We do not know what had happened with both Lien Shan and Kuei Ts'ang in the past. Except for the titles there is no trustworthy knowledge of the books today. The only book that survived is the Chou I or I Ching. Thus our attention should be directed to the River Map which was thought to have been secured by Fu Hsi.

The original map which Fu Hsi received from the Yellow River was thought to be lost in the eleventh century B. C. However, there was speculation that the map was reconstructed at the time of the restoration of the ancient classics during the Han Dynasty. If this was the case, it is questionable whether the reconstructed map was identical with the original one or not. However, the most reliable map was to be developed out of the so-called school of "Five Elements" or Wu Hsing in the Han era. The following map is commonly accepted as the identical map of Ho T'u, which was originally found from the Yellow River:

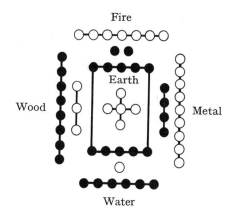

Since there is no way to verify the authenticity of this map, let us suppose that it was the authentic map with which Fu Hsi was acquainted and formed the eight trigrams. In the map there is a distinction between the black and white circles. Furthermore all the dark circles are even numbers such as 2, 4, 6, 8, and 10, while all the light circles are odd numbers such as 1, 3, 5, 7, and

9. According to Ta Chuan, "The number 1 belongs to heaven, 2 to earth, 3
to heaven, 4 to earth, 5 to heaven, 6 to earth, 7 to heaven, 8 to earth, 9
to heaven, and 10 to earth" (Sec. I, Ch. 11). Here, earth represents even
numbers or yin numbers, while heaven the odd numbers or yang numbers. It
goes on to say, "The heavenly numbers are five, and the earthly numbers are
also five. The numbers of these two series correspond to each other, and
each one has another that may be considered its complement. The heavenly
numbers amount to 25, and the earthly to 30. The numbers of both heaven and
earth amount to 55. Because of these numbers, the changes and transformations
are achieved, and the spiritual powers are moved" (Sec. I, Ch. 9). The total
numbers of heaven, the addition of 1, 3, 5, 7, and 9, amount to 25, while those
of earth, the addition of 2, 4, 6, 8, and 10, amount to 30. Thus the total
numbers of both heaven and earth amount to 55, which represent all the spiritual
powers in heaven and earth. Heaven represents the Great Yang or Great Brightness, and earth the Great Darkness or the Great Yin. Everything in the universe
is regarded as the product of the interaction of both heaven and earth. Heaven
and earth were represented by the sun and moon. This idea is implicit in
the word "I" 易   . As we see, it is the combination of two words of " 日 "
and " 勿." The former implies the "sun," while the latter could be the old
word of " 月 ," the "moon."[1] From the analysis of the word "I" it is possible
that the great yang came to be symbolized by the sun and the great yin by the
moon, for heaven and earth were thought to be governed by the sun and moon.
The correlation of heaven and earth with the sun and the moon is quite evident

---

[1]Legge, tr., op. cit., p. 38, note 1.

from the following accounts: "There are no greater images than heaven and earth. There are no greater cohesions then the changes of the four seasons. There is no more brightness than the sun and moon" (Ta Chuan, Sec. I, Ch. 11). Therefore, the title of the I Ching is harmony with the basic principle of the River Map, which became the basis of the eight trigrams.

The question is then how could the eight trigrams be formed out of this map" First of all, it is an hypothesis that Fu His, if he was really the author of the eight trigrams, failed to construct the trigrams with the circles of the map. He then decided to replace the circles with lines for convenience. The whole or undivided line (———) is used for the light circle, and the divided line (— —) for the dark. Then, all odd numbers became whole lines which signify yang forces, and all even numbers became divided lines which signify yin forces. The transition from circles to lines was the initial stage in the development of the trigrams. If we observe the map carefully, we will get some idea of how the trigrams were formed out from the map. We see that the circles on the outer sides of the map are divided into four groups; two groups of dark circles and two groups of light circles. The group of dark circles which represents the water is number 6, because of 6 circles. The group of dark circles which represents the wood has the number 8, because of 8 dark circles. Thus both 6 and 8 are even numbers and represent yin forces. The number 6 is assigned to the "old yin," which is ymbolized with two broken lines (⎺⎺ ⎺⎺), while the number 8 is assigned to the "young yin," which is symbolized with a broken line above and an unbroken line below (⎺⎺___). In a similar manner we have two groups of light circles which represent fire and metal. The group which represents fire has 7 light circles, and thus it has the number 7. The group which represents the metal has 9 light circles, and therefore it has the number 9. Both 7 and 9 are odd numbers and represent the yang forces. The number 7 is assigned to the "young yang," which is symbolized by the unbroken line above and the broken line below (___), and 9 the "old yang," symbolized by the two unbroken lines (___). These four lineal symbols represent not only the four seasons of the year but the foundations of the eight trigrams. By adding another line to these basic symbols the eight trigrams are formed. The process of the evolvement of lines to the eight trigrams is stated as follows: "Therefore, the I is in the Great Ultimate Beginning. The two primary powers produce the four symbols. The four symbols (images) produce the eight trigrams" (Ta Chuan, Sec. I, Ch. 11). The great ultimate beginning is identical with the Tao, the source of all things. The two primary powers, which present yin and yang forces, are the products of the Tao. Through the interaction of both yin and yang forces the four symbols (or images) are produced. The four symbols imply the old yang, young yang, old yin, and young yin. These four symbols again produce the eight trigrams. They are Ch'ien (≡), K'un (☷), Chen (☳), Li (☲), Tui (☱), Sun (☴), K'an (☵), and Ken (☶). The addition of one more line of either yin or yang, which represents man, to the two primordial lines of heaven and earth completes the trinity of cosmic principles. Thus the trigrams are the complete symbols of the universe. They are arranged according to the seasons to rule the universe: "Heaven and earth determine the position. The powers of mountain and lake are correlated. Thunder and wind meet each other. Water and fire do not meet each other. Thus the eight trigrams are mutually intermingled" (Shuo Kua, Ch. 2). The trigram Ch'ien or heaven and K'un or earth determine the north and south axis. Ken or mountain and Tui or lake attract each other.

Chen or thunder and Sun or wind work together for the rain which arouses all things to grow. And K'an or water and Li or fire do not go together. In this way the eight trigrams are correlated with the cosmic principles of the universe.

The third stage deals with the creation of hexagrams and the composition of the appended judgments or kua tz'u. According to the tradition, the authorship of the hexagrams is attributed to Fu Hsi, Shen Nung, Hsia Yu or King Wen.[1] Was Fu Hsi, who formulated the eight trigrams out of the Ho T'u or the River Map, responsible also for the creation of the sixty-four hexagrams? It is provable that Fu Hsi could construct the hexagram through the combination of the trigrams, even though the present form of arrangement of the hexagrams in the I Ching is commonly attributed to King Wen. The existence of different arrangement of hexagrams was evident even prior to King Wen, who, being a great diviner, was acquainted with some forms of divining system. Legge also believes in the existence of hexagrams prior to the time of King Wen. Out of these existing forms of hexagrams, Legge says, "King Wen takes them up, one after another, in the order that suits himself, determined, evidently, by the contrast in the lines of each successive pair of hexagrams, and gives their significance."[2] Even though there is not enough evidence to prove whether Fu Hsi or someone else was responsible for the formation of the hexagrams, it is quite clear that King Wen had something to do with the present arrangement of hexagrams and the addition of the appended judgments. As Chai eloquently puts it, there is no recent scholar who con-

---

[1] See Chu Chü-sheng, op. cit. "重卦者 或言伏羲 或言神農夏禹文王 四説."

[2] Legge, tr., op. cit., p. 10.

siders that King Wen had anything to do with the I Ching.[1] It is, of course, perfectly possible that the I Ching might be attributed to King Wen, since it used to bear the name of Chou I. There is some evidence to support the view that the Judgments were appended by King Wen: "At the end of Yin dynasty and the rise of Chou dynasty, the I was given. This was the time when King Wen and the tyrant Chou Hsin were fighting against each other. Thus the judgments of this book often warn against danger" (Ta Chuan, Sec. II, Ch. 11). It is a commonly held view that the judgments to the hexagrams were composed by King Wen when he was held captive by the last ruler of the Yin dynasty. According to a popular belief in China, King Wen was in captivity for seven years. During this time he was able to arrange the sixty-four hexagrams and prescribed the judgments to them. There is an interesting story which attempts to illustrate the tragedy of the great diviner King Wen. According to the story, his power of divining was tested by the tyrant Chou Hsin while he was in prison. In order to test his divining ability Chou Hsin brought him a bowl of soup, which was made of the flesh of his own son who had been murdered. Realizing this he took the soup in order to spare his life. While he was in prison, King Wen was deeply involved in the study of lineal figures. The arrangement of hexagrams and the composition of the judgments came to him, according to the tradition, not in a manner of logical anaysis but more or less like the visions which many prophets have experienced in the past. In both the Old and the New Testaments of the Christian Bible, especially in the Books of Daniel and Revelation, visions embodying divine truth to the prophets.

---

[1]Ch'u Chai, op. cit., pp. xxviii-xxix.

If this was the case of King Wen, the hexagrams and the judgments in the I Ching could be more than a mere product of human wisdom but the supreme gift of an extraordinary insight. From the psychological point of view, they could be understood as the revelations of cosmic unconsciousness which are not available to the human situation under ordinary conditions. Some modern scholars, who are scientifically inclined, may say that the I Ching is nothing but the product of hallucinations which came to King Wen amid the devastating conditions of his imprisonment. Whatever the mental condition of King Wen was at the time of his study, the I Ching has been regarded in past centuries as the supreme product of Chinese mentality. The greatness of Chinese mentality does not lie in its logical system of thought but in the intuitive insight derived directly from the nature of spiritual reality. Perhaps, the visions expressed in the hexagrams can be the creations of such mentality.

The final form of the I Ching which we have today was thought to have been completed by the Duke of Chou, the son of King Wen, who was responsible for the formulation of the texts for the individual lines of the hexagrams. The Duke of Chou, Tan, succeeded the regency for his nephew when his brother King Wu died. The brilliance of his leadership was not questioned. He was not only a great ruler but also a great philosopher who succeeded in his father's work and completed it as a tribute of filial piety. Even though this tradition has often been questioned by modern scholarship, it is certain that this textual stratum belongs to the early Chou period.[1] Furthermore,

---

[1]Hellmut Wilhelm, Change: Eight Lectures on the I Ching, tr. by Cary F. Baynes (Princeton: Princeton University Press, 1960), p. 11.

the texts for the individual lines of the hexagrams are done in harmony with the judgments on the hexagrams as a whole, so that the author of the texts for individual lines or _hsiao tz'u_ must be informed with the judgments on the hexagrams or _kua tz'u_. Even though it is questionable whether Tan had enough time to go through every line of the hexagrams and formulate the texts, it is reasonable to believe that the whole work of the _I Ching_ might be done in the Chou court under the leadership of the Duke. It is also worthless to argue about the authorship of _hsiao tz'u_, for we do not have any clear evidence to affirm or deny the traditional assertion that the Duke of Chou was responsible for the texts. As we have already stated, from our observation on the symbols and situations depicted in the texts on the individual lines of the hexagrams we do not need to question that the final form of the _I Ching_, not the inclusion of the Ten Wings, must come from the early Chou period. The traditional name of this book, _Chou I_, also suggests the idea that it was originally a Chou manual on divination. Therefore, we can safely conclude that the final form of the _I Ching_ was completed sometime in the early Chou dynasty, about three thousand years ago.

What I have attempted so far is to reconstruct the authorship of the _I Ching_ according to the Chinese tradition. As we have observed, there is no way to make any conclusive statement about the authorship of this book. I like to look at the _I Ching_, not as the product of specific individuals in history, but as the unique creation of Chinese civilization. It is a natural treasure which belongs to the very expression of Chinese culture. Even though the tradition has attributed the authorship of this book to particular persons, like Fu Hsi, King Wen, and the Duke of Chou, we must not think that they alone were responsible for it. Fu Hsi, for example, was a legendary figure who rep-

resents the very foundation of Chinese civilization. He is the symbol of
the begiing of Chinese culture. Just like Tan Kun, who was the legendary
figure representing the beginning of Korean civilization, and Amaterasu
Omikami, who was also the legendary emperor of Japanese civilization, Fu
Hsi became the symbol for the birth of Chinese civilization. Thus we can
say that the origin of the I Ching was in the origin of Chinese civilization.
The authorship of the I Ching can be compared with that of the five books of
Moses or the Pentateuch in the Hebrew Old Testament, which went through many
years of oral transmission and revision until they were finally written down
and canonized. Just like the Pentateuch was attributed to a great leader
like Moses, so the I Ching was attributed to great figures like Fu Hsi, King
Wen and the Duke of Chou. Like any other great national epic, the I Ching
probably went through various revisions and refinements through the centuries
of experiments in divination until it was finally completed and written down
about the time of the early Chou dynasty. Thus in the final analysis the
authorship of the I Ching belongs not to the several individuals whom we have
mentioned, but it belongs to the corporal community of early Chinese people.
Certainly, men like King Wen and the Duke of Chou who are credited with the
formulation of this book are not in any way separated from the community of
those who shared the tradition of Chinese civilization which is the real
source of this book. It is not only the product of Chinese history but an
intrinsic part of Chinese life. For this reason, even though it became the
first book of the Confucian classics, it never identified itself with the
Confucian schools only. It has become a source of inspiration and challenge
to all the people in the history of Chinese civilization.

3. Concerning The Origin Of The Ten Wings.

Let us now return to an examination of the authorship of the Ten Wings, which are supplementary commentaries to the main texts of the I Ching. There is no reason to doubt that the Ten Wings were written much later than the main texts. However, the question is how late they were written. Tradition assigns them to Confucius. A great deal of discussion on the authorship of the Ten Wings has been made in history. Since the writings of Confucius are available in our time, it is possible for us to make a critical examination of the traditional claim in the light of his writings. In the main texts of the I Ching, as we have already observed, there are not sufficient materials to make critical study of their authorship. However, in the case of the Ten Wings, we are able to use textual criticism to test the claims of traditional authorship.

Confucius once said, "If some years were added to my life, I would give fifty to the study of the I, and might then escape falling into great errors."[1] When he said it, it is believed that he was near the end of his life. Since he was fond of the I Ching and much interested in the study of it, tradition indicates that he decided to write various appendixes to the I Ching. Most of these appendixes come to us as the Ten Wings, except those portions which were corrupted and lost. The question is whether Confucius had time to write the Ten Wings, for he is believed to have begun his study of the I Ching in his seventies. We may take up each book of the Ten Wings and critically examine the authenticity of Confucian authorship.

The first two wings are the T'uan Chuan, the commentary on the judgments

---

[1]Analects 7:16.

or decisions. In this commentary we do not find any superscription of Confucius. Nevertheless, we do not find any convincing evidence to deny that it was written by Confucius. The commentary is well organized and an extremely valuable piece of work which helps us to understand the inner structure of the hexagrams in the I Ching. As Richard Wilhelm said, "The Chinese ascribe it to Confucius. I see no reason for doubting this ascription, inasmuch as it is well known that Confucius devoted much thought to the Book of Changes, and since the views expressed in this commentary nowhere conflict with this view."[1]

The third and fourth wings, which are known as the Hsiang Chuan or the Commentary on the Symbols, do not contain any clear evidence which would deny the traditional assertion that they were written by Confucius. There is no real difference between the T'uan Chuan and Hsiang Chuan in their treatise on the hexagrams except in their approaches. The T'uan Chuan interprets the hexagrams on the basis of the judgments, while the Hsiang Chuan approaches the hexagrams in terms of their images. Therefore, we do not have real evidence to affirm or to deny the traditional view that Confucius was responsible for the Hsiang Chuan. Again, Wilhelm makes a sound judgment in regard to the authorship of this commentary: "It is certain that they are very old and originated with the Confucian school, but I should not like to say definitely how close the connection with Confucius himself may be."[2] As in the case of the T'uan Chuan, it is impossible for us to make any definite statement on

---

[1] Richard Wilhelm and Cary Baynes, tr., The I Ching or Book of Changes (Princeton: Princeton University, 1967), Third Ed., p. 256.

[2] Ibid., P. 258.

the authorship of the Hsiang Chuan.

The fifth and sixth wings constitute essays which present some difficult problems in their authorship. They are called Hsi Tz'u Chuan or the
Commentary on the Appended Judgments, which is also known by the great his-
torian, Szu-ma Ch'ien, as the Ta Chuan or the Great Treatise. The traditional
claim that Confucius was responsible for this commentary is challenged. The
difficulty of maintaining the traditional authorship of this commentary is
much greater than those of the preceding commentaries. The difficulty is,
first of all, the original title of this commentary, that is, Hsi Tz'u Chuan
or the Commentary on the Appended Judgments, does not correspond to its contents. If the commentary is, as the original title indicates, for the appended
judgments, it should comment on the judgments specifically rather than on the
work of the I Ching in general. Moreover, there is the commentary on the
judgments, the T'uan Chuan, which belongs to the first and second wings. Thus
there is no reason to have another commentary besides this. Another difficulty
with the Hsi Tz'u Chuan has to do with frequent occurrences of the formula "The
Master said." This formula occurs about twenty-three times in this commentary.
The question is, if Confucius had written it, he could not introduce himself
with this formula. There must be someone else who wrote this commentary on behalf of Confucius. Therefore, it is rather difficult to attribute this work
to Confucius himself, even though it seems to contain traditional materials
of the Confucian school.

The seventh wing, which is called Wen Yen or the commentary on the
words of the text, also has almost the same problem that we have in the Hsi
Tz'u Chuan. The same formula "The Master said" occurs often but not as much
as in the Hsi Tz'u Chuan. The Wen Yen which we have now in the Ten Wings is

believed to be the remnant of a whole series of commentaries on the hexagrams
of the I Ching. It is rather unfortunate that we cannot make an extensive examination of this matter because the materials on both the Ch'ien and K'un
hexagrams are available to us. An added difficulty with this commentary has
to do with the collection of several commentaries. We notice that the first
three paragraphs of Wen Yen could be much older than the rest of the material.
Therefore, it is very difficult to attribute this work to Confucius. I am in
sympathy with Legge, who said, "I am obliged to come to the conclusion that
Confucius had nothing to do with the composition of these two Appendixes (Ta
Chuan and Wen Yen) and that they were not put together till after his death.
I have no pleasure in differing from the all but unanimous opinion of Chinese
critics and commentators."[1]

The eighth wing, Shuo Kua or the Discussion of the Trigrams, is a brief
but very important section. This commentary, like the previous one, contains
more than a single contribution. It is believed to be the combination of
several writings. Some of them may go back much further than Confucius himself.
For example, the third paragraph which deals with the sequence of the so-called
Earlier Heaven may go back as far as to Fu Hsi himself. In the fifth paragraph
we find the different arrangement of trigrams. This arrangement is known as
the Inner-World Arrangement, which is differentiated from the Earlier Heaven.
The Inner-World Arrangement is attributed to King Wen. Moreover, there is some
Taoistic influence on the commentary, especially in the first paragraph. There-
fore, it is very difficult to say that this commentary was written by Confucius.

---

[1] See Legge's translation, p. 30.

The ninth wing, _Hsu Kua_ or the Sequence of the Hexagrams, and the last wing, _Tsa Kua_ or Miscellaneous Notes on the Hexagrams, are somewhat inferior in their presentation of materials. Justifications for the sequence of the hexagrams in the _Hsu Kua_ are often arbitrary and inconsistent. The Miscellaneous Notes on the Hexagrams do not add much to our understanding of the hexagrams. As Creel said, "These two treatises are extremely brief and utterly superficial; there is no reason to suppose that Confucius would have bothered even to read, much less to write, such trifles."[1]

As a result of our examination it is clear that the traditional view on the authorship of the Ten Wings is questionable. However, this does not mean it can be rejected totally. On the other hand, it is difficult to affirm it. I believe that the total rejection of traditional authorship is as wrong as the complete acceptance of it. Some of those who are trained in textual criticisms go so far as to conclude that Confucius had nothing to do with the Ten Wings of the _I Ching_. Let us critically examine the objections to Confucian authorship. We may take each of them and examine them carefully in the light of the sayings of Confucius, mainly as found in the _Analects_.

First of all, one of the obvious objections to the Confucian authorship of the Ten Wings is, as we have already pointed out, the frequent appearance of the familiar phrase,"The Master said." This phrase or formula occurs only in two commentaries, the _Ta Chuan_ and _Wen Yen_. The appearance of this formula in both commentaries makes it rather obvious that they were not written by Confucius himself. Confucius could not introduce himself with this formula.

---

[1] H. G. Creel, _Confucius and the Chinese Way_ (Harper and Row, 1960), p. 199.

Thus they must have been written by some one other than the Master himself.
Creel said, "the words 'The Master said' evidently referring to Confucius;
this fact in itself indicates that he was not their author."[1] After denying
the authorship of Confucius, Creel indicates further that this formula was
applied by the Taoists who were actually responsible for the Ten Wings.
"These same words appear verbatim in the Taoist work, Chuang Tzu; it seems
perfectly clear that they were lifted from that source and put into the mouth
of Confucius."[2] I believe it is a rather weak argument to conclude that Confucius had nothing to do with the Ten Wings, because of the use of the formula
"The Master said." This formula, of course, denies that Confucius himself
wrote these commentaries but this does not deny that his words were accurately
recorded. The same argument can be applied to the Analects, where the same
formula "The Master said" also appears frequently. If the Analects were not
by Confucius, then certainly the Ten Wings of the I Ching may not be his.
It is better not to make a definite statement on the authorship of the Ten
Wings unless more convincing evidence can be found.

Secondly, it is argued that Confucius did not write the Ten Wings because they are pervaded with a philosophy which is absent from the Analects.
There is a certain validity to this criticism. Especially, the Ta Chuan and
Shuo Kua are full of metaphysical language and deal with more abstract ideas
which are not found in the Analects. However, this is not the case in the
other commentaries of the Ten Wings. For example, the T'uan Chuan and Hsiang
Chuan deal more with political and social images. Therefore, it is not only

---

[1]Creel, op. cit., p. 199.

[2]Ibid, p. 201.

an exaggeration but also a generalization to say that all the Ten Wings are metaphysically oriented.

Thirdly, the easy and simple way to know the world phenomena, which is described in the I Ching and in the Ten Wings, is foreign to the teachings of Confucius. Therefore, Confucius was not responsible for the Ten Wings. This argument seems to have some validity. In the Analects we do not find Confucius teaches an easy and simple way. Rather he teaches that knowledge is a hard thing won through experience and discipline. However, this does not prove that the Ten Wings have nothing to do with Confucius. If the I Ching was of interest to Confucius in his later years, this idea of the easy and simple way might come later. It is also probable that he rejoiced in knowing the I Ching, because it is an easy and simple way to know the things in the universe.

Fourthly, the dualistic concept of yin and yang, which occurs in all of the Ten Wings, is unknown to the pre-Confucian literature and does not occur in the Analects. Thus Confucius was not responsible for the Ten Wings. Even though the words "yin" and "yang" do not appear in the Analects they are implicit in it. For example, Confucius said, "There is no greatness like the greatness of Heaven... So boundless was it that the people could find no name for it; yet sublime were his achievements, dazzling the insight is of his culture!"[1] Here, the heaven is quite similar with the concept of heaven in the I Ching, where it is understood as Creativity. In his ethical principle of reciprocity and social relationship between the ruler and the ruled, parents and children, husband and wife, etc., the concept of polarity predominates all

---

[1] Analects 8:19

the way. The harmony and the mean presuppose the correlation of the creative *and the responsive* or active and passive relationship. As Smith has pointed out, "Already in the *Ch'un Ch'iu* period (720-479 B. C.), according to the <u>Kuo Yü</u> and <u>Tso Chuan</u>, the eight trigrams were being thought of as the symbols of heaven and earth, mountains and marshes, wind, fire, water and thunder. The cosmologies of the I Ching based their speculations on the analogy of the conception of human beings. A primeval unity manifested itself in two complementary forces, namely the <u>yin</u> and <u>yang</u>."[1] It is also possible that the reason why the <u>yin</u> and <u>yang</u> symbols are not explicit in Confucius' <u>Analects</u> might be that he was not acquainted with the <u>I Ching</u> at that time. Moreover, if we believe that the <u>Ho T'u</u> or the River Map was found in the time of the Hsia Dynasty, and the map was primarily the constitution of light and dark circles to signify the <u>yin</u> and <u>yang</u> forces, we cannot see why the concept of <u>yin</u> and <u>yang</u> was not known at the time of Confucius. Confucius makes reference to the River Map in his <u>Analects</u>.[2] As a result I believe that the concept of <u>yin</u> and <u>yang</u> was implicit in the mind of Confucius, even though it is questionable whether the technical terms such as "<u>yin</u>" and "<u>yang</u>" were unknown to him. Therefore, I am not convinced that the concept of <u>yin</u> and <u>yang</u> is foreign to the <u>Analects</u>.

Fifthly, Confucius not only disagreed with the philosophy of divination but denounced it. Thus the Ten Wings, which are primarily concerned with the

---

[1] H. D. Smith, <u>op</u>. <u>cit</u>., p. 91.

[2] <u>Analects</u> 9:8.

practice of divination, cannot have been written by Confucius.[1] This criticism is based on the passage of the <u>Analects</u> 13:22, where "The Master said,
'The people of the south have a saying--A man without constancy cannot be
either a wizard or a doctor.' Good! Inconsistent in his virtue, he will
be visited with disgrace. The Master said, 'This arises simply from not at-
tending to the prognostication.'" It is often misunderstood that by this
statement Confucius denounced the practice of divination. The statement
"Inconsistent in his virtue, he will be visited with disgrace" (不恒其德
或承之羞) is a direct quotation from the text on the third line of the
hexagram 32, <u>Heng</u> 恒 or Enduring. Confucius does not criticize the <u>I
Ching</u> here but he stresses the importance of "constancy," which means firmness of character and the unchangeable principle of changes. About the prognostication, "Chang K'ang-ch'ang says: 'By the <u>I</u> we prognosticate good and
evil but in it there is no prognostication of people without constancy.'"[2]
As we observed, the statement in the <u>Analects</u> 13:22 does not imply that Confucius did not favor the practice of divination but he criticizes the misuse
of it merely for the sake of divination alone. Even Hsun Tzu said that those
who know the <u>I Ching</u> well do not use it for divination. If Confucious denounced
the I Ching because of divination, he was not bothered to make use of a passage
from it. I believe that Confucius respected the <u>I Ching</u>, for he quoted it to il-

---

[1] For those who believe that Confucius disfavored the practice of divina-
tion through the use of the <u>I Ching</u>, see H. G. Creel, <u>Confucius and Chinese Way</u>,
p. 200; Fung Yu-lan, <u>A History of Chinese Philosophy</u>, <u>I</u>, p. 381; Honda Seishi,
"Tso I nien tai k'ao" 作易年代考 in Hsien Ch'ien Chi K'ao 先秦經籍考 ;
Homer H. Dubs, "Did Confucius Study the <u>Book of Changes</u>?" in <u>T'oung Pao</u> XXXV
(Leiden, 1929), pp. 82-90.

[2] James Legge, tr., <u>The Four Books</u> (N. Y.: Paragon Book, 1966), p. 188.

lustrate the importance of "constancy."

Finally, one of the most crucial arguments against the traditional view is that the <u>Analects</u> made no mention of the <u>I Ching</u>. This argument is centered around the passage of the <u>Analects</u> 7:16: "The Master said, 'If some years were added to my life, I would give fifty to the study of the <u>I</u>, and then I might come to be without great faults'" (子曰加我数年五十以學易可以無大過矣). The affirmation of this passage as being that of Confucius is to endorse his interest in the <u>I Ching</u>. In other words, this passage is much more like the passage of Matthew 16:18: "Thou art Peter, and upon this rock I will build my Church; and the gates of hell shall not prevail against it." Just as Matthew 16:18 is the key to the establishment of the Roman Papacy, the <u>Analects</u> 7:16 is the key to the understanding of the attitude of Confucius towards the <u>I Ching</u>. Just as some New Testament scholars believe that Matthew 16:18 was thought to be inserted by the early Church, <u>Analects</u> 7:16 is also believed to be interpolated later. The basic issue in this passage is centered around the word "<u>I</u>" (易). The word "<u>I</u>" (易) in the present text of Confucian <u>Analects</u> does not conform to the Lu text in the <u>Ching Tien Shin Wen</u> (24:8a), where the word "亦." is used instead of "易." The alternation of this character makes the passage quite different in its meaning. Since we cannot prove that the Lu text was correct, it is impossible to make a definite statement about the alternation of the word "亦." with "易." Moreover, <u>Analects</u> 9:8, "The phoenix does not come, the river puts forth no chart; I am finished," is also regarded as a Taoist interpolation. Here, the River Map or <u>Ho T'u</u>, which became the basis for the formation of trigrams and hexagrams, comes under suspicion. However, there is one passage in the <u>Analects</u> which can clarify our doubts concerning the attitude of Confucius towards the

I Ching. That passage is Analects 7:5, where Confucius said, "Extreme is my decay. For a long time, I have not dreamed, as I was wont to do, that I saw the Duke of Chou." It is, to me, the affirmation of the interest of Confucius in the I Ching, which was to be completed by the Duke of Chou. Confucius seemed to respect the Duke of Chou for his brilliant achievement in the texts on the lines of hexagrams. Confucius wanted to see the Duke of Chou in a dream before his death. His longing for the Duke of Chou, who was responsible for the completion of the I Ching, indicates definitely that Confucius did not denounce the I Ching.

All that I have attempted to do so far is provide enough room for both groups; those who claim that Confucius had nothing to do with the Ten Wings and those who rely on the traditional view that Confucius was responsible for them. I have not said that the traditional view on the authorship of the Ten Wings is either right or wrong. It is difficult in my view to find enough evidence to prove that the traditional claim is wrong. Furthermore, we do not have sufficient proof to support the traditional view either. Therefore, we cannot make an irresponsible statement such as "Confucius had nothing whatever to do with the Book of Changes."[1] I would like to see the Ten Wings as the product of many people who were both Taoists and Confucianists. The I Ching transcends religious sectarianism. It served as a bridge between Confucianism and Taoism. As Chai has pointed out, "We find when we come to examine them that there are many respects in which the main thesis of the I Appendices corresponds with that of the Chung Yung (Doctrine of the Mean). Moreover, the I Appendices borrow many ideas from the Lao Tzu (i. e.,

---

[1]See H. G. Creel, op. cit., p. 105; Fung Yu-lan, A History of Chinese Philosophy, I, pp. 381f.

<u>Tao</u> <u>Te</u> <u>Ching</u>), so that they have a good deal in common with Taoism."[1] It is,

therefore, unjust to attribute the work of the Ten Wings to the Taoists alone.

As we have seen the Ten Wings consists of many different forms of manuscripts.

Some of them are older than Confucius himself and others are much later. The

authorship of the Ten Wings can be compared with that of the Gospels in the

New Testament. Just as the Ten Wings have multiple authorship the Gospels

are collections of various forms of literary works. Moreover, a strikingly

similar formula "Jesus said" in the Gospels is also found in the Ten Wings,

where the formula is "The Master said." Just as the formula "Jesus said" in

the Gospels is not an empty phrase, the formula "The Master said" in the Ten

Wings may not be completely foreign to the sayings of Confucius. I do not

believe that Confucius was responsible for the whole appendices but he had

something to do with making them. The actual edition might take place in the

latter part of Chou dynasty or even in the early Han dynasty, but the mater-

ials in them might come from many years before. Therefore, I am in agreement

with Hellmut Wilhelm, who said:

> We know that Confucius did occupy himself intensively with the
> <u>I Ching</u> for even in the remnants of his conversation that have
> come down to us, we find it mentioned several times. The most
> plausible assumption is that he discussed this book with his
> disciples, just as he did other classics, and told them his
> thoughts about it.[2]

---

[1]Ch'u Chai with Winberg Chai, ed., <u>I</u>. <u>Ching</u>: <u>Book</u> <u>of</u> <u>Changes</u>, tr. by
James Legge (N.Y.: University Books, 1964), p. xxxix.

[2]Hellmut Wilhelm, <u>Change</u>: <u>Eight</u> <u>Lectures</u> <u>on</u> <u>the</u> <u>I</u> <u>Ching</u> (N.Y.: Harper
Torchbooks, 1960), p. 12.

4. The Legacy Of The I Ching.

Let us now consider the place of the I Ching in Chinese civilization.
The I Ching is not only the product of Chinese culture but also a key to the
understanding of its development. As one of the Confucian classics the I
Ching affected the life of many Chinese people. Its significance in Chinese
civilization is quite evident when we realize that this book alone was spared
from the burning of books under the tyrant Ch'in Shih-huang-ti in 215 B.C.
At that time all the scholarly books including the classics were completely
destroyed with the exception of the I Ching. Thus the I Ching has been transmitted to us without any serious interruption in its history. There were two
epochs which were most significant for the I Ching in Chinese civilization.
They were the Han and Sung dynasties. In both epochs the I Ching became the
center of intellectual development. During the Han dynasty the Taoists were
attracted to the I Ching, while during the Sung dynasty Confucian scholars
were interested in it. Both schools of thought approached it in different
ways. The Taoists made the I Ching fit their own way of thinking. Confucianists initiated a revival movement, the movement of Neo-Confucianism, through
the study of the I Ching. Thus in the history of Chinese civilization the I
Ching served both schools of thought.

During the former Han period (206 B.C. - A.D. 24) the Taoists were
able to bring the I Ching and the yin-yang school together. The yin-yang
school seems to have had its origin in the Ho T'u or the River Map, which as
we have already observed, became the source of the I Ching. The concept of
yin and yang was thought to be adopted from the dark circles and light circles
of the River Map, which also became the basis for the five elements--water,

fire, wood, metal and earth. Thus it is believed that the yin-yang principle and the concept of the five elements were developed independently from the same source, in which the I Ching also has its origin. The yin-yang school was interested in correlating the five elements with the seasons of the year, the directions of the world, the notes of musical scale and almost everything in the world. Its interest in numerology and in the I Ching contributed to calendaring and to music as well as to medical science in China. The Ta Chuan seems to suggest the relationship between the five elements and the yin-yang school of thought: "The heavenly numbers are five, and the earthly numbers are also five. When they are fixed among the five places, each may be considered as its complement. The sum of the heavenly numbers amounts twenty-five, and that of the earthly numbers amounts thirty. The sum total of heavenly numbers and earthly numbers amounts fifty-five" (Sec. I, Ch. 9). The numberical correlation between yin and yang or heaven and earth is clearly suggested in the Ta Chuan. The five heavenly numbers and five earthly numbers seem to correspond to the five elements. Just as the combination of five earthly and heavenly numbers constitute all the maryads of the universe, the combination of the five elements of yin and yang produces all things in the world. The coincidence of the yin-yang school and the Ta Chuan could be regarded as the initial stage of the amalgam between the yin-yang school of thought and the I Ching.

From the middle of the former Han dynasty most scholars devoted thmselves to the study of the I Ching and wrote the large body of so-called apocryphal literature which was differentiated from both the commentary and the texts of the I Ching. The word "wei" 緯, which is used for the apocrypha, means literally "woof" or a fabric, while the word "ching" 經, which is used for the main texts of the I Ching, means literally "wrap." The word

"Ching" when used in the classics signifies the wrapping of words. Both the word "wei"and "ching" are used in apposition to each other metaphorically to denote the latitudinal and longitudinal threads of knowledge, which, woven together, were regarded by the Chinese as a unified fabric covering all human knowledge.[1]   In this respect the apocryphas were significant contributions to the understanding of the I Ching during the Han dynasty. Perhaps one of the most important apocryphas was the I-wei ch'ien tso-tu 易 緯 乾 鑿 度, a Discourse Inspired by the Hexagram i, Ch'ien. According to this apocrypha, both Ch'ien and K'un or Creativity and Responsivity have their origins in the formless or wu hsing 無 形, which is the primal change, a primal beginning and the primal origin. When the form and matter are not yet separated there comes chaos. Thus the chaos becomes an order when the Ch'ien and the K'un or Creativity and Responsivity come together through the primal change. In this primal change there is no division into forms. Through the transmutation of the principle of changes there comes the form of heaven and earth. Through the interaction of both heaven and earth all things originate. Things originating from heaven and earth have three periods of life; the beginning, maturity and the end. Therefore, Ch'ien and K'un have three lines each, and the combination of two are similar to that of yin and yang. In this way the apocrypha tries to explain something when the I Ching or the Ten Wings fail to give an adequate explanation. The apocrypha explains the principle of changes in terms of yin and yang as interplay, which have their origins in the Supreme Ultimate or T'ai Chi 太 極. Thus the apocrypha provides the concept of the Supreme Ultimate, the source of heaven and earth, which in turn form the

---

[1]Fung Yu-lan, A History of Chinese Philosophy, II, pp. 88-89.

basis for all other existence in the universe. The concept of the Supreme Ultimate became very important to the Neo-Confucianism movement in the Sung dynasty.

There soon appeared the so-called Old Text school or <u>Ku Wen Chia</u> 古 文學 which had denounced the doctrine of the New Text school that was based on the apocryphas and other writings of the <u>yin-yang</u> and five elements schools. The Old Text school intended to go back to the Confucian classics directly without reference to superstitious numerology. However, the prevailing mood of the time did not make it necessary for the Old Text school to divorce itself from the <u>yin</u> and <u>yang</u> school. One of the great philosophers of that time was Yang Hsiung 揚雄 who lived around the beginning of the Christian era. Yang Hsiung went further than the New Text school in establishing all-embracing and all-controlling essence which was expressed in the word "<u>hsuan</u>" 玄 or the dark mystery. He composed the <u>T'ai Hsuan</u> 太玄 or the Great Mystery which consisted of four-line complexes or tetragrams. The lines were not only whole and divided but also twice divided. The triple division of lines signifies the trinity, the <u>yin</u> and <u>yang</u> joined with the Mystery. The four places corresponded to family, district, province and the country. Thus the tetragrams were based on the hierarchy of distributions in geography. Yang's writing of <u>T'ai Hsuan</u> or the Great Mystery was primarily based on the <u>I Ching</u> and <u>Tao Te Ching</u>. The concept of the Great Mystery was not too much different from the Great Ultimate or the formlessness of the New Text School. Therefore, it did not help in the new understanding of the <u>I Ching</u>.

As we have observed, an attempt was made during the Han era to bring the prevailing pre-scientific notion of <u>yin-yang</u>, <u>five elements</u> and the <u>I Ching</u> together. However, the <u>I Ching</u> became the center for the application of various principles and numerology. It was unfortunate that the I Ching was misused by various schools of thought. They created an unhealthy image of the I Ching through the use of magics and mysteries. As Richard Wilhelm said, "For the Han commentators were in the last analysis sorcerers, or were influenced by theories of magic."[1]

After the Han dynasty the period of disunity came. During this period of disunity the growing interest of people in the Taoistic doctrines and continuing spirit of the Mysterious Learning was evident. Among the best known scholars in that period were Wang Pi and Kuo Hsiang, who were interested in the writings of both Lao Tzu and Chuang Tzu. They were regarded as great Taoist or Neo-Taoist philosophers. Nevertheless, they accepted Confucius as the great sage. In this period both Taoism and Confucianism came together through the works of these men. Perhaps, Wang Pi was one of the greatest scholars to whom we must pay attention. Wang Pi wrote one of the famous commentaries on the I Ching as well as on Lao-Tzu. His commentary on the I Ching was Chou I, which means simply the I Ching. In this commentary he stressed non-being as the final source of all beings. This non-being or mu 無 is equivalent to the Supreme Ultimate or T'ai Chi of the I Ching and the Tao of the Tao Te Ching. This non-being does not manifest itself through non-being but through being or yu 有 . In the process of divining, the one which is to be taken away from 50 stalks is identical with this non-being:

> In the expansion of the numbers of Heaven and Earth, 50 is (the round number which is) taken as a basis. But use is made only of 49, so that 1 is not used. It is not used, but through it the use (of the other numbers) takes place; it is not a number (like other numbers), but through it the numbers are formed.

---

[1]Richard Wilhelm and Cary F. Baynes, tr. op. cit., p. lxi.

> Thus this (oneness) constitutes the super-ultimate of the
> process of change; 49 constitutes the ultimate of numbers.
> Non-being (Wu) cannot be made manifest through non-being;
> this must be done by means of being (yu). Therefore
> through the ultimate of existing things, the origin from
> which these come (i.e., oneness of non-being) is always
> made manifest.[1]

Even though Wang Pi was only twenty-three when he died, he had contributed
a great deal toward an understanding of the philosophy of the I Ching. Especially, his exposition of symbols or hsiang exemplifies the brilliance of
his philosophy:

> Symbols (Hsiang or hexagrams) serve to express ideas. Words
> serve to explain symbols. For the complete expression of
> ideas there is nothing like symbols, and for the complete
> explanation of symbols there is nothing like words. The
> words are intended for the symbols... Therefore the purpose
> of words is to explain the symbols, but once the symbols
> have been grasped, the words may be forgotten. The purpose
> of symbols is to preserve the ideas, but once the ideas have
> been grasped, the symbols may be forgotten.[2]

The relationship between words and symbols is analogous to the relationship
between yin and yang. They mutually complement each other. One cannot exist
without the other. As Hellmut Wilhelm said, "To Wang Pi, the I Ching is no
longer a compendium of superstition or playground for speculation, but the
book of wisdom from which precepts for action and endurance are derived."[3]
Wang Pi's creative approach to the I Ching was soon neglected by the Chinese
who were preoccupied with the foreign intruder, Buddhism, during the following centuries.

It was in the period of the Sung Dynasty (960-1279) that the I Ching

---

[1] Wang Pi, Chou I 7:8.

[2] Ibid., 10:9-10.

[3] H. Wilhelm, Change, p. 88.

again became the focal point of intellectual movement. This movement came to be known as Neo-Confucianism. The new era of the I Ching research had begun with this movement. Almost all the great Neo-Confucian scholars of that period dealt in one way or another with the I Ching. The apocryphas on the I Ching, which were largely written during the Han era, were banned as unorthodox. Wang Pi's work was forgotten. The intensive study on the I Ching began with the discovery of a mystic diagram, which may have been formulated by the Taoists during the Han dynasty. Chou Tun-Yi (1017-73) was said to have come into possession of one of these diagrams which was recomposed by him. It was called the T'ai Chi T'u 太極圖 or the Diagram of the Supreme Ultimate. This map explains the origins of the principle of changes and the process of cosmic evolution. This discovery marked the initiation of the Neo-Confucianism intellectual movement during the Sung dynasty.

Chou Tun-Yi's illustration of the Diagram was obviously inspired by the I Ching. In Ta Chuan there is clear evidence to support his application of this diagram to the I Ching: "The Supreme Ultimate is in the I. It produces the two forms. These two forms produce the four symbols(hsiang), and these four hsiang produce the eight trigrams. The eight trigrams determine good and bad fortune, and this good and bad fortune produce the great works" (Sec. I, Ch. 11). Chou followed this process in his diagram. The two forms were attributed to yin and yang, evolved from the Supreme Ultimate. Through the interaction of yin and yang the five elements, instead of the eight trigrams, were developed. From the five elements everything in the world was born. However, this Supreme Ultimate is also of the Ultimateless or Wu Chi 無極. The influence of this Diagram of the Supreme Ultimate to the rise of a Neo-Confucian movement was related to the study of the I Ching. The following account illustrates the relationship between Chou's diagram and the I Ching to the rise of Neo-Confucianism during the Sung dynasty:

> In borrowing from the Taoists, however, Chou reinterpreted what he took. His resulting "Diagram," together with its exposition (the Diagram Explained), became the first systematic product of Sung and Ming Neo-Confucianism. Its great importance lies in the fact that it came to be accepted by virtually all the Neo-Confucianists as the basis for their own cosmological speculations... The fact that the latter treatise (T'ung-shu, Explanatory Text) was originally known as the I T'ung (Explanation of the Changes) shows that in it, as in his discussion of the Supreme Ultimate, Chou was writing with the Book of Changes very much in mind.[1]

Another great scholar of the Sung period was Shao Yung (1011-77). He was a speculative genius, who brought the study of "emblems" and "numerology" together. His interest in numerology led him to work out a different I Ching table, which was arranged according to a natural system. His arrangement of hexagrams was based on the process of cosmic evolution. He started first with the arrangement of the eight trigrams and then proceeded to the sixty-four hexagrams. In arranging the eight trigrams, he began with the two primary lines--the dark or yin and the light or yang lines and then added each again to both. The dark line produced two lines of both the light and the dark. The light line produced another two lines of both the light and the dark. Thus they became four two-line complexes. Each line of the four again produced both the dark and light lines and then created 8 trigrams. From the 8 trigrams he, in the same way, obtained the 64 hexagrams in the process of natural evolution.

---

[1]Fung Yu-lan, A History of Chinese Philosophy, II, p. 442.

Shao Yung's arrangement of lineal figures to the trigrams according to the process of natural evolution can be illustrated as follows:

Using the same process of evolution the 64 hexagrams are to be arranged as follows:

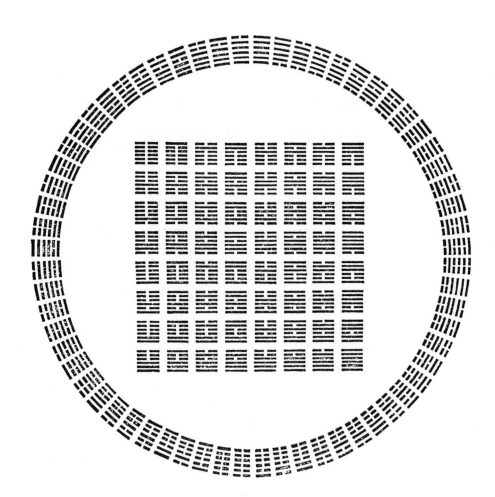

About six hundred years later this diagram fell into the hands of Leibniz through the agency of Jesuit missionaries. The diagram was precisely the same system which Leibniz independently constructed. Shao Yung used the hexagrams to construct the binary system which Leibniz worked out independently through the use of numbers. Shao Yung's system corresponded from point to point with Leibniz's binary system. However, the difference was the inverted order, which parallels the cultural patterns in the East and West. Thus, as Wilhelm said, "For a long time Leibniz had been trying to validate spiritual truths in mathematical terms, thus making them, as he thought, irrefutable."[1]

Shao Yung's interest in numerology brought him a new insight that influenced him to relate the numbers of the Changes to the cosmological chronology. In his Observation of Things or Kuan-wu P'ien he makes the following statement: "When the numbers of the Changes reach the end (of their evolution), Heaven and Earth complete a cycle. It may be asked: 'Do Heaven and Earth, then, also pass through a cycle (like other things)?' I reply: 'Since growth and decay exist (for all things), why should they not have such a cycle? Although Heaven and Earth are large, they too consist of form and matter (ch'i), and thus constitute two objects'" (Pt. IIb, 12b, 18). He expresses the period of time in terms of what he calls yüan 元 or cycles, hui 會 or epochs, yün 運 or revolutions, and shih 世 or generations. They are related as follows: 12 generations = 1 revolution; 30 revolutions = 1 epoch; 12 epochs = 1 cycle. Since one generation is equal with 30 years,[2] we get

---

[1]Hellmut Wilhelm, Change, p. 91.

[2]The Chinese word "shih" 世 is identical with three "shih" 十 .

the following foruma: 1 cycle = 12 epochs = 360 revolutions = 4,320 generations = 129,600 years. He coordinates this cycle with the pattern of natural evolution portrayed in his circular diagram of the 64 hexagrams. In this way he not only introduces the evolutionary process of expansion and contraction but also applies the hexagrams to the cosmic cycles of time.

Chang Tsai (1020-1077) was well known during the Neo-Confucian movement with his book, Cheng Meng or Discipline for Beginners. Like Chou Tun-Yi and Shao Yung he took as his point of departure certain ideas in the I Ching. He began his book with the study of a favorite passage in the Ta Chuan: "The Supreme Ultimate is in the I (Changes). It produces the two primal forms" (Sec. I, Ch. 11). Chang Tsai said that the Supreme Ultimate is the one and the Great harmony which is also equivalent with the Tao or the Way. This Great Harmony is used by Chang Tsai to imply his favorite word "ch'i" 氣 , which might be interpreted as "energy" or "vitality." In order to describe the state of this energy or ch'i, he makes use of a special term, "t'ai hsu" 太虛 or Great Void, which is the source of all things. The concept of Great Void was influenced by Taoism and Buddhism. However, Chang Tsai's contribution to the development of Neo-Confucianism was in the establishment of schools of thought by two Ch'eng brother: Ch'eng Hao (1032-1085) and Ch'eng Yi (1033-1108). Ch'eng Hao was responsible for Hsin Hsüeh or a school for the study of mind, while Ch'eng Yi was responsible for the establishment of Li Hsüeh or a school for the study of principles. The former is called the Lu-Wang school, for both Lu Chiu-yüan (1139-1193) and Wang Shou-en (1472-1528) expounded Ch'eng Hao's theory. The latter is called the Ch'eng-Chu school, for Chu Hsi (1130-1200) expounded Ch'eng Yi's doctrine. Both schools, even though philosophical rivals, had dealt with the I Ching. That is why it is almost impossible

not to mention the _I Ching_ when the philosophy of Neo-Confucianism is introduced. The influence of Taoism and Buddhism was secondary to that of the _I
Ching_ in the development of Neo-Confucianism. The _I Ching_ not only nourished
the wisdom of great scholars in that period but gave them inspiration to
study. The crowning work of Neo-Confucian scholarship, by Chu Hsi (1130-
1200), would not have been possible without the _I Ching_. Thus the _I Ching_
became the background for the study of Chinese philosophy during the Sung
dynasty.

Neo-Confucianism continued to dominate the intellectual life of China
during the Ming dynasty (1368-1643). During this period the _I Ching_ was
never forgotten. It continued to be the center of philosophical development.
When the bibliography of the Chinese classics was published in 1692, more
books were written on the _I Ching_ than any other book. The _I Ching_ had been
favoured by the Chinese from the beginning of their civilization to the present time. It became not only the basis for the intellectual movements of
the past but a practical book for the common people. Until recent times the
Chinese, Korean and Japanese turned to the _I Ching_ for guidance whenever
crucial issues arose in their life. On street corners and on temple steps
we still find the _I Ching_ surrounded by the crowd of people who seek its wisdom. Even under Communist rule the _I Ching_ has never left the sentiments of
its people. Scholars on the mainland of China are still engaged in creative
disputes about this book. We do not know what the future will bring to this
book. As the conglomeration of the East and the West takes place, the _I
Ching_ may become the focal point of our investigation. We cannot predict
the place of the _I Ching_ in the coming age of world civilization but the im-
petus of this book has been self-authenticated through the countless testi-

monies of human experiences in the past. If the book can transcend itself in time and space, as it has done in the past, it will continue to be respected and loved by all the people of both the East and the West.

CHAPTER II. THE PRINCIPLE OF CHANGES

The core of the I Ching is no doubt the principle of the "I." The Chinese word "ching" 經 signifies merely a book or a classic of literature. Thus the I Ching means nothing other than the book about the I, which is translated into English as the change or the changes. The 64 hexagrams which constitute the main framework of the I Ching are based on this principle of changes. Thus the principle of changes is the central issue as well as the main theme of our discussions on the I Ching. The theoretical foundation of the I Ching is based on this principle of changes. To understand this principle is to realize the philosophical background of the changes. Let us begin our investigation of the principle of changes with its source.

1. The Source Of Our Knowledge Of The Principle Of Changes.

Where does the principle of changes come from? Before defining the meaning of changes, we may question the source of this knowledge of changes. Where did the early Chinese get the idea of changes? Did this idea come from careful research conducted in laboratories and libraries? Certainly not since they did not have laboratories and libraries such as we employ in our research. How could they then find the principle of changes without these facilities? However, we must understand that the key to careful research is the precision of observation. Today scientists attempt to discover the principle which comprehends all the phenomena of the world through a careful observation of various specimens. The giant telescopes bring the universe into the laboratory and the sophisticated microscopes reach the infinitesimal dimension of the world and bring it to our eyes. The early sages of China also received the knowledge of the principle of changes through careful observation but they did not have the elaborate tools which we have in our time. They did not know the contemporary method of experiments. But they could carry out their research for the understanding of the universe. For them nature itself became their finest laboratory. They did not have modern tools for research but they had the sensitive intuition to apprehend the key to the mystery of the world. They did not know how to conduct the experiments which we use in our time, but they knew how to examine their lives which became living experiments. As Ta Chuan says, "The holy sages could observe all the movements under heaven. They carefully surveyed how these movements were met and interpenetrated, in order to know the certain trends of movements" (Sec. I, Ch. 8). The Holy sages knew that they must be with nature in order to find the principle which governs the nature. They did not take small pieces of isolated material as a means of knowing the whole. Rather, they wanted to know the whole through the study of the whole universe. To know the law which governs nature is to be a part of it. To be a part of that which rules the whole is to be a part of the whole. Thus they became part of nature in order to understand what nature is. They lived in nature and worked with nature so that they became one with nature. Did they really know the law of gravity or the principle of relativity? The laws and principles we have discovered through scientific research were not strange to them for they lived with what is natural. However, they were unable to put them in a mathematical formula as we do but knew them as a whole and undifferentiated continuum. The principle of changes must be inclusive of all other laws which are to be discovered.

We may then question why we who also live in nature do not know much about this principle. Perhaps our answer can be either we do not live in nature or we are not sensitive to observe what is a part of us. It is questionable whether we live in nature, even though we think we do. No one denies that we are in nature. We may be in nature but we want to live outside of it. This is a dilemma which a modern man has to face in our time. We want to create something that is un-natural and to live in it. At the same time we cannot get away from nature, because we are inherently of nature. Even though we are essentially of nature we do not know what is natural because of our desire to be un-natural. This desire to be un-natural becomes one of the strongest forces underlying the creation of technical civilization today. We want to be un-natural by avoiding what is natural. We avoid the cold northern winters by escaping to the south, we avoid the hot summer with an air-conditioner, we avoid the natural light with sun-glasses, we avoid the natural water and air through pollution, we avoid natural death through the power of medicine. We cannot know what is natural because we avoid it through what is un-natural, that is, what is created by man. We are essentially of nature but we think as though we are not of it. That is why we do not know things as natural.

Even though we think we are in nature, we are not sensitive enough to comprehend directly what is natural, that is, what is as is. We do not know how to observe nature, because our sensitivity is directed to what is un-natural. We are sensitive to the power of controlling nature without knowing it. We are born in the society of un-naturalness. The desire for un-naturalness, which is a basic orientation of contemporary man, is interested in power over nature. Man's desire to dominate nature is the root of sin.

Because he wants to dominate it, he does not understand it. Moreover, modern science is interested in empirical analysis. It wants to see pieces separately and to generalize the whole from the observation of separate pieces. We observe that the day is bright but do not observe that the brightness is followed by the darkness. We see the sun during the day but don't see it during the night also. We observe our life only in a time of living but never observe that death is also a part of our life. We do not see that darkness is a part of the light and light a part of darkness. When we see a short distance of earth, the earth looks flat. Nevertheless, when we see it as a whole, it is round. Because we want to be un-natural, we observe what is partial. Just like the blind men touching different parts of an elephant and understanding different parts, if we look at the pieces separately we never get the whole truth. The holy sages who comprehended the principle of changes were able to be in nature and to observe it as a whole. They lived in nature so that they were one with nature. Just like the Taoist painter who cannot paint without being one with what is to be painted, the sages could not understand what is natural unless they were one with nature. The I Ching, therefore, is similar to the painting of nature which is represented in the hexagrams. The sages not only observed nature but contemplated it so that nature and they were united. In this oneness the inner nature of what is natural is to be understood. Thus nature becomes the source of our knowledge of the principle of changes when we are united with nature.

2. The Meaning Of Changes.

What is the principle of changes? Perhaps, one of several possible approaches to the understanding of the idea of the I is etymological. This approach is congenial to us because Chinese in particular has its origin in symbols and images. The word "I" 易 can be analyzed from the point of view of a pictogram. The archaic pictogram of this word is believed to be like this 𩇕 . It looks like a round head, a sinuous body and a number of legs. Thus it originally meant "lizard" in an old Chinese dictionary. The peculiar characteristics of the lizard are easy mobility and changeableness. The lizard is believed to change its color twelve times a day. Moreover, it can easily detach its body from its tail when it is necessary. Because of its easiness and changeableness, the word "I" was believed to have been adopted for I Ching. Another etymological explanation of the meaning of "I" is based on the analysis of this word " 易 " into two parts: " 日 " which means the sun, and " 勿 " which means to give up. The word " 勿 " is often understood as the old form of " 月 " which means the moon. From the analysis of this word, it seems possible that it has its origin in both the sun and the moon. This idea is indirectly expressed in the Ta Chuan: "Heaven is above, and the earth is below. Thus the Ch'ien and the K'un are determined. In reference to this difference between the below and above, inferior and superior positions are established" (Sec. I, Ch. 1). Here, the relationship between heaven and earth is analogous with the relationship between the sun and moon. Just as "Heaven is above," the sun " 日 " is above the moon. Just as "the earth is below," the moon " 月 " is below the sun. This relationship between the sun above and the moon below is fundamental to the word "I" 易 . Since the sun and moon, just like the heaven and earth, are two fundamental forces, the principle of changes seems to presuppose the relationship between yin and yang forces. In other words, the concept of yin and yang comes from the principle of changes.

An objection to this explanation is that the concept of <u>yin</u> and <u>yang</u> appeared much later than the formation of the <u>I Ching</u>. It is true that technical terms like "<u>yin</u>" and "<u>yang</u>" came much later than the concept of the <u>I</u>. However, the concepts of <u>yin</u> and <u>yang</u> were implicit in the idea of heaven and earth as early as the beginning of Chinese civilization. Furthermore, it is not the <u>I</u> which presupposes the existence of <u>yin</u> and <u>yang</u> forces but it is the latter developed from the former. Finally, according to the study of recently discovered material, it has been suggested that the word "<u>I</u>" could be derived from the concept of the fixed and straight.[1] This meaning is somewhat contrary to the pictographic meaning of lizard as easiness and changeableness. To summarize our etymological approach to the understanding of the principle of changes there are three characteristics which are mutually inclusive. First of all, the <u>I</u> has the meaning of easy which is characterized by the pictogram of the lizard. Secondly, it has the meaning of change and transformation which comes from both the pictogram of the lizard and the interplay of the sun and moon. Finally, it has the notion of constancy and changelessness which comes from both the etymological meaning of the fixed and straight and the constant interplay of the sun and moon. All these three characteristics of the <u>I</u> are mutually interrelated to one another. It looks almost coincidental to see that these three meanings are already described in one of the well known apocryphas, <u>I-Wei</u> <u>Ch'ien-tso-tu</u>. According to this apocrypha, the <u>I</u> has three distinctive meanings: <u>I Chien</u> 易簡 or easy and simple, <u>Pien I</u> 変易 or transformation and change, and <u>Pu I</u> 不易 or changelessness.

---

[1]Hellmut Wilhelm, "The Concept of Time in the Book of Changes" in <u>Man and Time</u>: <u>Papers From the Eranos Yearbooks</u> (N. Y. Pantheon Books, 1957), p. 212, note 2.

These three meanings are not independent but mutually inclusive. If we observe the three meanings of I, in all the word "I" appears. In the first meaning the word I is used in relation to Chien or simple. In the second the word I is used in relation to Pien or transformation, and finally, it is used in relation to Pu or its negation. The word I is common to all three definitions, and, therefore, they are mutually interrelated. If we put these characters together, we may attain the concept of I as simple, transforming and unchanging. The method of changes or I is simple, the process of changes is transformation, and the background of changes is unchanging. Its method is simple and easy, because all things are explainable through yin and yang interplay. Its process is transforming because changes take place through the trans-formation of lines of hexagrams. Its background is unchanging, because the principle of changes itself is the Tao, the Way. Before we discuss these three aspects of changes, we must make clear what we mean by changes. Thus let us first focus our attention on the meaning of changes.

What is the meaning of the changes itself? Why is the principle of changes a key to the understanding of the universal phenomena? Perhaps one of the most significant words which is common to all things in the world is the word "I" or "changes." It is significant because everything is changing. Nothing is without change. Every moment is in the process of change. Nothing can remain the same forever. Everything is conditioned by change. Even time and space are conditioned by change. It is not time which effects the change, but it is the principle of change which moves time. The principle of changes penetrates all existing things whether matter or spirit whether external or internal dimensions of life. Change affects all. This is why the principle of changes is the key to the understanding of all things in the universe. The sages of China learned the principle of changes through the careful observation of nature. The very essence of nature became their teacher. In heaven the sun and the moon change their directions. When the sun reaches its zenith, it begins to decline. When the moon is full, it wanes again. When night reaches its peak, the day begins to expand. On earth high mountains become valleys, and the valleys become hills, and the hills become fields. Trees grow and die, flowers bloom and decay. The winter is followed by the spring, just as the decay is followed by new life. Man cannot stop aging. Pride brings him down and modesty wins love. Man's way of thinking changes and his pattern of behavior also changes. Customs change just as fashions change from time to time. Nothing is the same forever. From the movement of solar systems to the motion of electrons in the magnetic field of atoms, the principle of changes is working. Everything is changing but the change itself is unchanging.

The best example of the principle of change is running water. It was the great sage, Confucius, who, standing by a river one day, said: "Like this river, everything is flowing on ceaselessly, day and night."[1] Running water does not stand still. It moves always from the higher to the lower place. It never stays in the same place, for it moves constantly. It never repeats the same course. Everything in the universe can be compared with running water. The universe itself is in flux. It moves constantly to create from old the new and from the new to what is newer than the new. It moves all things to trans-form other so that the new may be created. Just like the water everything is in transition. Nothing is permanent. Nothing

---

[1]Analects 9:16.

is absolutely sure and right. Everything is relative and conditioned by the principle of changes. Changes are effected to all, but the principle of changes itself is changeless.

Change is more than mere movement. It moves to transfer what was to what is and from what is to what will be. It transfers things to create something anew from the old, and to create something old from what is new. The opposite of change is not what is unchanging but movement in an opposite direction. Change is natural movement but the opposite of change is movement against nature. To move according to what is natural is spontaneous. Thus change is spontaneous and natural. Since anything that is natural is spontaneous what is spontaneous is change. The change is expressed by both external and internal phenomena. There is a continuity between what is internal and what is external. The inner movement is conditioned by the external change just as the latter is conditioned by the former. Change has the power to transform and recreate all things in the universe. Wherever the production and reproduction or growth and decay are evident in the world, they are the signs of change.

Things in the universe are always in a state of flux but never in a state of chaos. They are in order, because the principle of changes moves them according to definite trends and courses. "Events are arranged according to their kinds. Things are classified into definite classes... Images are formed in the heaven, and forms are shaped on earth. In this way change takes place" (Ta Chuan, Sec. I, Ch. 1). The change takes place in a definite course because it is based on the procreation of life. The change is "the begetter of all begetting." It is the source of all that procreate and recreate. It is also the power which renews itself and gives the strength of transformation to all. It is the life-giving to death and the life-taking to the living. In change life and death are one. From life to death and from death to life change renews and transforms all according to their respective trends and natures. Change brings forth the recurrence but never the repetition of the same. Things come and go and man is born and dies again and again but there is no repetition for all things are relative.

Everything is subject to the eternal principle of changes. Our way of thinking, our attitude, our looks and our relation to others are changing. The order and disorder, the success and failure, the progress and decay, the joy and sorrow, the glory and tragedy, indeed every moment of our existence, is subject to this principle of changes. Nothing can escape from the principle of changes. As John Cage said,

> That moment is always changing. (I was silent: now I am speaking). How can we possibly tell what contemporary music is, since now we're not listening to it, we're listening to a lecture about it. And that isn't it. This is "tongue-wagging." Removed as we are this moment from contemporary music (We are only thinking about it) each one of us is thinking his own thoughts, his own experience, and each experience is changing, and while we are thinking I am talking and contemporary music is changing. Like life it changes. If it were not changing it would be dead, and, of course, for some of us, sometimes it is dead, but at any moment it changes and is live again.[1]

Even contemporary music, art, education and life are changing. What we think of contemporary phenomena is only a static form in our thought. Even our thinking is changing. It is not the now which we possess but the moment which possesses us. The now moment is also possessed by the change. We are the slave of time, and time is the slave of change. Nothing is absolute but

---

[1]John Cage, Silence: Lectures and Writings (Cambridge: M.I.T., 1961), p. 44.

change itself is absolutely unchanging.

The way of change is easy and simple. It is easy, because it is simple. It is simple, because it is easy. As it is said in the Ta Chuan:

> The Ch'ien knows through the easy. The K'un does things
> through the simple. It is easy, because it is easy to
> know. It is simple, because it is simple to follow. He
> who is easy to know makes friends. He who is simple to
> follow performs good works. He who possesses friends can
> endure forever, and he who performs good works can become
> great. To indure is the power of the sage, and greatness
> is the affair of the sage. By means of the easy and the
> simple the laws of the whole world are known. When the
> laws of the whole world are known, the sage makes his posi-
> tion in the middle (Sec. I, Ch. 1).

The easy is the counterpart of the simple, just as Creativity is the coun-

terpart of Responsivity. Creativity acts easily, for Responsivity responds

simply. Just as Creativity and Responsivity are gates for all things in the

universe the easy and simple are the ways of change. Everything changes

according to what is easy and simple. The simplicity of changes arises

out of pure responsivity while the ease of changes arises out of direct

action. What is natural is pure and direct. What is pure and direct is spon-

taneous, and what is spontaneous is simple and easy. The way of changes is

simple and easy because it is only a slight transference of a line of hexagrams.

All the changes in the universe essentially result from the uniting and the

dividing lines of hexagrams. It is analogous to an electron jumping out of

its own magnetic field and moving into another field so that the structure of

atoms changes. There is nothing simpler and easier than this method. To unite

the divided lines and to divide the united lines are the simplest and easiest

way of change. Certainly, the way of changes is easy and simple.

The way of changes is also constant and invariable. The water never

flows from lower to higher ground, the sun never rises from the West, the moon never comes out druing the day time. The father is seated and the son bows before him. The ruler rules and the servant serves. Creativity acts and Responsivity responds. The principle of changes is constant and irreversible. The ways of heaven and earth are observed correctly, and the ways of the sun and moon emit their light. Thus all the movements under heaven are constantly subject to this one and the same rule" (Ta Chuan, Sec. II, Ch. 1). The constancy and regularity of changes are the very essence of the eternal and invariable principle of changes. Everything in the universe results from this irreversible principle of changes. The change that is unchanging is the principle of changes. As William Ernest Hocking has pointed out, "As a first principle, the changeless is of course insufficient. Our Ultimate Reality must have qualities of both changelessness and change."[1] The change that is changless is the Tao of heaven and earth: "The tao of heaven and earth is constant and unceasing. It is advantageous to turn in any direction. If there is end, there must be beginning. The sun and moon acquire heaven and shine constantly. The four seasons are changed and transformed to produce all things... When this constancy is understood, the nature of heaven and earth and all things can be known" (T'uan Chuan, Sec. II, Hex. 32). Again, we read from T'uan Chuan: "Heaven and earth show that docile obedience in connection with movement, and hence the sun and moon make no error (in time), and the four seasons do not deviate (from their order). The sages show such docile obedience in connection with their movements, and hence their punish-

---

[1]William Ernest Hocking, The Meaning of God in Human Experience (New Haven: Yale University Press, 1912), p. 188.

ments and penalties are entirely just, and the people acknowledge it by their submission" (Sec. I, hex. 16, line 3).[1] The constancy and irreversibility which are the very essence of changes are the mystery of the principle of changes. The mystery of change is precisely "change that is the unchangeable." This mystery presents the best meaning of the change in the I Ching.

3. The Basic Constituents of Changes

When, then, are the basic constituents of this principle of changes? As we have already indicated the holy sages discovered the principle of changes through a careful observation of the phenomena of the world. Nature became their teacher and the world their laboratory. Society became the place to apply the principle gained from nature. Therefore, what constitutes the changes is known in nature. They saw that changes were produced through the interaction of two opposite poles. Everything in the universe has to do with the polarity of opposites. On earth day and night bring light and darkness. Summer and winter bring heat and cold. Solids and liquids are dry and wet. Everything has its opposite. There are male and female, positive and negative, creative and Responsive, and active and passive. Nothing can exist without its counterpart. Even in natural science cosmic polarities are seen. Cause and effect become effective tools for the study of nature. Chance and causality as well as rest and motion are the basis for the understanding of cosmic principles. Polarities are the basis for all things. Even in our mind creative thinking is often possible through the polarity of opposites. Love and hate,

---

[1]Legge's Translation.

attraction and repulsion, reason and faith are necessary for creative minds.
Without contraries there is no progression. This was why Hegel constructed
the system of dialectical method, the synthesis of counterpoles, which produces progression. Polarities occur even in our experiences. Our experience
of the sacred presupposes that of the secular. Our experience of the ultimate
is counterbalanced with that of the penultimate. What is painful cannot be
comprehended without the experience of pleasure, and what is sorrowful is known
only when what is joyful is experienced. What is good cannot be understood
without what is not good. The counterpole of right is wrong, and that of pride
is humility. If there is a master, there must be a servant, and if there is
parent, there must be a child. If there is a teacher, there must be a student.
Polarities are also expressed in art and architecture as well. If there is light,
then there must be shade. When there is form, there is content. There are polarities of symmetry and variation, unity and diversity, and strength and delicacy. In sculpture and painting these contrasts are the basis of beauty.
The greatness of music comes from the contrast of sounds. Drama and literature become alive through the contradictions, counter forces, and paradoxes
of expression and emotion. Dancing combines poise and movement. There is
nothing in the world that does not have its opposite. This is the way of
nature. Everything comes in opposites. Even invisible atomic structure consists of a polarity of electronic charges. These polarities are the basis
for all things which exist in the world. However, this polarity is not possible without unity. As Chang Tsai said, duality is impossible without unity
and the unity cannot exist without duality.[1] Duality is necessary for the

---

[1]Chang Tsai, Collected Works, Book 2, Section 1.

unity of all polarities and unity is essential for the polarities of inter-relationship. "Opposition may well be," as Royce held, "a necessary step in search for the whole truth."[1] The movement of duality toward union and that of separation from that union create changes. The process of changes is, therefore, simple and easy because it is the change within the counterpoles of movement. This idea is often expressed as "contrapletion," which implies that two poles of thought, while they stand over against one another (contra), at the same time fulfill one another (plere).[2] The principle of changes is nothing other than the relationship between the counterpoles, which came to be known in China as yin and yang polarity. The counterpoles of yin and yang are the basic constituents of the principle of changes which affects all things. The constant movement of yin and yang makes the constant flow of the universe possible. Therefore, Ch'en I in the time of the Sung Dynasty said, "There is only one system of action and response. What we call yin and yang are everywhere. Take, for example, the front and rear. The front is yang and rear is yin. Or take two sides. The left is yang and the right is yin. Or again take the above and below. The above is yang and the below is yin."[3] Since everything in the universe can be reduced to a relationship between yin and yang, the principle of changes is certainly easy and simple.

It is very difficult to trace the origin of the idea of yin and yang relationship even though the concept of yin and yang became technical around

---

[1] Josiah Royce, Lectures on Modern Idealism (New Haven: Yale University, 1919), p. 96.

[2] Louis William Norris, Polarity: A Philosophy of Tension Among Values (Chicago: Herry Regnery, 1956), p. 8.

[3] Ch'eng I, I-shu (Surviving Works) 15:7b.

third century B.C. It was during the former Han dynasty when the relationship of yin and yang became prominent through the rise of the so-called
"Five Elements" or "Five Stages of Movement" school. However, the concept
of yin and yang was implicit in the relationship between heaven and earth
in the most primitive stage of Chinese civilization. As we have already
noted, in the Ho T'u or the River Map, which was thought to be available to
the legendary king Fu Hsi, we find the implicit notion of yin and yang or
the light and dark dots.   The question is whether this map was a recreation
of the yin-yang school or not. Whether or not it was, the concept of polarity was known by the Chinese much earlier than the yin-yang school of thought.
The eight trigrams already presuppose the existence of a heaven and earth relationship as the primordial principle of all other existence. The trigrams
heaven (☰) and earth (☷) are the basis for other trigrams. Furthermore, the hexagrams Ch'ien and K'un become the basis for the formation of all
other hexagrams in the I Ching. The concept of the yin and yang relationship

was implicit in the idea of heaven and earth which was shared by both the
Confucian and Taoist schools of thought. The relationship between heaven and
earth is the most inclusive symbol of Chinese civilization and represents the
foundation of metaphysical speculations. The word "heaven" or t'ien 天 has
an inclusive meaning. It includes the idea of both sky and personal God. The
concept of God in China came from the concept of a personified heaven. On the
other hand, the concept of earth came to be used in China as a counterpart of
heaven. The earth was used to denote not only the soil but the mothergod
figure. The most primitive form of the Chinese word for earth, t'u 土 , is

similar to the meaning of soil. It might have been possible for the primitive people of China to personify the soil or earth as the Great Mother who produced and raised trees, crops and flowers through the recption of rain from the personified heaven. Earth and heaven were personified. Earth receives rain from heaven and produces all things. The relationship between earth and heaven was analogous with that of Mother and Father or Female and Male. In Ta Chuan it is said: "The Tao of Creativity (heaven) produces the male. The tao of Responsivity (earth) produces the female" (Sec. I, Ch. 1). The interaction between heaven and earth can be compared with intercourse between a father and mother or between a male and female. The polarity between the above and the below or between heaven and earth is to indicate the relative position of the male and female. The sexuality of hexagrams is clearly shown in the shapes of the lines. The straight or firm line (———) symbolizes the male sex organ while the divided or weak line (— —) symbolizes the female sex organ. The sex symbols of both the firm and yielding or the straight and divided lines are clearly expressed in their movements. The Creativity which represents the firm line or yang line moves forward, while the Responsivity which represents the yielding or yin line opens for Creativity. It is stated in the Ta Chuan: "In a state of rest the Ch'ien (Creativity) is concentrated, and in a state of motion it is straight. Thus it produces the great. The K'un (Responsivity) is closed in a state of rest, and it is open in a state of motion. Thus it produces the vast" (Sec. I, Ch. 6). The commentary to this passage makes such clear: "The movement of the Creative is a direct forward movement, and its resting state is standstill; the movement of the Receptive (Responsivity) is an opening out, and in its resting state it is closed. In resting, closed state, it embraces all things as though in a vast womb. In the state of movement. of opening, it allows the divine light to enter, and by means of this light illuminates everything."[1]   Intercourse between heaven and earth or male and female procreates all things, just as the interaction between _yin_ and _yang_ creates everything which exists in the universe. Here, we find that the origin of human life is taken as an example to illustrate the origin of all things. The genital influence of heaven and earth as procreation of another existence is not different from the interplay of _yin_ and _yang_ forces as the basis of all phenomena in the universe. Certainly the symbols of _yin_ and _yang_ were implicit in those of heaven and earth.

Yin, like earth, possesses female qualities such as tender, passive, receptive and quiescent character, while _yang_, like heaven, possesses male qualities such as the strong, active, positive and creative. Both _yin_ and _yang_ seemed to bear impersonal categories. The word "_yin_" 陰 signifies "overshadowing," while the word "_yang_" 陽 literally means "brightness." The constrast between _yin_ and _yang_ originally came from the conept of the northern and southern slopes of a mountain. The mountain slope where the sun shines is the _yang_ side, while the northern slope which is overshadowed is called _yin_ side. _Yang_ then represents what is bright or light, while _yin_ represents what is dark and shadowy. In the _Ta Chuan_ Creativity is identified with the light thing, and Responsivity with the dark thing: "Creativity and Responsivity are the gateways to the changes. The Creativity represents light things and the Responsivity dark things. In the union of both the dark and the light, the firm and weak (lines) reveal themselves. In this way the phenomena of heaven and earth come to manifest and the power of spirits is clearly perceived"

---

[1] R. Wilhelm, tr. _op._ _cit._, p. 387.

(Sec. II, Ch. 6). Here, the Creativity and Responsivity or the Heaven and Earth become the prototypes of the light and the dark or the yang and the yin. Therefore, the category of yin and yang becomes the microcosm of heaven and earth.

Just as the interaction of yin and yang becomes the basis for Chinese cosmology, it is also the origin of Japanese cosmology. According to Japanese mythology, "everything in this cosmos as well as all the deities were produced by the creative spirit of the two kami, namely, the kami of High Generative Force and the kami of Divine Generative Force."[1] The kami of High Generative Force is analogous to the Creative force of Heaven, and the kami of Divine Generative Force can be compared with the Receptive energy of Earth in the I Ching. The former is the male deity known as Izanagi, and the latter the female deity known as Izanami. According to the creation myth of Shintoism both of them were responsible for the procreation of the island of Japan and the myriad of all other things in the world. The story about the union of these two deities for the procreation of the Japanese islands is mixed with a considerable amount of humor:

> The Divine couple (Izanagi and Izanami) decided onto this island, where they built a sacred Bower with a high thick pillar at its center. Around this pillar the Female Deity turned from the right to the left, while the Male Deity turned the same from the left to the right. When they met in this way, she first addressed herself to him: "Oh, what a fine and handsome youth you are!" Whereupon he courteously responded to her amorous call, saying: "How pretty and lovely a maiden you are!" When they thus became united in marriage, they begot a misshpen leech which they straightway placed in a reed-boat and sent a

---

[1]Motoori Norinaga, Complete Works of Motoori Norinaga, p. 546; J. Kitagawa, "Religions of Japan" in Great Asian Religions (N. Y.: Macmillan, 1969), p. 296.

lift to the sea.[1]

As the story indicates, the concept of the yin and yang symbolizes the center of cosmic regeneration in Japan.

A similar idea is also expressed in Indian Cosmology. In the later development of Hinduism, for example, the Samkhya system of thought speaks of Prakriti, the feminine creative power, and Purusa, the male creative power. Moreover, the polarity of both male and female powers is implicit in the concept of male and female gods in India. The idea of polarity is much more clearly evident in the category of Indian thinking. "India is ever reluctant to accept any one-sided statement. One of her fundamental axioms is that of polarity, which implies that one part of a pair of opposites cannot be exclusively taken into account. Each statement is based on the simultaneous acknowledgement of its counter-statement."[2]

It becomes clear then that the axiom of polarity as the basis of cosmology is not merely a Chinese idea but an Oriental concept. This category of Oriental thinking, which is very clearly expressed in the I Ching, is different from the concept of polarity in the West. In the West the dichotomy between the opposing poles is so sharply divided that they are irreconcilable. The West seemed to follow the Zoroastrian notion of the ultimate dichotomy between the Good and Evil. This dichotomy leads Western man to think in terms of "either/or" category. In the East, especially in the I Ching, the polarity between yin and yang is not in terms of a dichotomy but in terms of a complementary relationship. This idea of complementary relationship between the

---

[1]Chikao Fujisawa, Zen and Shinto: The Story of Japanese Philosophy (New York: Philosophical Library, 1959), pp. 5-6.

[2]Betty Heimann, Facets of Indian Thought (N.Y.: Schocken, 1964), p. 56.

opposing poles is quite different from the "coincidence of opposites" or
coincidentia oppositorum, which was introduced in the West by Nicholas of
Cusa. The latter coincides but does not complement. It is not a creative
unity in harmony as is in the relationship between yin and yang.

According to the mutual relationship between yin and yang in the
principle of changes, one cannot exist without the other. Both of them are
inseparable. Yin cannot exist without yang. In this kind of relationship,
"Union is sure to give place to separation and by that separation will issue
in re-union."[1] This idea of both unity and separation and separation in unity
is implicit in both the divided and undivided hexagram lines in the I Ching.
In the process of transformation, the whole line (or undivided line) pushes
outward and becomes thin in the middle and breaks in two to form the divided
line. The divided line, on the other hand, pushes inward and grows together
as a whole line. Thus the divided and undivided lines are not separate entities but one in two different aspects. The unity and separation of these
opposites are thus spontaneous and simultaneous. Since every moment is the
moment of transformation and the process of change, the trans-formation of
lines continues without ceasing. The constant change within the universe is
then nothing other than the constant trans-formation of lines from the whole
to the divided and from the divided to the whole. That is why the principle
of changes is easy and simple. The union and separation of yin and yang are
similar to the opening and closing gates of heaven and earth. Just as everything in the universe proceeds from heaven and earth toward interaction, all
things are the procreation of the union and separation of yin and yang forces.

---

[1]Legge, tr., op. cit., p. 55.

4. The Tao As The Source And Background Of Changes

We may now question the origin of the basic constituents of change, that is, the origin of yin and yang forces. To question the origin of yin and yang is to question the ultimate ground of all existence and the order of the universe. The origin of yin and yang, that is, the ultimate ground of all things, is attributed in China to "Tao," which literally means the Way. A specific reference to the relationship between the Tao and yin and yang is found in the Ta Chuan: "One yin and one yang are called Tao" (Sec. I, Ch. 5).[1] In the same chapter of Ta Chuan the idea of "Change" is expressed as similar to that of "Tao," the source of all things: "The begetter of all begetting is called the Change." A commentary on this verse makes clear the relationship between the Tao and yin and yang: "The dark (yin) begets the light (yang) and the light (yang) begets the dark (yin) in ceaseless alternation, but that which begets this alternation, that to which all life owes its existence, is tao with its law of change."[2] It is clear from this illustration that the word "tao" is interchangeably used with the word "change." However, the word "I" or Change is not identical with "Tao" or Way, even though they are interchangeably used in the Ta Chuan. Just as the Tao accomplishes great things without action,[3] "The Change has no thought, no action. It is quiescent and still" (Ta Chuan, Sec. I, Ch. 10). However, the

---

[1]This is the literal translation of " 一陰一陽之謂道 ." R. Wilhelm's translation of this passage is as follows: "That which lets now the dark, now the light, appear is tao."

[2]Richard Wilhelm, tr. , op. cit., pp. 299-300.

[3]Lao-tzu, Tao Te Ching, Ch. 63.

Tao and I or Change are not identical but one in two different dimensions.
The Tao becomes the background of the Change, and the Change the foreground
of the Tao. The Tao is the background which makes the interaction between
yin and yang possible, and the Change is the foreground which is the movement
of yin and yang itself. The concept of the Tao in relation to the Change is
best defined as "the change that is unchangeable." On the other hand, the
concept of the Change in relation to the Tao can be stated as "the Changeless
that changes." Thus they are one in two different aspects. Since both of
them cannot be separated one from the other, to mention the Tao is in fact
to mention the Change, and to mention the Change is to mention the Tao. Thus
the Tao implies the Change and the Change also implies the Tao. To illustrate this, we can compare the concept of the I or the Change in the Ta Chuan
and that of the Tao in the Tao Te Ching. According to the former, "The Great
Ultimate is in the I. It produces the two primary forms. The two primary
forms produce the four images. The four images produce the eight trigrams"
(Sec. I, Ch. 11). According to the latter, Lao-tzu remarks, "The Way
begot one, and the one, two; then the two begot three and three all else"
(Ch. 42).[1] The Great Ultimate or the Primal Beginning in the Ta Chuan seems
to correspond to the One in Tao Te Ching, the two primary forces to the two,
and trigrams (which consist of three lines) to the three. Here, we can
see the correspondence of the Tao with the Change, because they are mutually
complementing each other. It is reasonable to believe that Lao-tzu seems to
be aware of the principle of changes. He taught that all things move constantly
and restlessly but at the same time they proceed back to their own origin. Pro-

---

[1] R. B. Blankney's Translation.

ceeding back to their origin, that is, to the Tao, means quiescence. To be
quiescent is to be "all changing-changeless." Or it is, as we have said,
"the change that is unchangeable." Just as quiescence or silence is the
background of sound, the Tao becomes the background of change. Just as sound
is the foreground of silence, Change is the foreground of the Tao. Since the
Tao is the background of the Change, it is not known. As Lao-tzu begins his
Tao Te Ching with "The Tao that can be told of is not the absolute Tao," it
is not expressible. It is similar to the Indian idea of the so-called
"Attributeless Brahman," which becomes the background of continual changes
and transformations as well as the eternal source of cosmic waves. It can be
grasped only as neti-neti, "the not-this, not that." It is free from continuous flow and transformation but also a part of it. As Heimann said, "It
(Brahman) is bound to a double aspect: constant reality and yet changing
activity. Brahman is the satyasya satyam, the reality of all existent realities, i.e., the essentially constant factor within all changes."[1] Brahman,
like the Tao, becomes the background of the Change, that is, "the change that
is unchangeable." The Tao is also similar to the Western idea of "Logos,"
it is often understood as the reality of cosmic process or the life-principle
of all things. However, the concept of the Tao presupposes dynamism while
that of the Logos in Greek philosophy presupposes a static view of the universe.

Perhaps the relationship between the Tao and the Change is more
clearly expressed in the concept of "li" 理 and "ch'i" 氣, which appeared
with the development of Neo-Confucianism during the Sung Dynasty. Ch Hsi

---

[1]Heimann, op. cit., p. 61.

remarked that no ch'i exists with li. The word "li" literally means principle while the word "ch'i" means vitality. Their relationship is similar to the Aristotelian notion of form and matter, even though the former is based on a dynamic and organic view of the universe. However, it is a mistake to translate ch'i as matter. Rather it is similar to energy which is also matter since contemporary physics understands that energy and matter are one. If the ch'i is energy it is also the Change. On the other hand, li, the embracing principle of cosmos, is also the Tao. However, the li alone is not the Tao but the li with ch'i, just as the Tao alone is not the li but the Tao with the Change. This relationship cannot be described in the "either/or" category but only in the "both/and" category. As Chang suggests,

> The ch'i fills the Great Ethereal. It goes up, it comes down, or it flies high without cessation. This is what the I Ching refers to as the real secret of the Changes, or what is called by Chuang-tzu the dust flying like a wild horse. Ch'i, which sometimes goes up or at other times comes down, is the beginning of motion or rest. What goes up is the light, yang part, what comes down is the heavy, yin part. It can consolidate or dissolve in the form of wind and rain, snow and frost, mountains and rivers, and myriad other things.[1]

The part of the ch'i which moves is the yang, while that which remains quiescent is the yin. Both the yang and yin pertain to the ch'i, whereas the li becomes the background of these interactions. Chu Hsi said, "Within the universe there are li and ch'i. Li constitutes the Tao that is 'above shaped'; it is the source from which things are produced. Ch'i constitutes the 'instruments' (ch'i 器) that are 'within shapes'; it is the (material)

---

[1]Carsun Chang, The Development of Neo-Confucian Thought (N.Y. Boodman Associates, 1962), p. 172.

means whereby things are produced."[1] Chu Hsi believed that the concept of

li was used to mean the Tao, but used the ch'i as the instrument (which is

also ch'i 器) because the same pronunciation is difficult for the Western

mind to understand. The ch'i as the instrument means the material content

within the form, and not the form which receives the content. Here again we

are faced with the question of the form and content relationship which was

used by Greek philosophy. This relationship is good in so far as it pre-

supposes a dynamic and organic world view. Just as the form and content are

without each other, "in the universe there has never been any material force

(ch'i) without principle (li) or principle (li) without material force

(ch'i)."[2] Here, we see the relationship between li and ch'i is analogous

with that between the Tao and the Change. Using this analogy we may be able

to determine the priority of emphasis between the Tao and the Change.

According to Chu Hsi, "the principle (li) and material force (ch'i)

cannot be spoken of as prior or posterior. But if we must trace their origin,

we are obliged to say that principle (li) is prior. However, principle (li)

is not a separate entity. It exists right in material force (ch'i)."[3] Since

the principle (li) corresponds to the Tao and the ch'i to the Change, we are

also obliged to say that the Tao is prior to the I or the Change. However,

the Tao is not a separate entity from the Change. The distinction is merely

a functional one. Since the Tao is the background of the Change, it is rea-

sonable to believe the priority of the Tao if we have to make a choice. The

[1]Chu Si, Chu Wen-kung Wen-chi (Collected Writings of Chu Hsi), 58:5.
[2]Chu Hsi, Chu Tzu ch'uan-shu (Complete Works of Chu Hsi), 49:1a.
[3]Ibid., 49:1b.

priority of the Tao to the Change is consistent with that of yang to the yin. According to Ta Chuan, "there is in the I the t'ai chi (the Great Beginning). This generates the two primary forces" (Sec. I, Ch. 11). Originally, the word "chi" 極 meant the ridgepole--a simple line symbolizing the whole line (————). Thus t'ai chi 太極 means the great (t'ai) whole line, which means the great yang. This great yang or t'ai chi generates the yin and yang forces, which are symbolized by the divided and the whole lines. Thus the yang in principle has the priority of being just as the Tao has its priority over the Change.

What does the priority of the Tao to the Change mean? Since the Tao is the background of the Change it is prior to the beginning of all changes in the universe. The beginning of changes means the beginning of all beings because beings and changes are simultaneous. To be is to change and to change is to be. Thus the priority of the Tao to the Change means to be before all beings. To be before all beings means to be non-being. Thus the Tao can be described at its best in terms of non-being or Void which signifies the priority of all beings. However, we must be reminded that the Tao is not merely non-being only but always the non-being with being, for the former presupposes the latter. The idea of non-being or Void, which is attributed to the Tao, is a later development in Chinese philosophy. This concept was undoubtedly introduced by Buddhist scholars in the late Han era. The concept of Void or nothingness became convenient for Neo-Confucian scholars who constructed an intelligent argument concerning Chinese cosmology. The application of this idea, by Chou Tun-yi, was already seen in the early period of the Neo-Confucian movement. Chou Tun-yi is known as the forerunner of the intellectual movement which flourished in the Sung dynasty. He uses the term "wu chi"

無極 or the ultimateless to express its priority to the supreme ultimate. Even though Chou Tun-yi's use of this term "Ultimateless" was influenced by Buddhism, we can trace this idea back to Lao-tzu's concept of the Tao as the limitless and infinite. I believe that the concept of Nothingness or the Void came to be used through the synthesis of both Buddhist and Taoist notions concerning the origins of the Ultimate. Wang Pi in his commentary to the I Ching applies the concept of Non-being or Wu 無 prior to being or yu 有 . "Thus though Heaven and Earth, in their greatness, are richly endowed with the myriad things; though their thunder moves and their winds circulate; though their evolving operations the myriad transformations came to be--yet it is the silent and supreme non-being that is their origin."[1] In the process of manipulation of the fifty yarrow stalks for the consultation of the I Ching, one is set aside and never used. For this Wang Pi derives a special meaning. The one which is set aside and not used for manipulation represents the non-being, which manifests the beings of 49. One is not numbered but through it all numbers are formed. Because one is the basis from which all other numbers are built, it is non-being or the Tao. In this way Wang Pi provides the rationale to explain why one is set aside. Thus non-being which is not used signifies the priority of its origin to all other numbers which are used for manipulation.

As we have indicated, the concept of non-being or mu was first used by the Taoists who were influenced by Buddhism in China. The evidence for the concept of non-being in the early development of Buddhism is clearly apparent in the group of Buddhists known as the liu chia 六家 or six houses and ch'i

---

[1] Wang Pi, Chou I 3:4.

tsung 士宗 or seven schools during the period of Disunity. They began to speculate about the word "k'ung" 空 or "śūnyatā" as a substitute for non-being or wu. Tao-an (312-385), for example, expounded the concept of original non-being or pen-wu 本無 . He believed that the concept of śūnyatā or k'ung was identical with the origin of non-being. By definition k'ung is the void or emptiness, which is beyond all attributions. The concept of emptiness or void must not be conceived of as the Western understanding of nihilism. The concept of k'ung or original non-being is the affirmation of all existence through the negation of all. This seems like a contradictory statement. But in k'ung or void nothing opposes or excludes. It transcends all the possible opposites and includes both the affirmation and the negation of all existence. The Tao, like the concept of k'ung, also transcends the dichotomy between being and non-being or negation and affirmation. The Tao as the background of the Change means k'ung or śūnyatā.

Perhaps one of the best illustrations for our Western understanding of the concept of the Tao as the k'ung is the idea of zero which we use every day. It is more than a mere accident that the Chinese word "k'ung" also means zero in mathematics. Furthermore, the Sanskrit word "śūnyatā" means zero also. Actually, the term for zero in Sanskrit is nirvanām or śūnyatā. Therefore, it is perfectly acceptable to say that the meaning of the Tao as k'ung or śūnyatā is zero. We know that zero (0) is more than a mere symbol or number. It is non-being or void because it in itself is not a number. On the other hand, it is also the symbol of all numbers. Zero in itself is not a number but paradoxically has the potentiality of all numbers. It is, in other words, both non-number and all numbers. It is of both the positive and the negative. It is the matrix of all and none. It transcends all the differentiation between the negative and positive and between the expansion and the contraction. It does not exhaust either infinite expansion and contraction. It is like an embryo, the ever-swelling germ, which contains all the possible forms of productive potentiality. No matter how many fractional numbers and diminutive numbers we may add to it, it cannot be exhausted. No matter how many numbers we may combine or multiply we cannot make zero. No matter how many immeasurably minute numbers might be added together we cannot make zero. The invisible atom-like substance is still greater than zero. The productive potentiality of zero is beyond all arithmetical categories of addition, subtraction, division and multiplication. "Zero transcends all empirical data, all ciphers and forms, and yet, just because of this, it is the basis of all empirical data."[1] The transcendental nature of zero is identical with the Tao as the background of constant change and flow. Just like the zero the Tao is both incalculably great and small simultaneously. It transcends all possible opposites and dichotomies for it is the basis for the complementary relationship of both yin and yang. The Tao, the background of Change, is, like the zero, all-excluding yet all-embracing reality. This reality alone is absolute. Just like the zero is used with numbers, the Tao does not exist by itself but always with the Change. Thus the Tao is known to us through the Change, and the Change is active because of the Tao. Just like the number, the Change is the foreground of the Tao.

The Change as the foreground of the Tao is analogous to the number as the foreground of the zero. Zero is similar to the Tao and numbers to the changes. Zero not only has infinite possibility but also finite actuality.

---

[1]Heimann, op. cit., p. 99.

Zero presupposes numbers and the latter the former, just as the Tao presupposes the changes and the changes the Tao. Zero and numbers (from one to nine) complement one another. The limited numbers from one to nine can be expanded and contracted indefinitely when zero is added to them indefinitely. The limitation of numbers without zero is quite evident. The number 1 cannot exceed 9 unless zero is added to it. Without zero the changes in numbers are limited. Any number which is greater than 9 or less than 1 requires zero. Thus the changes within these limited numbers, from 1 to 9, must be either an expansion or a contraction. When the number reaches 9, it has to revert to its opposite. When it reaches one it reverts again toward nine. The constant changes of these numbers can be compared with the swing of a pendulum. Since these numbers, from one to nine, are the foreground of zero, and zero is the background of these numbers, both zero and the numbers are inseparable. The numbers presuppose the zero, and the latter the former. However, the numbers in themselves are limited, just like the Change in itself is limited. The Change is limited within the two poles of yin and yang, just as the numbers are limited within one and nine. The Change is confined within these two categories. Yin changes to yang, and yang changes to yin. When yin reaches its peak, it begins to change to be yang, and when yang reaches its peak, it changes to yin again. When yin is in its peak, it is called the old yin (— —), which changes to young yang (— —). The young yang is still growing or expanding toward the fuller life. When it is fully expanded and reaches its peak it becomes the old yang (———), which changes to the young yin (———) again. In this way the change between yin and yang takes place. This constant interchange according to expansion and contraction is the foreground of the Tao. This process of changes in terms of expansion and contraction or growth and

decay is conceived from the observation of the natural porcess of changes.
As is in Ta Chuan, we learn the principle of changes from nature. "When
the sun goes, the moon comes. When the moon goes, the sun comes. The alternation of sun and moon produces light. When cold goes, heat comes. When
heat goes, cold comes. The alternation of cold and heat completes the year.
What is gone contracts. What is to come expands. The alternation of contraction and expansion produces the advancement" (Ta Chuan, Sec. II, Ch. 5).

The principle of changes according to contraction and expansion, first
of all, presupposes the limitation of that which changes. Just like the numbers from 1 to 9, the foreground of zero, are limited in themselves, everything that is subject to change, the foregrcund of the Tao, is limited.
Nothing in the universe can either expand or contract indefinitely but can
both expand and contract infinitely. Since things cannot indefinitely either
expand or contract they must be limited. Things are within the limitation of
both expansion and contraction. This limitation can be applied to both microcosmic and macrocosmic changes. In microcosmic changes the expansion and
contraction are limited within the poles of yin and yang. In macrocosmic
changes the poles of expansion and contraction are limited within the universe.
This concept eventually draws a conclusion that the universe, the foreground
of the Tao, is limited. The traditional Western view of cosmos as infinitude
does not fit the cosmology of the I Ching. If the cosmos is infinite it can
either expand or contract indefinitely. It is then almost necessary to say
that the universe must be finite if the principle of changes in terms of expansion and contraction is valid. The universe is finite but its change is
indefinite. However, the finite universe is also infinite because of the Tao,

which is the background of the Change. In other words, the foreground of
the Tao is limited but the background of the Change is infinite. The finite universe is the foreground of the Tao which is infinite. Since the
Change is inseparable from the Tao, the universe is finite from the process
of changes in terms of expansion and contraction but is infinite because of
the Tao. The Universe is then both finite and infinite. It is contrary to
the "either/or" logic of the West but is a sound statement. The universe is
finite when it is seen in terms of the Change while it is infinite when it
is seen from the Tao. Moreover, the foreground of the absolute is transitory
and the background of the Change is unchangeable. Thus what is changeable
is limited and is inseparable from what is unlimited. The foreground of the
unlimited, that is, the limited, is subject to the principle of changes in
terms of contraction and expansion. We may take up a hexagram and examine
its limitation according to the changes in terms of expansion and contraction.
Let us take the first hexagram, Ch'ien or Creativity, which consists of

six unbroken lines. The principle of changes in terms of contraction and
expansion takes place within these six lines. The lines are counted from
the bottom up. The lowest line is to be taken first. According to the
hsiao tz'u or the text on the lines, the beginning line means a hidden dragon. This means the dragon is not yet revealed. The second line means the
dragon appearing in the field. This indicates that the dragon and his power
begin to emerge. It is the expansion of the power of the dragon, the light-
giving power, which is creative. The fifth line means a flying dragon in the
heaven. Here, a dragon reaches the highest and fullest manifestation of his

power. The top and last line mean that the arrogant dragon will have cause to repent. Here the dragon exceeds the proper limits and begins to lose his power. It is the beginning of its reversion to the opposite. Thus within each hexagram the principle of changes in terms of expansion and contraction is applied. Everything that reaches a certain peak must revert to its opposite. That is why the principle of changes presupposes the limitation of that which changes.

5. The Dynamics Of Changes And World Phenomena.

The principle of changes in terms of contraction and expansion presupposes that everything which changes is intimately related. The intimate relationship among all things is compared with organic unity. The universe which is in the process of continuous change is more or less like an organic whole. Because the world is conceived in terms of organism, the Change takes place according to production and reproduction. As Ta Chuan says, "production and reproduction is what is called (the process of) change" (Sec. I, Ch. 5).[1] The world as a gigantic machine is not possible in the frame of the principle of changes. If the process of changes is conditioned by expansion and contraction or growth and decay, nothing can be separated from organic wholeness. Hindu thought of the cosmos is very similar to the cosmology of the I Ching. The world for Hinduism is a living organism, the expression of a dynamic universe. For example, the Nobel Prize winner, Sir Jagadish Chandra Bose examined the beating pulse of the plant, following the Indian idea that everything in

[1]Legge's Translation.

the universe is a part of this living organism. Likewise, one of the great poets, Rabindranath Tagore adhered to the same idea of the intimate inter-wovenness of all cosmic forms to express his richness of imagery. Thus the world which both the I Ching and Hinduism describe is similar to the idea of a living organism. In the West, Teilhard de Chardin, for example, con-ceives the universe to no longer be a state but a process. Teilhard and Whitehead employ the category of becoming and process rather than of being and substance. The Change takes place in the world of becoming and process.

Because the universe which constantly changes is an organic whole, what one does affects others. In other words, the principle of changes in terms of expansion and contraction presupposes a relationship between cause and effect. The process of changes is the process of transition from the cause to effect and from effect to cause. The inter-relationship of both cause and effect is called the Change. However, this cause and effect prin-ciple is not rational or reasonable in terms of our common experience. Since the process of changes deals not only with the realm of our consciousness but also that of our unconsciousness, the cause and effect relationship in the process of changes is quite different from that in a scientific investigation. We may take up a few hexagrams and examine how one affects others. The hexa-gram 6, Sung or Conflict is followed by Shih or the Army. The cause for the

rise of the army was conflict. Thus in Hsü Kua or Sequence of the Hexagrams it is said, "When there is conflict, the masses surely rise up. Therefore there follows the Army. Army implies mass." The rise of the army was effected by the conflict which was the cause. Let us take the hexagram 10, Lü or Good

Confuct, which is followed by T'ai or Peace. In the Hsü Kua we read: "Lü

brings peace. Calm will prevail. Thus there follows peace. Peace means

interrelation." Here, we notice that the principle of changes is based on

mutual relatedness. One eventually affects others, for everything is inter-

related. The hexagram 14, Ta Yu or Great Possession, is followed by Ch'ien

or Modesty. The relationship between these two hexagrams illustrates much

better the understanding of mutual dependency. In Hsü Kua it is said,

"Great Possession can not make it too full. Thus there follows modesty."

Here, the concept of cause and effect is well illustrated. The Great Posses-

sion is the cause and Modesty is its effect. However, it also expresses the

principle of changes in terms of expansion and contraction. When the great

possession reaches its peak, it begins to move downward or revert to its op-

posite. The former hexagram exceeds the proper limits, that is, it is too

full; hence modesty follows. Finally, the last two hexagrams illustrate the

mutual relatedness in terms of the principle of changes. The hexagram 63,

Chi Chi or After Completion, is followed by the last hexagram, Wei Chi or

Before Completion. As we see these hexagrams, the latter is the reversion

of the former. The After Completion affects the birth of the Before Com-

pletion. This precisely in accord with the principle of changes in terms
of expansion and contraction. Hsü Kua explains that nothing can be exhausted
completely: "Things cannot exhaust themselves forever. Thus there follows
Wei Chi at the end." When things are complete they begin to decay. This is
the principle of changes which conditions all things.

The principle of changes in terms of contraction and expansion also
presupposes the significance of a center or mean in relation to all things
which change. The most favorable position of the movement of changes is the
center or the mean, chung 中 , between the two extremes. The word "chung"
or "the central" appears thirty-five times in the T'uan Chuan or the Commentary on the Judgments, and thirty-six times in Hsiang Chuan or the Commentary
on the Symbols. The concept of chung or a center represents the mean between
the utmost degree of expansion and that of contraction. To be in the center
of these two extreme poles of changes is to be in the most steady and safe
moment of transition. The significance of this mean or chung is clearly evidenced in the structure of trigrams and hexagrams. In the trigrams man occupies the center of the three lines. In the hexagrams the second and fifth
lines are the most important among the six lines because both of them occupy
the center of trigrams. The importance of the mean or chung in the structure
of the hexagram is well illustrated in the hexagram 11 and 12. The hexagram 11,
T'ai or Peace, consists of two trigrams: the trigram K'un or the Earth above,

and the trigram Ch'ien or the Heaven below. This hexagram is in a favorable
position because both trigrams move toward each other to the center. The
heaven, which is below, moves upward and the earth, which is above, moves

downward. Thus the image is: "Heaven and earth unite in peace. Thus the ruler fashions and completes the way of heaven and earth. He regulates the gifts of heaven and earth in order to aid the people." The hexagram 12, P'i

or Stagnation, consists of the trigram Ch'ien or heaven above and the K'un or earth below. As we observe, this hexagram is the reversion of the preceding one. The heaven which is above draws farther and farther away from the center. Thus the commentary on the Symbols says: "Heaven and earth do not unite in Stagnation. Thus the superior man falls in danger but exercises his moral power, in order to escape the difficulties. He cannot be honored with wealth." The center is important not only within the hexagram but among the hexagrams. For example, the thirty-second hexagram, Heng or Enduring, occupies the central position of all other hexagrams in the I Ching. Because of its central

position, it is advantageous to move in both directions. The judgment says: "Heng means successful progress and no mistake. The advantage will come from being correct. Movement in any direction will be advantageous." The primary meaning of "Heng" is not duration but constancy. It does not mean the state of rest but the center of movement. It is the center of both directions, be- cause it occupies the mean of 64 hexagrams. Thus it is advantageous to move in both directions. Some of these illustrations help us to see the signifi-

because it occupies the mean of 64 hexagrams. Thus it is advantageous to move in both directions. Some of these illustrations help us to see the significance of the central position in the principle of change.

Since the central position represents the steadiness and integration of changing movements, it is used as the norm for human affairs. Chung Yung or the Doctrine of the Mean begins with the definition of chung or the center: "Being without inclination to either side is called Chung." It is the central position where the movement of both expansion and contraction takes place. It is thus the state of harmony and equilibrium. When the mean or chung is applied to personal life, it is the situation in which there are no stirrings of pleasure, anger, sorrow, or joy. When those feelings have been stirred, and they act in their due degree, there ensues what may be called the state of harmony. This mean is the great root from which all the proper human behaviors grow in the world.[1] The mean is simply the middle way between the extremes. In the second section of Ta Chuan (Ch. 5), the onesidedness of human behaviors is warned against:

> He who keeps danger in mind is he who will rest safe in his seat; he who keeps ruin in mind is he who will preserve his interests secure; he who sets the danger of disorder before him is he who will maintain the state of order. Therefore the superior man, when resting in safety, does not forget possibility of ruin; and when all is in a state of order he does not forget that disorder may come.[2]

Much the same idea is expressed in the teachings of Jesus in the New Testament. For example, Jesus said, "If any one would be first, he must be last of all and servant of all" (Mark 9:35). In another place Jesus said similar

---

[1] Chung Yung 1:4

[2] Legge's Translation (Sec. II, para. 39).

words: "He who is greatest among you shall be your servant; whoever exalts himself will be humbled, and whoever humbles himself will be exalted" (Matthew 23:11, 12). These passages of the New Testament are not too much different from those of the I Ching. Jesus knew that anything that exceeds the proper limits must revert to its opposite. The concept of the golden mean which had been taught as early as the time of Aristotle is nothing strange to the West. To avoid the extremes is a way of attaining the mean which brings harmony of opposites in human life. However, the uniqueness of the I Ching is the concept of time connected with the mean. In other words, in the I Ching the concept of time is correlated with means. The mean is relative to time, because everything changes with time. It is not absolute and cannot transcend the realm of transition. Thus moral and ethical absolutism does not apply to the I Ching. Nothing has absolute value in itself, except the Tao, the change that is unchangeable. In the I Ching time and changes are intimately related.

The principle of changes in terms of expansion and contraction, therefore, presupposes the importance of time or timing. The word "shih" 時 or "time" originally meant "sowing time" which came to be related to season in general. The meaning of the word "shih" becomes much clearer if we analyze it. The Chinese word "時" may be derived from three different parts: "日" or the sun, "土" or soil, and "寸" or a small unit of measurement (Korean inch). As we will see, these three ideas are included in the concept of time. The sun has to do with the seasons, the soil with sowing, and the small unit of measurement with the section or unit of the season. The word "寸" was used in its early form as "sole of the foot" for the unit of measurement. Since the sole of the foot was related to the planting of seeds in a field, the word "shih" or time was used as a unit of a season set apart for a certain activity. Later this idea was extended to the four seasons and then to years. The concept of time then came from this very concrete idea which could be immediately experienced and perceived. It does not represent merely the principle of abstract progression. It is primarily a segment or unit of concrete event which takes place in the process of changes. This segment of event is represented by the situation in the hexagram as a whole. The situation which is signified by time changes according to expansion or contraction, increase or decrease and emptiness or fullness. Since the situation differs according to the process of changes, time also differs according to the situation. Each different situation represents different time. In the main texts of the I Ching the word "shih" or time appears only once in the fifty-four hexagram, Kuei Mei or the Marrying Maiden. The Image of this hexagram is: "Thunder over

the lake is the marrying maiden. Thus the superior man comprehends the transitory in the eternal end." The concept of time is implicit in the image but the explicit word "shih" appears in the fourth line of the hexagram. It says "The marrying maiden draws out the opportunity. Time will come for a late marraige." The literal translation of the last sentence should be: "A later marriage possesses time." It is clear from the literal translation that the concept of time here is not chronological time but the opportune time or the appointed time. Time is an occasion rather than the abstract succession of movement. It is the occasion of fulfillment. Thus the time expressed in the I Ching is similar to the Biblical concept of time as Kairos, the fulfilled

time. It is different from clock time, the chronos, which is the succession
of passing moments. In the I Ching time is kairos, the opportune time. To
act according to time is to be in accord with the proper situation for action.
Illustrations of the relationship between time and situation are seen in the
Commentaries to the I Ching. In the thirty-third hexagram, Tun or Withdrawal,
the Commentary on the Judgments says, "The firm is in the proper place which
is appropriately correlated. Thus it moves according to time." Also in the
first hexagram, Ch'ien or Creativity , we find a similar expression of time.
In the third line, the Wen Yen or the Commentary on the Words of the Texts
says, "The superior man advances in virtue and cultivates his duty. He does
not make mistake, because he intends at the time." In both cases time signifies the idea of kairos, the opportune time. Harmony in the situation is also
harmony with time. To have the right time is to have the right situation in
which to act. To have the right situation is to have the right time for changes.
Each situation has its own time, the proper time of its own. In the second
hexagram, K'un or Responsivity, the Wen Yen says, "The way of K'un is smooth.
It receives heaven into itself and acts at the proper time." Each situation
has its appointed time. This idea is very clearly expressed in the Book of
Ecclesiastes in the Old Testament. The following passages from Ecclesiastes
describe the concept of time, which is practically similar to that of the I
Ching:

> For everything there is a season, and a time for every
> matter under heaven: a time to be born, and a time to
> die; a time to plant, and a time to pluck up what is
> planted; a time to kill, and a time to heal; a time to
> break down, and a time to build up; a time to weep, and
> a time to laugh; a time to mourn, and a time to dance;
> a time to cast away stones, and a time to gather stones
> together; a time to embrace, and a time to refrain from
> embracing; a time to seek, and a time to lose, a time
> to keep, and a time to cast away; a time to rend, and a
> time to sew; a time to keep silence, and a time to speak;

a time to love, and a time to hate; a time for war, and a
time for peace (Ecclesiastes 3:1-8).

These appointed times are different situations which are decided according
to the course of heaven and earth. The principle of changes corresponds to
the four seasons (Ta Chuan, Sec. I, Ch. 6). Just as the interaction of yin
and yang corresponds to that of sun and moon, change conforms to a definite
duration: "Their changes and penetrations should correspond with the time"
(Ta Chuan, Sec. II, Ch. 1). Thus a superior man waits for a proper time to
act. In the 40th hexagram, Hsieh or Liberation , the Ta Chuan says, "The
superior man maintains the means in his own person. He waits his time for
action" (Sec. II, Ch. 5). The superior man who knows the principle of
changes can wait for the right time for his decision for action. In the 49th
hexagram, Ko or Revolution, the Commentary on the Symbols says, "Fire in the
lake is revolution. Thus the superior man sets the calendar and makes
the time (or season) clear." To miss the time is unfortunate and brings misfortune. In the 60th hexagram, Chieh or Regulation, the Commentary on the
Symbols says concerning the second line: "Don't go out the gate and the
court yard! It will bring misfortune, because one misses the crucial time."
The importance of time in changes is much more emphatically expressed in the
forty-eighth hexagram, Ching or the Well. On the first line of the hexagram
the Commentary on the Symbols says, "No animals can come to an old well, for
time forsakes it." Here time is not a mere empty succession of movement but is
filled with the possible energy of creativity. Time and the situation of the
hexagram correspond to each other. Time does not eixst in itself without
changes. The process of changes does not exist without time either. Both
time and change make possible the formation of the germinal situations as ex-

pressed in the 64 hexagrams of the I Ching. The essence of time consists of changes, while the sequence of changes is possible because of time. Through the process of production and reproduction the perennial movement of time is sustained. Zero is the symbol of eternal time. It corresponds not only to infinite situations but also with the infinite variableness of time. Time never comes to an end because of eternal time, which is of the Tao. Time never repeats itself but always renews itself through the recurrences of similar cyclic patterns. The recurrence of fulfilled possibilities is not a repetition of the same but the renewal of the cyclic movement. Time is the expression of changes, and the principle of changes is the essence of time. Therefore, an eternal time is the background of time, that is, "the timeless-ness that is timely."

CHAPTER III.   SYMBOLIZATION OF CHANGES

The I Ching is a book of symbols about the principle of changes. It
gives symbols to express various situations of changes. The basic symbols
of changes are the 64 hexagrams. Each hexagram represents a germinal situation which is complete in itself as a unit. The 64 hexagrams then represent
the 64 germinal situations which complete the microcosm of the universe.
However, the hexagram is the combination of two trigrams. The trigrams are
the basis for the hexagram. Moreover, the bases of the trigrams are lines.
Since the lines are the basic symbolization of both trigram and hexagram in
the I Ching, let us begin our discussion with the symbolization of lines.

1.   Symbolization Of Lines.

There are two basic symbols, the undivided and the divided lines,
which are combined in various ways to form the hexagrams in the I Ching.
What do these lines represent? They represent both yin and yang forces.
Since the principle of changes is based on these two forces, it is not really
surprising that these two lines become the bases for the hexagrams. As we
have already seen in the preceding chapter, the origin of these two symbols
may go back to the origin of these two forces. If we believe that the concept of yin and yang came from the contrast between light and dark or between
the active and passive, we notice that their symbols were also contrasting
ones. In other words, yang represents the active principle which is symbolized
by the light, while yin represents the passive principle which is symbolized by
the dark. Since the sun represented the day and the moon the night for the

primitive mind, it could be possible that yin and yang or the dark and the
light correspond to the sun and moon. As the Ta Chuan says, "The yin(dark)
and yang (light) are correlated with the sun and moon" (Sec. I, Ch. 6). It
seems to believe that the light principle was called yang and the dark principle yin. The sun was later known as t'ai yang or the great light, while
the moon as t'ai yin or the great dark. Because of these two principle forces,
we have indicated that the concept of the "I" 易 was derived from the combination of both the sun 日 and the moon 月 which was believed to come from
the old pictogram of 勿 . It is probable that the principle of yang came
to be used as the symbol for the sun and that of yin as the symbol for the moon.
The sun and moon became the prototypes of yin and yang. The symbol of the
sun was a light circle, while that of the moon was a dark circle. This idea
was implicit in the Ho T'u or the River Map, which was believed to have originated at the hand of Fu Hsi, the legendary king. As we have mentioned in the
first chapter, this map consists of both light and dark circles. Those circles
which have odd numbers are light, and those numbers which are even are dark
circles. The dark circles represent the moon-like character of yin. The light
circles represent, on the other hand, the sun-like character of yang. Thus in
this map the yang principle was symbolized by a light circle o, while the yin
principle was symbolized by a dark circle ●. It is possible, as we have indicated,
that Fu Hsi was unable to combine the circles successfully. Thus we believe that
he substituted the lines for circles. The light circles were replaced with
the undivided lines, and the dark circles with the divided line. Thus both
the undivided line (———) came to signify yang and the divided line (— —)
yin. What is then the significance of these two lines?

The significance of these lines is, first of all, in their simplicity. The line is perhaps the simplest symbol. An efficacy of symbolism lies in its simplicity. A complex symbolism tends to distort the real meaning which it signifies. The simpler the symbol is the easier it is to understand its meaning. Since the forces of yin and yang are considered to be the primary categories of all other existence, they must be expressed by the primary units of other symbolisms. Lines are the bases for other symbols. Just as yin and yang are the basic categories of all other existence, the lines are the primary expressions of all symbols. The words which we use consist of lines. For example, the word "change" is the combination of many lines. The Chinese language is full of lines. Without lines we cannot communicate. Shapes and forms of all things are lines. Paintings, sculptures, and pictures are of lines. Likewise, everything in the world is of yin and yang forces. Just as no symbolism is adequate without lines, nothing can exist without yin and yang forces. Thus the lines are the simplest but the most profound symbolisms, which are in return the bases for all other symbolisms.

Secondly, the significance of using the lineal symbols of both the divided and undivided is in their paradoxical character, that is, the complementary of opposites. The divided and undivided lines symbolize the opposing characters, just as yin and yang represent the opposing poles. The divided line, which symbolizes yin, is quite different from the undivided line, which symbolizes yang. The former represents even numbers, while the latter represents the odd numbers. Even numbers themselves never become odd numbers and odd numbers themselves never become even numbers. They are distinctive in their characters but they have at the same time their essential nature. The divided line is the division of undivided line, and the undivided line is the line before the division. Likewise, _yin_ and _yang_ are distinctively different in their characters but are complementary to each other. What is not divided is the undivided line and what is divided is the division of the undivided line. Also, what is _yang_ is not _yin_ and what is not _yin_ is _yang_. They are both different and the same at the same time. They are not in relationship of "either different or same." Since _yin_ and _yang_ relationship is in the category of "both/and" description, the absolute distinction between them is unacceptable. The symbolism of black and white or light and dark circles is closely associated with the category of "either/or" rather than of "both/and." Using the divided and undivided lines this absolute dichotomy of the "either/or" idea could be easily overcome. Here, we see again the advantage of using lines of the divided and the undivided rather than circles of the dark and light.

Thirdly, the significance of using the divided and undivided lines is historically conditioned. The _I Ching_ had its origin with the book of divination. Before the elaborate method of consulting the oracles as described in the _I Ching_, there was a primitive method of consulting the oracles. The most primitive method of consulting the oracles seemed to have been the drawing of lots. In drawing lots the long and short stalks were used. The long stalks represented the positive and affirmative answer to the question asked. The short stalks symbolized the negative and denial of what was questioned. This kind of method is still used in Asia. Instead of using stalks matchsticks were often used in drawing lots. A drawing is often made from the mixture of both long and short matchsticks to get the answer. Even in America we use the lottery system to draft our youth into military service. Tossing a coin in the air to find an answer is not much different from the primitive practice of consulting the oracles. It is probable that the long stalk which represents the positive answer came to be identified with the _yang_ force. At the same time the short stalk which represents the negative answer came to be known as the _yin_ force. As Hellmut Wilhelm says, "At the first the method seems to have been a sort of drawing of lots, wherein long stalks meant a positive answer and short stalks a negative. Then, because of the equality in rank of the two fundamental forces, and probably also because of the old conception that heaven is one and earth two, two short stalks were made equal to one long stalk and were used to symbolize the _yin_ force."[1]

Fourthly, the significance of these lines lies in their fertility symbolism. As we have already said, the whole or undivided and the divided lines could be the sex symbols of both male and female. Since the undivided line symbolizes the essential force of male, it represents the reproductive organ of the male. On the other hand, the divided line seems to stand for the reproductive organ of the female. Since the reproductive organs of both male and female are the basis for production and reproduction, the importance of these sexual symbols was hardly questioned by the primitive Chinese people. Moreover, the idea of fertility symbolism is compatible with an organic view of the cosmos and the principle of changes in terms of production and reproduction. The movements of these lines make much clearer the possibility of their genital symbolisms. The undivided line, which represents the Creative power of the male organ, moves straight forward and backward, while the divided line, the Receptive power of the female organ, opens and closes (_Ta Chuan_, Sec. I, Ch. 6). The mysterious power of procreation through the harmony of sexual relation is symbolized in the relationship between the divided and un-

---

[1]H. Wilhelm, _Change_, p. 32.

divided lines. The divided line (— —) symbolizes its willingness to receive the coming of the undivided line. It is the symbol of openness for the opposite. On the other hand, the undivided line (———) is the symbol of straight forwardness and movement to that which is open. Thus both of them complement each other to complete the change, that is, the procreation of others. Certainly the principle of changes in terms of creation and procreation has its implicit meaning in the sexual symbolism of both the divided and the undivided lines.

Finally, the significance of using the divided and undivided lines comes from the distinctive characteristics of both male and female. The distinctive character of the divided line or the yin line is the softness, while that of the undivided line or the yang line is the firmness. Softness and tenderness are atributes of the feminine character, while firmness and hardness are attributes of the male character. Yang is the undivided line, because of its hardness. On the other hand, yin is the divided line because of its tenderness. It is the natural tendency of the male to be strong and aggressive while that of the female is to be soft and tender. The notion of responsive and creative comes from the characteristics of male and female nature. In correlating these two symbols, the male strength is equivalent with the double strength of female power. The single line of the undivided, that is the male power, is correlated with the two lines of the divided, which represent the female power. Both male and female powers are correlated, so that one is not in any way better than the other. It is, therefore, questionable whether we should translate the yin and yang lines as the yielding and firm lines. The Chinese word for the unbroken line is kang hsiao 剛爻 , which literally means hard or firm line. The Chinese word for the divided line is jou hsiao 柔爻 , which means the soft or tender line. The word "kang" is in apposition to "jou." The former is a typical expression of man's character, while the latter that of the female character. The characteristic of softness or tenderness is not that of weakness but of reception. The distinctive characteristic of hardness or firmness is an outward appearance but weakness is an inward strength. Thus the hard line is easily broken and becomes the divided line. On the other hand, the tender line is similar to the tender shoot of a tree which grows together inwardly to be strong. In this way the hard line changes to the soft line and the soft line changes to the hard line. The firm line pushes outward, and becomes thin in the middle and breaks in two to form the divided line. The tender line, on the other hand, pushes inward and then grows together into an undivided line. In this manner the process of changes and transformations take place.

2. Symbolization Of Duograms.

The significance of the use of these lineal symbols becomes much clearer when we come to discuss the trigrams and hexagrams. However, before discussing the trigrams, let us briefly look at the duograms, which do not occupy an important place in the I Ching. What we can learn from the duograms is the time element in the process of changes. The duograms indicate the progressive evolvement of changes from yang to yin and from yin to yang. The combination of both the undivided and divided lines makes four duograms possible as follows: 1) Yang is in its peak or in its peak or in its greatness the old yang (————). The old yang begins to change to the young yin. 2) The young yin results from the change of one line from the old yang. In the young yin the lower line of

old <u>yang</u> changes to <u>yin</u> line. Thus the young <u>yin</u> consists of a <u>yin</u> line below and a <u>yang</u> line above (———). 3) When the young yin grows to its greatness, it changes into the old <u>yin</u>. In the old <u>yin</u> all the lines are <u>yin</u> (—— ——).
It begins to change again. This time the newly changed line remains and the old
<u>yin</u> line changes to <u>yang</u> line. 4) When the old <u>yin</u> line of the old <u>yin</u> changes
to the <u>yang</u> line, it becomes the young <u>yang</u> (—— —). Again the old <u>yin</u> line of
the young <u>yang</u> changes into the <u>yang</u> line, and then the old <u>yang</u> (———) is to
be formed. In this way they evolve in a systematic fashion. The movement of
time in the process of changes can be illustrated in a picture as follows:

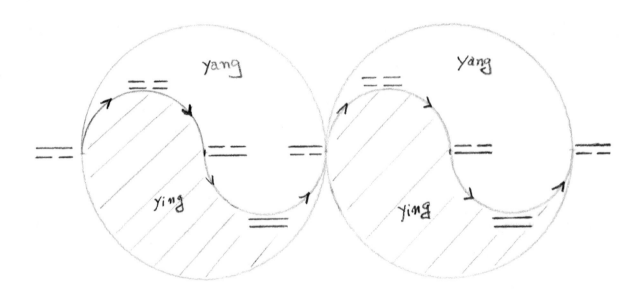

The changing time of the duograms can be related to four seasons of the year.
As we relate the movement of changes with the seasons we see more clearly the
principle of changes in terms of contraction and expansion. If we begin with
young <u>yin</u>, which represents the autumn, we see the expansion of the young <u>yin</u>

(‾‾) toward the old yin (‾ ‾), which represents the peak of the yin
force. The old yin thus represents the winter season. When the yin force
reaches its peak, it loses its power. Thus the movement of changes is downward. The cold winter begins to lose its coldness and reverts toward warmth.
Thus it is followed by the spring, which is represented by the young yang
(‾‾). The young yang is placed at the center between the old yin and the
old yang. Thus spring is the season of moderation between the cold and the hot.
As the spring expands its warmth, the power of yang also expands. When the
yang force reaches its peak, it is called the old yang (‾‾), which represents
the summer. As the old yang begins to lose its warmth it returns to the
young yin again. Just as the summer reaches its peak, it loses its warmth
and eventually becomes autumn, the old yang gradually changes into the young
yin again. from the young yin, the autumn, the new cycle starts again. From
this constant cyclic evolution of yin and yang forces according to expansion
and contraction, the process of changes takes place. Just as the divided and
undivided lines produce the duograms, the four duograms again procreate the
eight trigrams. Thus the Ta Chuan says, "The two primary forms (forces) produce the four images (which mean the four duograms). The four images produce
the eight trigrams" (Sec. I, Ch. 11).

3. Symbolization Of Trigrams

The trigrams are the prototypes of hexagrams. The hexagram is a mere
combination of two trigrams. Thus the eight trigrams are called in Chinese
as pa kua 八卦. The word "pa" means number "eight," and "kua" here means
"trigrams." The hexagram is often called as chung kua 重卦, which means

"double kua" or the "double trigrams." From the analysis of these two words we notice clearly that the hexagram is identical with the double trigrams. Even though the word "Kua" is indiscriminately used in referring to both trigrams and hexagrams, in a strict sense kua seems to be intended for the trigrams only. Let us therefore take the word "kua" to mean the trigrams rather than hexagrams. We can then say that the kua or the trigrams are the basis for the formation of the 64 hexagrams. Moreover, they represent the basic units of all possible situations in the universe. The kua or the tri-gram consists of three lines. This means an additional line is necessary to the duograms. If yin and yang lines are needed for the procreation of all things, why do we need another line to complete the microcosm of the universe? Does this signify that the double lines in themselves are incomplete? These questions are to be answered if we believe that the trigrams are the básic units of world phenomena.

a. The Trigrams And The Yin-Yang Relationship.

There is no doubt that the relationship between yin and yang, or the combination of the divided and the undivided lines, constitutes the basic category of all existence. Nothing can exist without both of them. They are the basis for all ontic structure of existence. Without yin and yang nothing can exist. They are the essence of all beings whether spiritual or material. Nothing can assert its own existence without both yin and yang together. Thus the duograms, the combinations of two lines, become ontological foundations for all other existence. If this is the case, the question is: "Why do we have to have another line to complete the unit of situations?" An immediate response to this question is simply that we do not add any "new" line or a new constituent to make the trigram. Another line which is added to two already existing lines is nothing new but one of either the divided or the undivided lines (yin or yang line). In this respect the addition of another line does not change the basic fact that yin and yang are the foundations of all the ontic structures of the universe. Then the addition of another line to the duograms is not ontic but functional. Why are three lines necessary to perform the function which makes all things possible?

According to the principle of changes, yin and yang become the ontological basis for changes and transformations. However, the functional process of changes has to do with expansion and contraction through production and reproduction. The concept of production and reproduction becomes very important in understanding the functional nature of changes. The yin and yang interplay by its very nature procreates either yin or yang so as to continue the process of changes. Procreation is conditioned by the yin-yang relationship, and the latter is accompanied by the former. One cannot exist without the other. They are mutually inclusive and dependent. Procreation is necessary for the process of change which is based on the yin-yang relationship. From the relationship between the procreation and yin-yang interplay, we soon notice why the trigram is necessary for the completion of situations. The duograms which consist of two lines symbolize the basic constituents of changes. However, the very existence of these two constituents conditions the existence of another, because of the necessity of procreation. In other words, two lines which symbolize both yin and yang are always accompanied with the procreation of either young yin (the divided line) or young yang (undivided line). Without the procreation of another line of either yin or _yang_ the process of changes cannot continue. The addition of this other line, which is procreated, to the duogram makes the trigram possible. Since that which is procreated and that which procreates are inseparable in the process of changes, the former is incomplete without the latter and the latter without the former. This complementary relationship between the one and the two makes it possible to create the trigram as the basic unit of all possible situations in the universe.

b. The Trigrams And Family Life.

The concept of threeness is deeply rooted in Chinese tradition. The origin of this concept may go back as far as the time when the concept of the trigrams was established. For the primitive Chinese people heaven and earth became the symbols of their father and mother. The idea that "the heaven is my father and the earth is my mother" is not strictly confined to the Chinese people. The earth as a mother-god figure was almost universal. Moreover, the frequent use of such a phrase as, "our heavenly father," in the Lord's Prayer as well as in many places in the Bible, has the profound implication that heaven is not only the place where God dwells but it is the symbol of God Himself. In China, heaven and earth were the sources of life. Man was their procreation. Thus heaven, earth and man constitute the Chinese trinity. Heaven and earth are prototypes of _yin_ and _yang_, and, therefore, they become the source of all things. The uniqueness of man in China is that he is not only the product of the same substance as heaven and earth but also their son. In China man is often called _t'ien tzu_ 天子 or the son of heaven. If heaven and earth are the source of all things they seem to be self-sufficient. Never-

theless, in China, no living organism, in fact everything in the world that
is understood as an organism, is sufficient without its own procreation.
Heaven and earth are insufficient without their child. A good illustration
of this is to be found in the relationship between the husband and wife.
Heaven and earth are analogous to the husband and wife. In China the husband
and wife can be compared with yang and yin. They are incomplete without a
child or children. In the West the family life stresses the horizontal relationship, that is, the relationship between the husband and wife. In the
East the family structure is based on the vertical relationship, that is, the
relationship between the father and son or between the parent and children.
The oriental way of life is also expressed in the various narratives of the Old
Testament. For example, Abraham's desire to possess his child was stronger than
the idea of monogamy. Thus he goes to Hagar, his maid servant, to conceive a
son. Just as the husband and wife are insufficient without their child, the
relationship between heaven and earth, that is, between yang and yin, is incomplete without man, their procreation. Fork's words are quite appropriate
here: "One yin and one yang, that is the fundamental principle. The passion-
ate union of yin and yang and the copulation of husband and wife is the
eternal rule of the universe. If heaven and earth did not mingle, whence
would all the things receive life? When the wife comes to the man, she bears
children. Bearing children is the way of propagation. Man and wife cohabit
and produce offsprings."[1] The relationship between yin and yang is complete
through the procreation of either yin or yang. That is why the concept of

---

[1]A. Fork (tr), World Conception of the Chinese (London: Arthur
Probsthain, London, 1925), p. 68.

threeness became important in Chinese thought. Trigrams are then the symbolization of threeness as the basic unit of life. In the trigram the bottom line is understood as the way of earth. The middle line represents the way of man, and the top signifies the way of heaven. Man is the center of both heaven and earth, so that the middle line becomes important in the trigrams. As Ta Chuan says, "The I is a book which is vast and great and contains everything. It has the tao of heaven, the tao of the earth, and the tao of man. These three primal powers are doubled and make six lines. The six lines are nothing other than the tao of the three primal powers" (Sec. II, Ch. 10). The central position of man seems to be recognized by the physical sciences of our time. It is more or less a coincidence that man's size is about 10^{-30} times of the universe, and the atom's size is about 10^{-30} times of man. If the universe represents the heaven and the atom the earth, man is certainly the center of them in size. However, our interest is not the size of them but the functional relationship among them. The central line which represents man is similar to a child who is surrounded by his parents. Perhaps the life of the oriental family can be compared to this relationship of the child as the center of attention. A child grows up with his mother's milk, that is, the fertility of the earth, and with his father's wisdom, that is, the will of heaven. The trigrams thus depict the typical family life of the Chinese people. It is a universal longing of man and woman for a child who can succeed them. In this respect, the I Ching expresses the natural inclination of all people.

c. The Trigrams And Social Life.

The trigram is not only the complete symbol of family life but also
that of the social and political life of man. In every form of social structure there are basically three groups of people. In China, as in Plato's
Republic, the sages or the wisemen occupied the upper class of people. The
sages interpreted the will of heaven to those who rule the people. The people
of the ruling class occupied the central position. The mass of the people who
were ruled belonged to the lower class. These three groups of people are
still essential for the form of government. Even though three power structures of our democratic form of government, that is, the executive, judicial
and legislative powers, were not known in that time, the trigram serves as a
useful function of balance of these powers for a creative purpose. In social
life there are also three basic classes of people: the people who belong to
the upper class, middle class and the lower class. In China the gentry occupied the upper class. The common people occupy the middle class, and the
serfs and servants occupy the lower class. The trigram could serve in allo-
cating the people according to their qualifications.

d. The Trigrams And Personality.

As to the structure of personality, the trigram symbolizes the three
distinctive levels of existence. As Culling said, "In the Western world is a
prevailing tenet several centuries old: 'man is a threefold being, body,

mind, and soul.' The _I Ching_ said it a thousand years ago."[1] The threefold personality in terms of the soul, mind and body is analogous with the trigram. However, the distinction among the three parts of human nature is questionable and vague. However, it is important to notice the psychic strata of man in relation to the trigram. The psychological implication of the _I Ching_ is very important, because of its nature as an oracle book. The oracle of the _I Ching_ operates through the disclosure of our unconsciousness. Thus the relationship of our psychic structure with the trigrams is worth examining here. In the structure of the trigram, the bottom line represents our subconsciousness, the central line the consciousness, and the top line the superconsciousness. The state of subconsciousness or the bottom line of the trigram is suppressed by the state of consciousness which occupies the central line. The state of superconsciousness, which is represented in the upper line of the trigram, is disclosed at the moment of enlightenment or liberation from the finite self. The function of conscious realm through the demands of superconsciousness. In other words, the superconscious can be compared with the heavenly realm, and the subconscious with the earthly realm. Between them, the conscious, which is to be compared with the human realm, occupies the most important place. The psychological value of the _I Ching_ in the understanding of our psychic structures cannot be denied. The place of the _I Ching_ in our psychic strata is implicated in _Ta Chuan:_ "It receives one's fate like an echo, whether he is neither far nor near, neither dark nor

---

[1]Louis T. Culling, _The Incredible I Ching_ (Toddington, Cheltenham: Hellios Book, 1965), p. 14.

deep. Thus he knows of the things that are coming" (Sec. I, Ch. 10). Here, the subconscious is expressed in terms of the dark and the deep in man, and the superconscious in terms of far and near. The conscious enters into relationship with the unconscious and the superconscious. Moreover, the trigram indicates the three distinctive aspects of self; the passion, mind and will. Passion occupies the bottom line of the trigram, the mind the central position of the trigram, and the will the upper line. The relationship of passion, mind and will is not really different from Thomas Aquinas' idea that the mind controls the passion to attain the will which is good. In China, the normative Confucianism has maintained the intrinsic goodness of human nature. Because man is good in his very nature, what he wills is also good. Thus the mind can direct the passion, which is the power, to do the will of heaven. The moral philosophy which is based on the teachings of the I Ching is not totally strange to the Western mind.

e. The Trigrams and Cosmic Phenomena.

As we have said, the trigram can be applied to all the possible situations of human life. In India the Sāmkhya school also teaches that there are three constituents of all worldly phenomena. All our worldly activities are the mixture of three: the innate inertia (tamas), the driving force of tendency and passion (rajas), and the balance between both which is called the harmonizing medium (sattva). "In this way the special importance of the number 'three' is philosophically interpreted; a union between the two opposites is finally established by a third harmonizing element."[1] The philosophy of the Sāmkhya school is comparable to that of the trigram in which heaven and earth represent the opposing forces and man as the harmonizing medium. Thus in principle there is a common character between the Hindu and Chinese notions of a triad or of a cosmic drama. Since the triad, or relationship of the trigram, is understood as the basic unit of world events, to know the principle of the trigram is to know the hexagrams which represent the microcosm of the universe. Thus let us examine the nature of the pa kua or eight trigrams.

f. The Eight Trigrams.

The three lines of both yin and yang are combined to form the eight trigrams. In constructing the eight trigrams, the duograms are used as the foundation of the trigrams. You will recall the old yang (———) will change to the young yin (———) which then grows to be the old yin (— —). The old yin will change to the young yang (— —), which again becomes the old yang. In this way the four duograms or images are to be completed. By the addition of either yin or yang lines to these duograms, the eight trigrams are formed. Following the same order which we have used for the duograms, we can add the yang line (———) to the old yang (———) to make the trigram (———), which is called the Ch'ien or Creativity.   By adding the yin line (— —) to the old yang (———) we attain the trigram (———), which is called the Tui or the Joyous. Using the same procedure for the rest of the duograms we can obtain

---

[1]Heimann, op. cit., p. 96.

the following: the trigram <u>Sun</u> or Gentleness (☴) and <u>K'an</u> or the
Abyss (☵) are obtained from the young <u>yin</u> (⚏). The trigrams <u>Ken</u>
or Stillness (☶) and <u>K'un</u> or Responsivity (☷) are formed from
the old <u>yin</u> (⚏). The trigram <u>Li</u> or the Flaming (☲) and Chen or the
Awakening (☳) are derived from the young <u>yang</u> (⚎). These trigrams
are correlated with natural phenomena as well as the seasons of the year.
The trigram <u>Ch'ien</u> corresponds with heaven and <u>K'un</u> with the earth. The
trigram <u>Tui</u> signifies the lake and <u>Ken</u> the mountain. The trigram <u>Chen</u> is
correlated with thunder and <u>Sun</u> with wind. Finally, the trigram <u>K'an</u> is
correlated with water (or rain) and <u>Li</u> with fire. From these symbolic cor-
respondences we can imagine the world view of the primitive people in China.
The basic categories of world phenomena consist of eight natural objects.
They are heaven (<u>Ch'ien</u>) and earth (<u>K'un</u>), mountain (<u>Ken</u>) and lake (<u>Tui</u>),
thunder (<u>Chen</u>) and wind (<u>Sun</u>), and water (<u>K'an</u>) and fire (<u>Li</u>). If we observe
Chinese landscapes carefully, almost all of them are primarily based on a combination of these eight objects. In other words, the eight trigrams become
the primary objects of painting in China. If we construct a landscape out of
these eight objects, we may put them together in the following way: Between
heaven (<u>Ch'ien</u>) and earth (<u>K'un</u>) wind (<u>Sun</u>) gathers over the mountain (<u>Ken</u>),
the dark clouds produce the thunder (<u>Chen</u>) and lightning (<u>Li</u>), and then the
rain (<u>K'an</u>) fills the lake (<u>Tui</u>). In spite of the thunder and lightning,
the mountain is still and the lake is calm. The significance of these objects
is not only that they are the primal units of a primitive world view but also
their correlation with the trinity of world principles. The wind and thunder
commonly arise in heaven, the mountain and lake are of the earth, and fire

and water are most commonly used by man. Thus heaven is on top, earth on the bottom and man in the middle of the trigram.

g.   The Sequence Of Eight Trigrams.

The correlation of the eight trigrams with seasonal changes is discussed in <u>Shou Kua</u> or Discussion of the Trigrams: "Heaven and earth determine the position. The powers of mountain and lake are correlated. Thunder and wind meet each other. Water and fire do not meet each other. Thus the eight trigrams are mutually intermingled" (Ch.2). The above description is based on the sequence of arrangement in pairs which is often called Primal Arrangement or Sequence of Earlier Heaven. This arrangement is believed to be made by Fu Hsi himself. The Sequence of Earlier Heaven (or Before the World) is as follows:

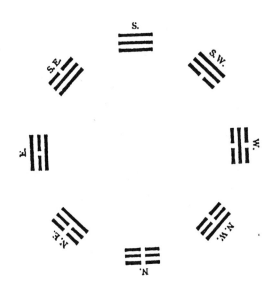

According to this diagram, Ch'ien or heaven and K'un or earth determine the direction of both north and south or both the summer and winter. They represent the poles of the universe. They correspond to the directions of both the old yang and the old yin of the duogram. Wind, (Sun) and thunder (Chen) arise from each other in heaven. The mountain (Ken) and lake (Tui) bring cosmic harmony on the earth. Both water (K'an) and fire (Li) balance each other in their opposing direction. They point to the west and to the east as well as to autumn and spring. The west corresponds to the young yin, while the east corresponds to the young yang. This Sequence of Earlier Heaven is a priori order or a mathematical order which is not relative to immediately experienced time and situation. This arrangement is similar to the arrangement of the duograms which we have already diagramed. The directions of the trigrams are conditioned by the intensity of the yin and yang forces. When yang forces are in their peak, they indicate summer, while when yin forces are concentrated on the trigram it is winter. Thus Ch'ien (☰) is south, while K'un (☷) is north. In the autumn there are more yin than yang and in the spring there are more yang than yin. Thus it is a logical and mathematical arrangement according to the proportion of yin and yang forces.

Later, King Wen was believed to have altered the arrangement of the trigrams. His arrangement is known to us as the Sequence of Later Heaven or the Inner-World Arrangement. In re-arranging the trigrams, King Wen removed them from their opposite directions and put them together according to the temporal progression of the cyclic year. This arrangement follows the immediately experienced situations of natural phenomena. It is described in the

<u>Shuo Kua</u>: "The ruler comes forth in the <u>Chen</u> and completes everything in the <u>Sun</u> (or Gentle). He causes things to see one another in the <u>Li</u> (or Flaming), and causes them to serve one another in the <u>K'un</u>. He gives them joy in the <u>Tui</u>, and battles in the perfection in the <u>Ken</u>" (Ch. 5). The arrangement of the trigrams, according to the Sequence of Later Heaven (or Inner-World), is not in a logical sequence as is in the preceding arrangement. It does not correspond with the forces of <u>yin</u> and <u>yang</u> but with the attributes of the trigrams. The sequence of Later Heaven is known as follows:

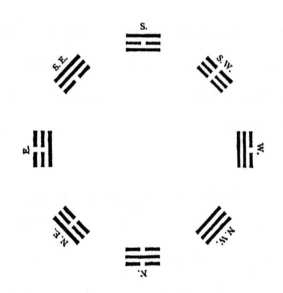

Everything begins with Chen, the Awakening, because of its symbol of thunder which produces electricity and sound to awaken all things under heaven and over the earth. All living things arise in the sign of Chen, because it stands in the East which is the symbolic location of new life. Thunder stands at the East because the day breaks from it. The East symbolizes not only spring but the new beginning of all things. That is why the Chinese calendar begins the New Year with the beginning of the spring. The spring symbolizes not only the beginning of new life but of the new year. All living things which begin with the Awakening are to be completed in the Sun, Gentleness. The Sun or Gentleness is to be compared with the midmorning of the day and with the transition between spring and summer. In this season of the year, all living things are completely formed and the seeds change to new forms. The mid-morning is the time of renewal and refreshment for the wind blows gently. The Awakening of seeds is completed in the season of Gentleness, for it is mid-way between spring and summer. Thus the Chen is completed by the Sun, which is followed by Li, the Flaming. The attribute of Li is light and brightness. Thus it is the trigram of the South. It also corresponds to the noontide of the day and the summer of the year. It is the midsummer which is regarded as the hottest time of the year. Since the trigram Li is the symbol of fire, and fire makes heat, it is in the direction of the south and the summer. South is always warmer than the north. For this reason the summer is correlated with the south. In ruling the brightness or fire represents the shining seal of power and glory. Thus the holy sages turned their faces to the south. The trigram Li is followed by K'un, Responsivity. It represents the mid-afternoon and the transition of the summer to the autumn. This is the time when all living things begin to bear fruit in their wombs which represents Responsivity. Bearing fruit is followed with the nourishment of motherhood. That is why Responsivity is also the symbol of nourishment as well as the reception of fruits. The Responsive is followed by Tui, Joy. The symbol of the Tui is the mid-autum as well as the direction of the west which also signifies the time of sunset. Autumn is the season of Joy for the fruits are ripe. It is the time of harvest. Tui is followed with the trigram Ch'ien or Creativity. It is the trigram of the north-west and the direction of movement toward the deeper darkness. It represents the time when the dark and the light struggle each other. The victory of yin power is certain but the final effort of yang is desperate. In the moment of final battle the creative energy of Ch'ien is radically manifest. The Ch'ien is followed by the trigram K'an, Abyss. The K'an is the depth of water and it is the trigram of the north. It is the symbol of the cold winter and midnight in which everything rests. After the toil and struggle comes comfort. Winter is the time of quiescence. The K'an is followed by Ken, Stillness. It represent the direction of the northeast. It is the symbol of mountain which signifies the transition of the winter to the spring. It is the beginning of the new day, the dawn. The hidden rest and comfort join with the new year. It is where both the beginning and the end meet together. The Ken is followed by the Chen, Awakening, again. In this way the Sequence of Later Heaven moves along with the cyclic recurrence according to the changes of the world. It represents not only the movement of seasonal changes but the cycle of experience in which the old and the new are linked together inseparably.

Why is the Sequence of Later Heaven distinctive from the Sequence of

Earlier Heaven? What are the distinctions between these two arrangements?
The characteristic difference between the Sequence of Earlier Heaven and
Later Heaven is very similar to Kant's distinction between "noumenon" and
"phenomenon." Just as the noumenon represents things in themselves, the
Sequence of Earlier Heaven is a priori order which is not conditioned by the
sense experience of man. It represents the logical and mathematical reality
which becomes the background of phenomenological appearance. On the other
hand, the Sequence of Later Heaven is analogous with Kant's notion of
"phenomenon" which is conditioned by our sense data. It is the order of
immediately experienced reality. It represents the posteriori order which
deals with the empirical nature of changes. Thus it is the foreground of the
Sequence of Earlier Heaven. Because of this relationship, both of them are
inseparable. The a priori order is different from the a posteriori order in
its arrangements but they mutually complement each other. The difference of
the arrangements signifies that what we can experience in changes is not always the same as that which we cannot experience in changes even though
they are mutually inclusive. To illustrate this, let us take a dream as the
revelation of a priori order or the archetype of unconsciousness. The dream
may correspond to the actual experience in a different way. In other words,
the symbols in the dream and those in actual experience may be different but,
if the dream was really the visual expression of unconsciousness, they can be
correlated meaningfully. Let us look at the trigram Li, Flaming , in the
Sequence of Later Heaven. The Li occupies the position of the south and the
summer which is also held by the trigram Ch'ien according to the Sequence of
Earlier Heaven. "To understand fully, one must always visualize the Inner-
World Arrangement (the Sequence of Later Heaven) as transparent, with the

Primal Arrangement (the Sequence of Earlier Heaven) shining through it.
Thus when we come to the trigram <u>Li</u>, we come at the same time upon the
ruler <u>Ch'ien</u>, who governs with his face turned to the south."[1] The correlation of both Sequences can be compared with the correlation of both
the unconscious and the conscious, the physical and spiritual, the seen
and the unseen aspects of phenomena. Thus the function of those two
different arrangements helps us to see the correlation between the two
polarities of abstract and concrete situations in the universe. In other
words, the phenomenal changes are different from the noumenal changes but
are correlated harmoniously.

h. The Attributes of Trigrams

Let us now discuss the attributes of each trigram. Since the trigrams
are the bases of hexagrams in the <u>I Ching</u>, knowing what the trigrams stand for
is helpful in knowing the symbolic significance of the hexagrams. To being
with, we have the pair of opposites, <u>Ch'ien</u> and <u>K'un</u>. The <u>Ch'ien</u> (———)
consists of three undivided lines, while the <u>K'un</u> (⚏) consists of three
divided lines. The trigram <u>Ch'ien</u> originally meant "dry," for the primary
meaning of "<u>Ch'ien</u>" 乾 is dry. The trigram <u>K'un</u> originally meant "moist."
Thus the combination of both the dry and the moist became the beginning of
creation. As we have seen in the Sequence of Earlier Heaven, the <u>Ch'ien</u> stands
for the south or the summer, the time of heat, which dries everything. On the

---

[1]Richard Wilhelm, <u>op</u>. <u>cit</u>., p. 271

other hand, the trigram K'un stands for the north or the winter, the time of coolness, which preserves moisture from evaporation. Heat is the symbol of active force while coolness is the symbol of rest and calmness. Thus the concept of yang and yin had already been implicit as early as the origin of the trigrams. The active force is the natural endowment of the male character while the passive force is the expression of the female nature. In this way the Ch'ien becomes the archetype of yang forces while the K'un the archetype of yin forces.

The concept of the Ch'ien and K'un as the heaven and earth may come from the original meaning of the dry and the moist. As Hellmut Wilhelm said, "What is pure and light rises up and becomes heaven; what is turbid and heavy sinks down and becomes earth."[1] Since the dry corresponds with the pure and light, it becomes the symbol of heaven. On the other hand, the moist corresponds with what is turbid and heavy and sinks down. Thus the moist becomes the symbol of earth. Heaven or Ch'ien is represented by the symbol of a dragon, which is often associated with the storm, thunder and lightning. The image of thunder and lightning in heaven is the symbol of power, creative energy and active movement. In contrast to the dragon, a mare belongs to the earth. The dragon gives rain to make the pasture green while the mare eats the green pasture. Thus the mare is the apposition to the dragon, just as the K'un is the apposition to the Ch'ien. The mare is the symbol of the vast expansion of the earth because she can run tirelessly over the green pastures. The mare is also the symbol of a gentle and submissive character. Thus she is

---

[1]H. Wilhelm, Change, p. 82.

receptive. The Ch'ien as heaven is the symbol of prince and father, while the K'un as earth is the symbol of mother and mass who are ruled from above. The Ch'ien is the symbol of the head, for the power of creativity manifests itself in the head, while the K'un is the symbol of the abdominal cavity, for receptivity takes place in the belly. Ch'ien is round, because heaven looks round. K'un is square and flat, for the earth appears to be flat and square. Ch'ien is the symbol of metal, for it is strong and solid, while K'un is for fragility for it is tender and soft. Ch'ien is jade, while K'un is cloth. Ch'ien is content, while K'un is form. Ch'ien is fruit while K'un is the trunk of the tree. The color of Ch'ien is a deep red which is the intensified color of the light principle. The color of K'un is black which is intensified darkness. The red activates the mind and emotion of people while the black receives. The combination of both Ch'ien and K'un procreates all things, for they are the archetypes of yin and yang, which are the basic categories of all existence. To relate them to the structure of family life, Ch'ien is father while K'un as mother procreates three sons and three daughters.

The trigram Chen (☳) is the first son who resembles his mother because the female searches first for the power of the male and receives a son (Shuo Kua 10). The trigram Sun (☴) is the first daughter who resembles her father because this time the male searches first for the power of the female and receives a daughter (Shuo Kua 10). It is no mere chance, therfore, that the son generally resembles his mother while the daughter resembles her father. We often ask when a child is born whether the child looks more like the father or the mother. We expect a baby boy to resemble his mother and a baby daughter to resemble her father. The reason for this is clearly expressed in the structure of trigrams. The trigram Chen, the first son, consists of two yin lines and one yang line. Thus it has more yin than yang, that is, it looks more like mother than father. On the other hand, the trigram Sun, the first daughter, has two yang lines and one yin line. Thus she looks more like her father than her mother. The attribute of Chen is the arousing, which means movement. The attribute of Sun is the gentle, which means penetration (Shuo Kua 7). Chen is compared with the foot of the body for it moves along the ground. Sun belongs to the thigh of the body, for food reaches it through the mouth. Chen takes from his father the symbol of the dragon and the horse, both of which are noted for their swiftness. Sun is symbolized by the cock, whose voice penetrates and pierces the stillness. Chen is decisive and vehement, while Sun is aggressive and retiring, that is, indecisive (Shuo Kua 11). Chen is bamboo that is green and young, while Sun is wood which grows long and high. Bamboo which grows fast represents spring, while wood which stands naked represents autumn. The color of Chen is dark yellow, which is a mixture of the dark heaven and the yellow earth, while that of Sun is white, which is the color of the yin principle.

The trigram K'an (☵) is the second son, who resembles his mother because she seeks a second time and receives the son. The trigram Li (☲) is the second daughter, who resembles her father because he seeks a second time and receives the daughter. Since the structure of K'an in its old form is the pictogram " 川 ", which came to be written as " 水 " or water, it is possible to suppose that K'an was derived from this earlier form. Since the trigram Li is the apposition to K'an, it is the symbol of fire. Water and fire do not go together. Thus the place of K'an is north (or as winter) for it is the apposition to fire. On the other hand, the place of Li is the south and summer. The deep water, the Abysmal, is also the symbol of K'an, for water forms the abyss.

Li is the symbol of the clinging, for fire clings together toward the burning point. K'an, or the abyss , in the body is the ear, for the ear is deep inside of the body. Li in the body signifies the brightness of the eye, for the eye is a shining part of the body. K'an is also ditches, ambush, bending, straightening out, bow and wheel, for they are analogous with the shape of the abysmal. Especially, the idea of "bending and straightening out" is the expression of flowing water. This uneasy movement of water is similar in man to melancholy, sick hearts, and of earache. On the other hand, Li as the symbol of flaming is the sun, lightning. The lightning and fire are also dangerous. Among men Li is the big-bellied because of its shape in the trigram. The color of K'an is red, which is the symbol of blood, for the blood is the fluid of the body. Its animal is the pig, which lives in mud and water. The animal of Li is the pheasant, which is like a firebird. Its sign is dryness because of fire. Thus it represents the shell-bearing creatures, such as the tortoise, the crab, the snail, the mussel, the hawkbill tortoise. Among trees Li symbolizes those which dry out in the upper part of the trunk. The sign of K'an is penetration, for water is easy to penetrate. Among wood it means that which is firm and endurable (Shuo Kua 11). The firmness and endurance of wood result from the constant penetration of water.

The trigram Ken (⚍) is the third son, who resembles his mother because she seeks for a third time and receives the son. The trigram Tui (⚌) is the third daughter, who resembles her father because he seeks for a third time and receives the girl. Ken is the symbol of keeping still because in its structure the upper line is firmly supported by the two lower lines. When the upper line, which represents the will of heaven, is strong and man and earth are receptive to it, it is steady and standstill. However, in the trigram Tui

the structure is reversed. The upper line, the will of heaven, is receptive
to the strong lines of both the middle and the bottom lines. Thus it means
the joy of immediate satisfaction for the fulfillment of man and the world.
In the body Ken symbolizes the hand which can hold firm. Tui is the joy of
the mouth, because she is interested in gossiping. It is thus the mouth and
tongue. The animal symbol of Ken is a dog that stands at the door to keep the
house. On the other hand, the animal of Tui is the sheep because the two parts
of the divided line at the top of the trigram correspond to the horns of the
sheep. Ken as the mountain is the symbol of the steady and Tui as the lake is
the joyous. Ken is the bypath, that is, the mountain path and little stones
along the side. Tui means smashing and breaking apart because the lake appears
to be smashed when a passing object breaks the water. Ken means doors and
openings because the structure of the trigram is in the form of a gate. Tui
symbolizes a dropping off and bursting open because its structure has an opening above. Because Ken is the door or the gate, it also means the door keeper
and watchman who guards the street and protects the people. Tui is the
concubine who is led by the immediate joy and regrets later life. Thus the
joy does not last too long.

i. The Trigrams and Sexuality.

The combination of Ch'ien as father and K'un as mother procreates three
sons and three daughters. The sex of a child is opposite to the parent who
seeks after it. Thus the sons have a strong resemblance to their mothers and
the daughters to their fathers. In other words, "The yang (light) trigrams
have more yin (dark) lines, the yin (dark) trigrams have more yang (light)

lines" (Ta Chuan, Sec. II, Ch. 4).   The light trigrams are the sons, and the dark the daughters. Ta Chuan explains it further: "What are they and how do they act? The yang (light) trigrams have one ruler and two subjects. That indicates the way of the superior man. The yin (dark) trigrams have two rulers and one subject. This indicates the way of the small man" (Ta Chuan, Sec. II, Ch. 4). The sons have two yin lines and one yang line while the daughters have two yang lines and one yin line. The superiority of man is that one yang can match with two yin forces or one master has two subjects. The characteristic of woman is that one yin can stand for two yang forces. Here, the strength of woman is in the power of yin or the Receptive while that of man is in the power of yang or the Creative. Thus both the sons and daughters as well as the Creativity and Responsivity are complementary to each other.

What we have said so far deals with King Wen's Sequence of Later Heaven or the Inner-World Arrangement which is the basis for the understanding of the present form of hexagrams in the I Ching. According to the Sequence of Earlier Heaven or the Primal Arrangement, which is attributed to Fu Hsi, the sex determinant is based on the unpaired line of trigrams. Thus, according to the Primal Arrangement of trigrams, the sons are Chen (☳), Li (☲), and Tui (☱). Here, both Li and Tui have altered their sex. Again, the daughters, according to the Primal Arrengement, are Sun (☴), K'an (☵), and Ken (☶). Here again we see the alternation of sex takes place to both K'an and Ken. Only those which have not altered their sex are Chen and Sun, the first son and the first daughter. Except these two trigrams, the rest

of the trigrams procreated by the Ch'ien and K'un can be sexually inter-
changeable. For example, the second son, K'an, in the Inner-World
Arrangement represents the water, which is of the lake, the youngest
daughter, Tui. Thus K'an changes to the second daughter and Tui the
youngest son in the Primal Arrangement. According to the Inner-World
Arrangement, Li is the second daughter, who symbolizes fire, the sun,
and lightning. These attributes of Li are those of yang which represent
male characteristics. Thus Li changes to the second son in the Primal
Arrangement. To understand fully the meaning of the eight trigrams, the
Inner-World Arrangement must be viewed in the light of the Primal
Arrangement. The correlation of both of them is needed to know the
attributes of these trigrams. As we have already indicated, the
Inner-World Arrangement of trigrams becomes the foreground of the
Primal Arrangement and the latter the background of the former.

4. Symbolization of Hexagrams

a. The Hexagrams and Trigrams

Let us now discuss the hexagrams. What is the hexagram?
What is the relationship between the trigram and hexagram? The hexagram
means simply the diagram which consists of six lines. The word "kua" 卦
is used to describe both the trigram and the hexagram. As we have already
indicated, for the distinction between the trigram and the hexagram, the
word "chung kua" 重卦 is often used for the hexagram. Chung kua means
simply the double kua or the double trigrams. Sometimes the word "ta
sheng kua" 大成卦 is used as an alternative name for chung kua or the

hexagram. To differentiate the trigram from the hexagram, the term
"hsiao sheng kua" is often used for the trigram. Ta sheng kua means
literally the great kua, and hsiao sheng kua means the small kua. Thus
there is no qualitative distinction between the trigram and hexagram
from the etymological understanding of these words. The hexagram is
the expansion of the trigram. The size of the hexagram is that of the
trigram doubled. For example, the first and second hexagrams, Ch'ien
and K'un,

are the expansion of both the trigram Ch'ien and K'un. The hexagram
Ch'ien is simply the trigram Ch'ien (☰) doubled, and the hexagram
K'un is the trigram K'un (☷) doubled. Thus it is quite appropriate
to say that the hexagram is chung kua or the double trigrams. It is
important to remind ourselves that the 64 hexagrams are the various
combinations of the pa kua 八卦 or the eight trigrams. When the eight
trigrams are doubled in every possible way the 64 hexagrams are produced.
We can thus say that the hexagram is nothing but a great trigram and
the trigram is nothing but a small hexagram. The hexagram can be reduced
to the trigram and the trigram can be expanded to the hexagram. Because of
this mutual relationship we can easily observe why the same word "kua"
is used simultaneously for both the trigram and the hexagram. The
distinction between them is not qualitative but quantitative.

The relationship between the trigram and the hexagram is similar
to the relationship between the interplay of yin and yang and the
structure of the duogram. Just as the duogram is the combination of

both yin and yang, the hexagram is also the combination of both trigrams. Just as yang does not exist without yin, one trigram alone cannot make the hexagram possible. As we have seen, the complementary relationship between yin and yang line makes the duogram possible. It is also true that complementary relationship between the upper and the lower trigrams make the hexagram possible. Just as the yin and yang are the inseparable whole, the hexagram is also understood as the inseparable unit. Even though the hexagram is the combination of two trigrams, it cannot be compartmentalized. The hexagram must be seen as a whole. It is complete in itself, just as the trigram is a complete unit. The uniqueness of the hexagram is in its completion, just as it is in the trigram. The trigram consists of three lines, which represent different functions. The upper line represents heaven, the middle the man, and the lower the earth. In the hexagram the same pattern is expanded. In it, the two upper lines (5th and 6th lines from the bottom) represent heaven, the two middle lines (3rd and 4th lines) man, and the two lower lines (first and the second lines) earth. To illustrate, let us quote the familiar passage of the Ta Chuan again: "The I is a book which is vast and great and contains everything. It has the tao of heaven, the tao of the earth, and the tao of man. These three primal powers are doubled and make six lines. The six lines are nothing other than the tao of the three primal powers" (Sec. II, Ch. 10). Since each force is represented in the hexagram by two lines or double forces, the hexagram is called the great kua. That is, the hexagram, is the expansion of the trigram but at the same time it is unique in itself.

The complementary relationship between the two constituting trigrams, just like the relationship between yin and yang, is commonly experienced in our every day life. For example,the power of electricity
is different from both the positive and negative current. However, the
combination of both the positive and negative currents makes electricity
possible. We often distinguish between time and space to describe our
existence in the world. If we think that we can describe our being in
terms of time and space, we can be the combination of both time and space.
However, we know that our existence is more than both time and space.
Our existence is unique from time and space, yet it is impossible without
both of them at the same time. In the hexagram the same principle is
applied. It is of two trigrams but is also unique from them. The hexagram has its own identity as the self which is autonomous in itself. The
hexagrams can be compared with atoms, which consist of both electrons and
a nucleus but are unique to themselves. Just like atoms, the hexagrams
are the germinal units of all possible situations in the universe. They are
the microcosms of the universe. Everything and every possible predicament
in the universe can be expressed within these 64 hexagrams in the I Ching.
That is precisely why the Ta Chuan says, "The I contains the measure of
heaven and earth. Thus it enables us to perceive the tao of heaven and
earth" (Sec. I, Ch. 4).

b. The Sixty-Four Hexagrams

Why do the hexagrams limit themselves to the number 64? It seems
possible to extend the germinal situations indefinitely by adding

indefinite numbers to both _yin_ and _yang_ lines. For example, the
combination of two lines of _yin_ and _yang_ makes the 4 duograms possible.
With the addition of one more line to the duograms the eight trigrams are
produced. Again by adding another line to the eight trigrams the sixteen
quartergrams are available. In this way it is possible to expand the
possible situations indefinitely. Why does the _I Ching_ stop at the
number 64? Why are the 64 hexagrams to complete all the possible situations
in the universe? These questions are answered only in relation to the
trigrams. Since the eight trigrams are the archetypal units of every
possible situation in the universe, every possible combination of those
eight produces the 64 hexagrams. It is based purely on mathematical logic.
We must come back again to the Chinese word "_kua_" 卦 to see the relationship between the trigram and the hexagram if we want to know why the
number 64 became the complete description of whole situations in the
universe. Since the hexagram is called the _ta sheng kua_ or the great _kua_,
the trigram which is the _hsiao sheng kua_ or the small _kua_ cannot expand
more than its own number of _kua_, that is, number eight. Thus each small
kua or trigram can expand as far as the number eight. It cannot go
beyond what is the intrinsically given number, that is, number eight.
Therefore, the small _kua_ can be extended to the great _kua_ by every possible
multiplication of eight. The great _kua_ cannot expand indefinitely, because
of the intrinsic limitation of the possibility of expansion in the small
kua. However, if we believe that the hexagram or the great _kua_ is
qualitatively different from the trigram or the small _kua_, it is possible
that the great _kua_ can grow indefinitely. Since the great _kua_ has no
qualitative distinction from the small _kua_, the former is limited to the

intrinsic limitation of the latter.

We may be able to get more enlightenment on the limitation of the 64 situations if we analyze the word "kua" 卦 carefully. The word "kua" 卦 has its origin in the practice of divination. If we separate the word into two parts, it is much easier to understand it. Kua 卦 is the combination of two words: kuei 圭 and pu 卜 . The word "pu" 卜 denotes divination by tortoise shell prior to the formation of the hexagram. According to the Book of Rites, "Kuei wei pu, ts'e wei shih" 龜為卜 筴為筮 , which means that pu method of divination using tortoise, while the shih method makes use of stalks. However, the word "pu" 卜 has been used to imply divination of all kinds. That is why the method of divination which makes use of stalks is often described as pu shih 卜筮 , which means the divination by stalks. Now, let us look at the other part of the word "kua." The word "kuei" 圭 is the combination of two identical words of t'u 土. The word "t'u" 土 means the soil but the shape and the structure of the word is similar to the structure of the trigram. The t'u 土 consists of three lines, two horizontal lines and one vertical line. Doubling the t'u, just as doubling the trigrams (one above and the other below) we have the word "kuei" 圭 . Thus kuei 圭 is analogous with the hexagram. We may have stretched our imaginations too much to illustrate the relationship between the trigram and hexagram through the analysis of the word "kua." However, it is not a coincidence that the word kuei has some relation to the hexagrams. Actually, kuei 圭 signifies a sundial, which is the measurement of seasons and changing situations. Kuei is also the name of the measurement which is divided into 64 degrees. The 64 divisions of kuei certainly correspond with the 64 hexagrams. Just as all the changing phenomena are to be measured by the 64 divisions of kuei, the

64 hexagrams represent all the possible situations in the universe. The 64 are the complete numbers which express the rounded whole of the universe.

However, it does not make sense to say that the 64 germinal situations can represent all the possible phenomena of the universe. It seems that there are many more possible situations in our life. Through the development of civilization and modernization new situations arise. It seems, therefore, impossible to deal with various situations through the use of 64 hexagrams. However, it is a grave mistake if we think that the 64 hexagrams are identical with the 64 actual situations in our world today. The hexagrams do not represent the actual situations but the germinal situations which are to be actualized in many different ways. The hexagrams are analogous with seeds which are to be grown. As Ta Chuan indicates, "To know the seeds is to know the divine. In his dealing with those above him, the superior man does not flatter. In his dealing with those beneath him, he is not arrogant. For he knows the seeds. The seeds are the slight beginnings of movement and the first indications of good fortune and misfortune. The superior man realizes the seeds and acts immediately without any delay of a single day" (Sec. II, Ch. 5). The hexagrams, which are analogous with the seeds, are identical with embryonic stages. They are the undifferentiated continuums, from which all kinds of actual situations will eventually evolve. They are potentialities which are not yet actualized in human experience. The 64 hexagrams are similar to the 64 different potentialities which could be realized in many different ways. If we believe that a single cell (or the germinal situation) can evolve, in its multiple dimensions,

into all the living creatures of our time, it is not difficult to believe
that the 64 germinal situations or the 64 undifferentiated continuums are
sufficient to summarize all the possible phenomena of the universe.

c. The Structure of the Hexagrams

The nature of the hexagrams becomes clear if we examine the structural
aspects of the hexagrams. We have already pointed out that the hexagram
is the combination of two trigrams. These two constituting trigrams are
called the primary trigrams, because they are primarily responsible for
the formation of the hexagram. The lower primary trigram consists of the
first three lines from the bottom of the hexagram, while the upper primary
trigram is formed with the 4th, 5th, and 6th lines of the hexagram. For
example, the hexagram 11, T'ai or Peace, is the combination of both

the primary trigram Ch'ien (━━━━) below and the primary trigram K'un
(══ ══) above. The trigram Ch'ien is called the lower primary trigram
of the hexagram T'ai, and the trigram K'un the upper primary trigram of it.
If we observe the hexagram T'ai carefully, it is possible to form two
more trigrams. If we begin with the line 2 upward, we get the trigram
which consists of lines 2, 3 and 4 (━━━━), the trigram Tui. Again we
can begin with the line 3 upward and get the lines 3, 4 and 5 which
constitute the trigram Chen (══ ══). Both trigrams are within the primary
trigrams and are called the nuclear trigrams, because of their structure
within the hexagram. The trigram Tui is called the lower nuclear trigram

while the trigram <u>Chen</u> is called the upper nuclear trigram. The function
of nuclear trigrams is rather limited within the function of the primary
trigrams. Moreover, the function of the primary trigrams is limited
within the function of the hexagram as a whole. The relationship between
the nuclear trigrams and the primary trigrams in the hexagram can be
compared with the relationship between children and parents in the home.
The relationship between the mother and father is analogous with the
relationship between the lower and upper primary trigrams of the hexagram.
The relationship between the daughters and sons is also analogous with the
relationship between the lower and upper nuclear trigrams of the hexagram.
Just as the parents delimit the function of their children, the two
primary trigrams also delimit the function of the nuclear trigrams. The
relationship between the mother and father sets up a norm of family life
for the children. However, this does not mean that the children are not
important. Many major crises of family life, such as the destruction of
harmony and the separation of parents, result from the unfortunate
relationship among the children. Likewise, the relationship between
the two nuclear trigrams can influence the destructive effects of the
hexagram. However, the function of parents is also conditioned by the
welfare of the whole family. Thus the function of the two primary
trigrams is confined within the hexagram as a whole.

d. The Hexagrams and the Attributes of Constituting Trigrams

Let us now examine how the attributes of the trigrams affect the
nature of the hexagram. We may return to the hexagram 11, <u>T'ai</u> or Peace,

for our examination. Let us first examine the relationship between the attributes of both primary trigrams, Ch'ien below and K'un above. Some of the main attributes of Ch'ien are creative, strong, heaven or the father, while those of K'un are the responsive, devoted, earth or the mother. We see the favorable correlation between these two trigrams in terms of their attributes. The relationship between the creative and responsive, between the strong and the devoted, between the heaven and the earth, and between the father and mother shows the harmonious co-existence of opposites. However, the correlation of these attributes is relative to the position of these trigrams. It is, in other words, important to know the position of the creative in relation to the receptive. The lower trigram always occupies the "below," "within," and "behind." On the other hand, the upper trigram occupies the "above," "without," and "in front." Because of these implications in the positions, the lower trigram stresses the idea of coming in while the upper trigram stresses the concept of going out. The lower trigram is inner-directed, while the upper trigram is outer-directed. As to the position of the trigrams, the center is also important. The trigrams can move closer together toward the center or move away from the center. With these preliminary remarks, let us now come back to the hexagram T'ai or Peace again. The lower primary trigram, Ch'ien, is in the position of below, within and behind the upper trigram, K'un. On the other hand, the upper primary trigram K'un is in the reverse position of the former, that is, in the position of above, without and in front of the trigram Ch'ien. The relationship between these two trigrams is relative to the direction of movement. The trigram Ch'ien moves upward,

because it is of light principle. The trigram K'un moves downward because
it is of heaven and inactive principle. Thus the lower primary trigram,
Ch'ien, moves toward the center, just as the upper primary trigram, K'un,
moves down to the center of the hexagram. It is a good sign that both
trigrams move close together toward the center. Thus the commentary on
this hexagram says, "The Receptive, which moves downward, stands above;
the Creative, which moves upwards, is below. Hence their influences meet
and are in harmony, so that all living things bloom and prosper."[1] There
is, therefore, no doubt why this hexagram is named T'ai or Peace.

The significance of the position of the trigrams becomes clear if
we examine the hexagram 12, P'i or Stagnation, which is the reversion

of the hexagram 11, T'ai or Peace. In the hexagram P'i the primary trigram Ch'ien (——————) is above and the primary trigram K'un (══ ══) is below. The attributes of both Ch'ien and K'un are identical in both hexagrams. However, the difference is in the position of how the trigrams
are constituted. In the hexagram P'i, the light principle, the trigram
Ch'ien, is above, so that it moves upwards. The trigram K'un, which is
below, moves downward. Thus both trigrams move away from the center. The
commentary on this hexagram remarks, "Heaven is above, drawing farther
and farther away, while the earth below sinks farther into the depths.
The creative powers are not in relation. It is a time for standstill and

[1]Richard Wilhelm, op. cit., p. 48.

decline."[1]   Here, we see the importance of the position of the constituting trigrams in relation to the nature of the hexagram. When the
trigram Ch'ien is above and K'un is below, as in the case of the hexagram P'i, it is the time of stagnation. When the trigram Ch'ien is
below and K'un is above, as in the case of the hexagram T'ai, it is the
time of peace and harmony.

Our discussion on the constituting trigrams has been centered
around the primary trigrams. Let us now focus our attention on the
nuclear trigrams within the hexagram T'ai or Peace. As we have already
pointed out, the constituting nuclear trigrams are Tui (———) below
and Chen (———) above. Some of the main attributes of the trigram
Chen are : awakening, movement, thunder, wood and the elder, while those
of Tui are: the joy, pleasure, lake, the youngest daughter. The trigram
Chen as the awakening moves upwards in the manner of his father Ch'ien,
and Tui as the joy also tends to move upwards because of its light principle. Thus both of them move upward from the center. Their influences do
not meet each other. This unhealthy circumstance, created by the relationship between the two nuclear trigrams, does not upset the harmonious
correlation between the two primary trigrams. The Judgment on the
hexagram points out the side effect which is caused by the two nuclear trigrams: "Peace. The small departs and the great approaches. It is good fortune and success." Here, "the small departs" is an unfarovable effect created
by the relationship between the nuclear trigrams. However, "the great approaches"
is a favorable situation which is created by the relationship between the two

---

[1]Ibid., p. 52.

primary trigrams. As we have seen, the significance of the relationship between the nuclear trigrams is delimited by that of the primary trigrams.

d. The Revealed and Hidden Hexagrams

In understanding the true nature of hexagrams, we must presuppose that there are hidden hexagrams which are opposite to the manifested ones. In other words, each hexagram we have obtained through the manipulation of stalks or coins has its opposite structure which is hidden. This idea is based on the principle of changes. According to the principle, yin and yang complement each other. Yin presupposes the existence of yang, and yang also presupposes the existence of yin. Since the hexagram is constantly in the process of changes and transformations, it presupposes the existence of its opposite. For example, the hexagram Ch'ien presupposes the existence of its opposite, the hexagram K'un, behind it. Behind the hexagram K'un is the hexagram Ch'ien also. It becomes much clearer if we look at the Diagram of the Great Ultimate, T'ai Ch'i T'u, where the two opposing symbols of primal monad are intertwined together. If we have not seen it before, we can easily draw the symbol. Take a circle and divide it into two equal parts by drawing an S-shaped curve from top to bottom. One part should be dark and the other light. A light dot can be placed in the middle of the dark part and a dark dot in the middle of the light. Here, we have attained a perfect symmetrical symbolism of changes and transformations. In this symbol what is light is also dark, because of the dark dot in it. What is dark is also light at the same time, because of the light dot in the dark. Just as the light principle presupposes the existence of the dark, each hexagram presupposes the existence of its

opposite which is not revealed. The hexagram changes to what is the
opposite of its own. When it changes completely to its opposite, it starts
to return again. For example, when the hexagram <u>Ch'ien</u> changes completely
to its opposite, the hexagram <u>K'un</u>, it starts to return to the former.
Even each line of the hexagram presupposes the existence of its opposite.
When the undivded line changes to the divided line, the former presupposes
the existence of the latter. Thus, lines, trigrams and hexagrams which
are not revealed are the opposites of those revealed.

f. The Hexagrams and the Principle of Changes

Let us now look at the lines of hexagrams in the light of the
principle of changes. The lines of the hexagrams also represent the process of changes. "The lines," said <u>Ta Chuan</u>, "are imitations of movements under heaven" (Sec. II, Ch. 3). As Wang Pi said, the hexagram expresses the time and the line the change of time. Time is the situation of the
hexagram for situation is of time. The situation which is expressed in
the hexagram changes just as the lines of the hexagram are transformed
from the divided to the undivided and from the undivided to the divided.
Just like the things on earth change while the earth itself is changing.
Thus the lines change within the changing hexagram. Thus it is said in
<u>Ta Chuan</u>: "The <u>I</u> is a book which is not far away. Its <u>tao</u> is forever

changing and transforming everything. It flows through the six empty

places of above and below. The firm and yielding transform each other.

They don't have to be confined within a rule, because the change is at work

here" (Sec. II, Ch. 8). Even though there is no certain rule of the

change of lines, there are fixed rhythms: the movement inward and outward

according to the principle of changes. The movement of lines from inward

to outward implies the movement of the lower trigram which represents the

position of the inward, to the upper trigram, the position of the outward,

of the hexagram. In this movement of changes from the inward to the outward

or from the bottom to the upper portion of the hexagrams, the lines change

constantly. "The I is a book which begins with the first (line) and are

summed up in the last (line)" (Ta Chuan, Sec. II, Ch. 9). The movement

of changes within the hexagram is compared with the process of building

which begins with the foundation and moves upward. The beginning line

or the bottom line is the foundation of the hexagram. This line is

difficult to understand because it represents the depth of the unconscious.

However, the top line or the last line is easy to understand, for it starts

to reveal the unconscious. The manifestation of unconsciousness moves from

the depth to the surface of the conscious. That is why the judgment on the

first line is tentative, while on the last line is complete. The beginning

line and the top line, which do not belong to the nuclear trigrams, set the

limitations of the hexagram. They delimit the most primitive stratum of

cyclic changes. The real evolvement takes place in the lines of two nuclear

trigrams. The four lines in the middle are active in the process of evolve-

ment. Since the beginning and the top lines are not participating in the

active process of evolvement, they represent the mass and the sages. The fifth line represents the ruler who is perhaps most active in the process of changes. The fourth line represents the minister who assists the ruler. The third line is the one who connects the central with the local government. The second is the official who is also very active in the process of changes. The fifth and second lines are most active because of their central positions in the primary trigrams. Each line is differentiated with the position of work, all of them work together for the process of changes. A fixed rhythm in the process of changes within the hexagram is a process of gradual evolvement from the bottom to the top line. Let us take up the same hexagram, T'ai or Peace, to illustrate this gradual evolvement of changing poitions. The beginning line means: "When ribbon grass is pulled up, it brings the sod with it. Advance will bring good fortune." Here the time of prosperity calls officials to lead the people. "Ribbon grass" implies the roots of the state which are the multitudes. The second line means: "One who is uncultured can cross the river without a boat and does not neglect the distant for his companions. Thus he can walk in the middle." Here the official is an able man who could manage to rule with the middle way for action. The first or beginning line calls for a man who could lead the mass of people so that the second line acts decisively on the request of the first line. The movement of action in the second line is clear but not violent. The third line means: "There is no peace that is not liable to be disturbed. There is no going that is not followed by a return. It is difficult to be right without blame. Do not blame about the truth: enjoy the blessings you still possess." The third line represents the transitional position, which is the difficult position to maintain. In this line we see that the changes are slow yet coming. It is hard work to change the mind of people. The fourth line means: "He flutters down and does not boast his wealth. He calls his neighbour in sincerity." This is the position of the minister, who in his respectful position does not boast of his position or his wealth. The fourth line expresses the attitude of the minister in time of peace. The fifth line means: "The king I gives his daughter in marriage. By doing this there will be blessing and great good fortune." The fifth line represents the ruler as is indicated here. It is the highest blessings and great good fortune to give his daughter in marriage. This line certainly represents the height of peace and prosperity. The top line means: "The wall returns into the moat. Don't use army. Announce your orders to the people of your own city. Firmness brings regret and humiliation." Prosperity and peace are not exceptions to the principle of changes. They are followed by the decline and humiliation. Everything is subject to the principle of changes. It is the time of reversion. Thus there is a certain trend of evolvement in changes. The line in each station is given a certain position, which is a part of the total situation of the hexagrams as a whole. All of them are subject to change and transformation.

g. The Hexagrams and the Position of Lines

The correlation of the lines of these hexagrams has to do with their character. The lines are either the divided or the undivided but their locations are either correct (or central) or incorrect (not central). The characteristic of the line is relative to its position in the hexagram. A line is correct when it stands in an appropriate place. For example, as a rule, a firm line (or undivided line) occupies the first, third or fifth place, while the tender (or the divided) line the second, fourth or sixth place. Yang lines properly occupy the odd places while the yin lines the even places. However, this kind of rule does not always work. When the time calls for receptiveness, the yin line is favorable irrespective of its position. Likewise, when the time calls the firmness, the yang line is favorable irrespective of its position. For example, in hexagram 19, Lin or Approach, the line in the second place ought to be the divided line according to the rule.

However, this particular time calls for the line of firmness in the second place. Nine[1] at the second place means: "Approaching together will bring good fortune and advancement." The fifth place, as a rule, is to be the yang line. However, in this particular time the yin line is appropriate. Thus six[2] in the fifth place means: "To know the Li is the duty of a great prince. It brings good fortune." In the hexagram 32, Heng or Enduring, the

yin line in the first place is not appropriate. Thus six at the beginning means: "Desiring Heng too hastily brings misfortune, even though it is correct. There will be no advantage." The yang line in the second place, as a rule, is not appropriate. Thus nine in the second place means: "Regret disappears." The yin line in the fifth place means: "Heng maintains right

---

[1]Nine is the moving number of yang line.

[2]Six is the moving number of yin line.

virtues. It is a good fortune for a woman, but misfortune for a man."
It is good for a woman, because of its divided line, but is unfortunate
for a man. To take another example, according to the rule of correct or
incorrect position of either yin or yang lines, let us observe the hexagram
16, Yü or Eagerness . The yin line of the hexagram is not in the central
position. Thus, six at the beginning means: "Proclaiming Eagerness

brings misfortune." The yin line in the second place is correct. The
judgment on the second line is good: "It is firm as a rock. It is not
a whole day. Correctness brings good fortune." In this line the Hsiang Chuan
or the Commentary on the Symbols says, "It is not a whole day. Correctness
brings good fortune, because it is central and right." The yin line in
the third place is not correct. Thus the judgment says, "Eagerness that
looks upward. If it is delayed, it brings remorse." Hsiang Chuan adds
a remarks: "Eagerness that looks upward brings remorse, because the place
is not appropriate." Thus the correlation of lines with appropriate places
in the hexagrams often violates the rule in a certain situation, but the rules
of correlation are reliable in most cases.

There is also a certain rule of correspondence of lines within the
hexagram. As a rule, yang lines correspond with yin lines only, and vice
versa. As we said, the first, third and fifth places are correct for the
yang line, and for the second, fourth, and sixth places are correct for the
yin line. Since a yang line corresponds to a yin line and the hexagrams consist of two primary trigrams, the first place (yang line) corresponds to the

fourth place (<u>yin</u> line), the second place (<u>yin</u> line), the second place (<u>yin</u> line) to the fifth place (<u>yang</u> line), and the third place (<u>yang</u> line) to the top place (<u>yin</u> line). Thus the first and fourth, the second and the fifth, and the third and the top lines are correlated. The most important correlation among them is the correlation of the second and fifth place. Their relationship is analogous with the relationship between offical and ruler, son and father, or wife and husband. The firm official corresponds to the yielding ruler and the yiedling official to the firm ruler. In the case of hexagram 4, <u>Meng</u> or Immature Youth, the second or the offical is firm while

the fifth or the ruler is yielding. Thus the judgment of the hexagram says, "<u>Meng</u> is successful." The same relationship is seen in hexagrams 7, 11, 14, 18, 19, 32, 34, 40, 41, 46, and 50. The relationship between the firm ruler and the yielding official is also favorable. For example, the hexagram 3,

<u>Chun</u> or Difficulty (or Uneasiness) , has some difficulty, but success is supreme. As the judgment says, "<u>Chun</u> is originating, penetrating, advantageious and correct." The hexagrams 8, 25, 37, 42, 45, 49, and 53 are like the hexagram 3, favorable, for they have the firm ruler and the yielding official. However, the hexagram 33, <u>Tun</u> or Withdrawal, as well as the hexagrams 39 and 63 are far less favorable. Therefore, we can conclude that the correlation of the second with the fifth place, whether either the <u>yang</u> line is in the second place and the <u>yin</u> line is in the fifth place or the <u>yin</u> line

is in the second place and yang line in the fifth place, is important for the hexagram as a whole. The correlation between the first and the fourth and the third and sixth places appears to be rather insignificant to the hexagram as a whole.

Another aspect concerning the relation among the lines within the hexagram is that of mutual dependence. This idea is well expressed in the hexagram 8, Pi or Uniting Together. As the commentary on this hexagram indicates, the principle expressed in this hexagram became the basis for the social organization of ancient China. The principle of mutual dependence or holding together is also applied to the relationships among the lines in the hexagram. The principle of mutual dependence deals with the relationship between the two adjacent lines of the hexagram. In the relationship between the adjacent lines, the lower line receives the upper line and the upper line rests on the lower line. In this mutual dependency the relationship between the fourth and fifth lines is the most important, for it represents the relationship between the minister and ruler. The mutual cooperation and confidence between the ruler and minister merely controls the destiny of the state according to the traditional concept of Chinese government. In the family situation the relationship between the husband and wife is the most important. It is most favorable when the fourth place is the yielding line and the fifth is a firm line. Let us look at the hexagram 8, Pi or Uniting Together, which symbolizes the principle of mutual dependence. The fourth line of the hexagram is yielding (minister of wife) and the fifth line represents the firm (ruler or husband). In the fourth place, "The subject seeks for union with his master." In the fifth place, "It expresses

the most illustrious instance of seeking union." Similarly, the hexagrams
9, 20, 29, 37, 42, 48, 55, 57, 59, 60 and 61 are favorable in the mutual
dependency between the firm ruler and the yielding minister. However, when
the relationship is altered, that is, the yielding ruler (fifth place) and
the firm minister (fourth place), it is rather unfavorable even though there
are some exceptions. For example, hexagram 30, Li or the Flaming, has the
firm line in the fourth place and yielding line in the fifth place. The

firm minister or wife in the fourth place means: "Its coming is sudden, as
if extinguishing fire and throwing away the dead." The ruler or husband in
the yielding line of the fifth means: "Tears flowing in torrents and la-
menting in sorrows. It will bring good fortune." The uniting together in
this case, that is, when the ruler is the yielding line and the minister is
the firm line, is less favorable than the former case. Other hexagrams
which have a similar situation of Li are the hexagrams 32, 35, 50, 51, 56
and 62.

In conclusion it should be pointed out that the fifth place is not
always the position of the ruler or the ruling line. There are some exceptions to it. For example, in the hexagram 16, Yü or Eagerness , the fourth

place is the ruling line, because it alone is the firm line in the hexagram.
In the hexagram 23, Po or Breaking Apart, the top line is the ruler, for

the same reason. The same principle can be also applied to the hexagram 24,
Fu or Return, in which the first line acts as the ruler. Often the distinc-

tion between the governing ruler and the constituting ruler is analogous to
the relationship between the executive and judicial branches of our government. Sometimes the governing ruler acts as the constituting ruler and at
other times each has different places in the hexagram. The governing ruler
of the hexagram is mostly in the fifth place but there is no definite rule
to determine the constituting ruler's place in the hexagram. We have to
rely on the Commentary on the Judgments or T'u Chuan to find out the position of the constituting ruler within the hexagram. The constituting line
is often the line which expresses most clearly the basic frame of a given
situation. It is to be compared with the justice of the supreme court who
is responsible for the correct interpretation of the constitution of the
government. In the hexagram 12, P'i or Stagnation, for example, the con-

stituting ruler is in the second place. It reads, "Bearing endurance,
the small man receives good fortune. The great man also attains success in
the P'i." Also in the hexagram 54, Kuei Mei or the Marrying Maiden, the

constituting ruler is in the third line. It reads, "The maiden marries as
a concubine." In both cases the constituting ruler expresses well the basic
feature of the hexagram as a whole. However, the constituting ruler does
not always express the constitution of the hexagram. For example, the hexagram 10, Lü or Treading, has the constituting ruler in the third place. It

says, "A one-eyed man can see a lame man who is able to walk. He treads on
the tail of the tiger, which bites him. It is misfortune. Thus a warrior
acts on behalf of his great ruler." Hsiang Chuan elucidates it saying, "The
misfortune in the biting of the man is due to the inappropriate place."
The judgment on this hexagram is the other way around: "Treading upon
the tail of the tiger, which does not bite him. It is successful." Thus
the constituting ruler of this hexagram does not represent the clear picture of the hexagram.

   As we have observed, there is no single rule which can apply to all
the hexagrams. There are many exceptions to the rules which we have mentioned, so that they are merely arbitrary devices for our understanding of
the hexagrams. If we believe that the hexagrams are expressions of unconscious strata which manifest themselves in our interpretations, they may
not be subject to the logical system of the conscious. Many of them do not
make sense to us at all. But they somehow express the inner orientations of
the world of phenomena which are not directly accessible to the world of the
conscious. Because they are inexpressible to our way of thinking they are
used with lines to reveal what is not known in words. Thus,"The Master said:

Writing cannot express words fully, words cannot express thoughts fully.
Is it impossible to see the thoughts of the holy sage? The Master said:
The holy sages made the symbols in order to express their thoughts fully.
They constructed the hexagrams in order to express fully what is true and
what is false. They appended judgments in order to express their words
fully" (Ta Chuan, Sec. I, Ch. 12).

CHAPTER IV. THE HEXAGRAMS IN WORDS

The hexagrams, as we have already seen, are symbolic of germinal situations which are correlated with the principle of changes. We have attempted to spell out some of the possible rules by which the hexagrams are to be realized. Some of these rules have been formulated on the basis of the appended words on the hexagrams. These words appended to the hexagrams are known to us in Chinese as "hsi tz'u" 繫辭, which literally means "appended words." The hsi tz'u or the appended words include both kua tz'u 卦辭 , the hexagrams in words, and hsiao tz'u 爻辭, the lines in words. Let us first consider the meaning of the word "tz'u" 辭 , before we discuss them separately.

1. The Meaning of " tz'u"

The word "tz'u" is commonly understood as "words" or "speeches." Is it then valid to translate the word as "judgments," instead of "words"? However, we find the word "judgments" in the Ten Wings, the Appendixes to the I Ching. According to T'uan Chuan, the word "tz'u" is identical to the word "t'uan" which literally means "judgments" or "decisions." Since the words "t'uan" and "tz'u" are used identically in this commentary, it is reasonable to believe that the concept of "tz'u" or "words" has been used interchangeably with the idea of "t'uan" or "judgments," at the time the commentary was written. As James Legge remarks, we do not know how the character "t'uan" arose and how it was named "t'uan".[1] In any case, the word "tz'u" came to be

---

[1]Legge, op. cit., p. 213-214.

known as t'uan or the judgments.

The meaning of tz'u, the words, is judgments (or t'uan) in T'uan Chuan, the Commentary on the Judgments. Let us observe the use of the word "tz'u" in Ta Chuan or the Great Treatise. As we will see, tz'u is used in Ta Chuan and other commentaries to mean the judgments. For example, the Ta Chuan says, "The tz'u or the word is appended to indicate good fortune and misfortune" (Sec. I, Ch. 2). Here the tz'u or the words are used for the judgments or the decisions (t'uan). A similar statement is found again in Ta Chuan: "the differentiation between good fortune and misfortune is dependent upon the tz'u (Sec. I, Ch. 3). In both cases the word "tz'u" means judgments or discriminations which include value judgments. In another place the tz'u means more than judgments. The following statement implies that the tz'u is not only judgments but also interpretations: "the tz'u is appended to give a clear interpretation as to either fortunate or misfortunate. In this way our doubts are resolved" (Ta Chuan, Sec. I, Ch. 11). The tz'u as interpretation is close to the feelings of the sages: "The feelings of the holy sages manifest themselves in the tz'u" (Ta Chuan, Sec. II, Ch. 1). Here, the feelings of the sages are analogous with their intuitive insights to discern the truth. The other meaning, which is associated with the word "tz'u", is stimulation: "The stimulation of all movements under heaven is expressed in the tz'u (Ta Chuan, Sec. I, Ch. 12). To summarize the meaning of tz'u expressed in the Ta Chuan, we can say it has three different aspects: judgments, interpretations and stimulations. Judgments presuppose an interpretation of the hexagrams and stimulations for actions on which the judgments are made. Thus judgments are inclusive of both interpretations and stimulations. Since they are different from the ordinary understanding of judgments, let us differentiate them by using the capital letter "J". Thus tz'u means the Judgment, which is to be used differently from judgment.

Our definition of the Judgment corresponds with the definition found in the Shuo Wen Chieh-tzu, a dictionary composed by Hsu Shen around 100 A.D. It defines the meaning as legal action or dispute. Its legalistic and judicial judgments are implicit in the sentence by the judge on the cases presented before the court. Since the process of making judgments in court needs a careful study and understanding, the judgments need precise interpretations. Also the judgment of the court is not a mere statement but includes an action for prosecution. The concept of tz'u (or the Judgment) is analogous with the judgment of a civil court, which is implicit in the interpretation of a given situation and the action for prosecution.

What is the relationship between the Judgments and the kua or the hexagrams? The concept of the Judgments becomes much clearer if we analyze them in relation to the hexagrams. The relationship between the Judgments and the hexagrams is stated in the Ta Chuan: "The holy sages appended the Judgments in order to define clearly good fortune and misfortune" (Sec. I, Ch. 2). Again in Ta Chuan the Judgments are compared with the hexagrams: "Therefore, the differentiation of the rich from the poor is based on the positions, and the distinction of the great from the small is based on the hexagrams, and the differentiation between good fortune and misfortune is based on the Judgments" (Sec. I, Ch. 3). In both cases the distinctive function of both the hexagrams and the Judgments is indicated. The function of the hexagram is to help us understand the phenomena while that of the Judgments is a decision for action on the basis of the hexagrams. The dynamic aspect of the

Judgment in relation to the hexagrams is much more clearly expressed in the following statement: "This is why there are the differentiation between the small and the great among the hexagrams, and the distinction between danger and safety in the Judgments. The Judgments indicate the trends of development" (Ta Chuan, Sec. I, Ch. 3). Again we see the contrast between the hexagrams and the Judgments in their functions: "The extreme appearance of many diversities under heaven depends upon the hexagrams. The stimulation of all movements under heaven is based on the Judgments" (Ta Chuan, Sec. I, Ch. 12). These passages present the contrast between the functions of the hexagrams and the Judgments. However, their contrast is not dichotomous but is complementary. The hexagrams represent the forms in which the complex phenomena of the world are patterned while the Judgments present the contents which are ever moving and changing aspects of world phenomena. The relation- ship between the hexagrams and the Judgments resembles the Greek notion of form and content. Form represents the symbol in a sense, while the content represents the movement in the sense of action and trend. The hexagrams indicate what the germinal situations are, while the Judgments signify what the situations become. Since being is not without becoming in the principle of changes, to talk of the hexagrams is eventually to talk of the Judgments. Both the hexagrams and the Judgments are inseparable. They are always in a complementary relationship.

The Judgments indicate the trend and movement of events which are actualizing themselves through the principle of changes. This trend or becoming is the source of our knowledge about fortune and misfortune. As Ta Chuan indicates: "Good fortune and misfortune, remorse and humiliation are produced by movements" (Sec. II, Ch. 1). The movements are the Judgments. The Judgments are best understood as indicators, which are sensitive enough

to tell us what is going to happen. Just as the indicators are the bases of
action for the future, the Judgments are also the foundations of our decisions.
Electricity flows and produces light but we do not know its flow without the
indicator or the voltmeter. To use this analogy, electricity is analogous
with the germinal situation itself, the light with the hexagram and the
voltmeter with the Judgment. The Judgment not only indicates the trend of
movement as expressed in the hexagram but also the possible outcome of the
future, that is, the trend of becoming. The Judgment forecasts future
possibilities as the indicator does. However, the forecast indicates only
the possibilities of becoming. It gives room for our decision to alter the
trend of becoming. That is why the Judgment stimulates the course of action.
The Judgment of the hexagram 5, Hsü or Waiting, for example, says, "Waiting.
Sincerity will bring you light and success. Correctness brings good fortune.
It is advantageous to corss the great river." Here the Judgment not only

forecasts the movement of this hexagram but tells us the way to attain
good fortune and to avoid misfortune. Just as the indicator helps us to
decide what to do with our future, the Judgment gives us room for a decision
to control our future within the possible trends of movement. This is precisely why the I Ching differs from other oracles or divination books. The
Judgment in the I Ching can be compared with the concept of hope, which is
much different from wishes. Hope is the direction of the present situation
toward the future while the wish is an expectation without the direction of
the present reality. Hope is based on decision and commitment to that which
is expected but the wish is based on illusion and longing for something new

without any commitment to it. Because of the Judgment which has the element
of hope, the I Ching is a unique book of divination.

2. The Names of the Hexagrams

Since the Judgments begin with the name of the hexagrams, it is helpful to mention them. The name of the hexagram or kua ming always proceeds
the Judgment. Thus let us examine it in relation to the Judgment. The Judgment on the hexagram 1, for example, begins with the word "Ch'ien", which is
its name. The Judgment reads, "The Ch'ien is originating, success, advantageous and correct." Here, the word "Ch'ien" with which the Judgment begins
is the name of this hexagram. It is difficult to notice in English translation that it is the name of hexagram. According to Wilhelm's translation,
the Judgment says, "The Creative works sublime success, furthering through
perseverance" (乾 元 亨 利 貞). Here the word "Creative" is "Ch'ien"
乾 , which is the first word of the Judgment and the name of the hexagram.
Let us look at the hexagram 5, Hsü or Waiting. The Judgment on this hexagram says, " Waiting. Sincerity will bring you light and success. Correctness brings good fortune. It is advantageous to corss the great river." Here,
we do not have any trouble understanding from the translation that "Waiting"
or Hsü, the name of the hexagram, is added in the beginning of the Judgment.
The names of hexagrams are autonomous in themselves and not dependent
upon the following sentences of the Judgment. However, there are at least
four hexagrams in the I Ching which do not have their names in the Judgments.
Let us examine each of them separately.

The hexagram 10, Lü or Treading, does not have its name in the Judgment.

From the English translation we can hardly notice this. According to Wilhelm's translation, we read the Judgment as follows: "Treading. Treading upon tail of the tiger. It does not bite the man. Success." Here the word "Treading" is added by the translator. Thus the original text of this hexagram ought to be: "Treading upon the tail of the tiger, which does not bite man. Success" (履虎尾不咥人亨). If we take away the word LÜ 履 from the Judgment, the sentence is incomplete. In other words, without the word "Treading" we have the following construction in the Chinese sentence: 虎尾不咥人亨, which does not make sense at all because it is incomplete. Since the Judgment without the word "LÜ" or "Treading" does not make sense, it is possible that the name of this hexagram was lost. The name which we have now might be replaced with the first word of the Judgment in the later period.

The hexagram 12, P'i or Stagnation, also lacks the name in the Judgment. Again we cannot notice this in the translation. In both translations of the I Ching by Wilhelm and Legge the word "P'i" 否 is added to the Judgment. Thus the Judgment reads, Standstill. Evil people do not further the perseverance of the superior man. The great departs; the small approaches."[1] According to the original text, it reads, "The evil people do not advance (or further)..." (否之匪人 ...). Again, if we take the word "P'i" 否 away from the Judgment as a part of the name of the hexagram, the sentence does not make sense at all. It is, therefore, possible that the name of this hexagram was lost udring the long period of transmission and replaced later with the first word of the Judgment.

The hexagram 13, T'ung Jen or Fellowship, also does not have its name

---

[1] R. Wilhelm's translation.

in the Judgment. At this time we do not have much trouble in understanding this from the translation. The Judgment on the hexagram says, "Fellowship is possible in the open. Success. It is advantageous to cross the great river. The correctness of the superior man brings advantage." If we take the name of the hexagram, "Fellowship," from the Judgment, the sentence is incomplete. Thus it is probable that the name was lost and replaced later with the first words of the Judgment.

Finally, we see the same example in the hexagram 52, Ken or Stillness, which does not have the name in the Judgment. In the translation the name of the hexagram is often added to the Judgment: "Ken or Stillness. One keeps his back still so that he no longer see his body..." According to the Chinese text, it reads as follows: 艮其背不獲身...." The word "ken" 艮 is not repeated in the Chinese text. Again, if we remove the first word of the Judgment, the rest of the sentence is incomplete and does not make sense at all. Therefore, we presume that the name of this hexagram was lost and replaced later with the initial word of the Judgment.

There are two more hexagrams which we cannot put in the same category as those previously discussed. They are the hexagram 14 and 61. Both of their names consist of two Chinese character. In the hexagram 14, Ta Yu or Great Possession, the Judgment says, "Great Possession has supreme success." As we have already indicated the name of the hexagram, "Great Possession," should be, as a rule, included in the Judgment. If we remove the name from the Judgment, the main text of the Judgment is: "Supreme success." It is questionable whether the name was included as the text of the Judgment or not. "Supreme success" alone is not sufficient for the Judgment even though it can stand by itself as a proper use of Chinese words. However, it is most probable that the first two words of the Judgment were originally parts of the Judgment. If this was the case we can presume that the name of the hexagram was lost and replaced later with the first two words of the Judgment.

The same problem is raised with the hexagram 61, Chung Fu or Inward Trust. The Judgment on this hexagram reads, "Inward Trust. Pigs and Fishes have good fortune. It is advantageous to cross the great river. Correctness brings advantage." If we take out the name of the hexagram, "Inward Trust," from the Judgment, the rest of it is: "Pigs and fishes..." This sentence is sufficient by itself but it can be improved if we add the name of the hexagram, "Inward Trust," as a part of the Judgment. It is again questionable whether the name was part of the Judgment or not. Just like the hexagram 14, this hexagram does not indicate whether the name came from the Judgment or not. It is probable, just as in hexagram 14, that the name of this hexagram was lost and replaced later with the first two words of the Judgment.

We have dealt with the names of hexagrams which might have their origins in the Judgments or kua tz'u. The rest of the names of hexagrams may possibily have their origins in hsiao tz'u or the Judgments on the lines. In order to differentiate the hsiao tz'u from the kua tz'u, let us abbreviate the former as the lines rather than the Judgments on the lines. If the hexagrams were named after the formation of the lines (or hsiao tz'u), it is possible to believe that the names of hexagrams which do not have their origins in the Judgments might be derived from the lines. Let us first analyze the words of the lines which are identical with the names of the hexagrams. Those names of hexagrams which are identical with the lines (or hsiao tz'u) are so numberous that we cannot make a detailed examination here. However, those names which are identical with the words of the first lines are

found in the hexagrams 4, 5, 7, 8, 10, 13, 15, 16, 18, 19, 20, 22, 23, 24, 25,
27, 29, 31, 32, 33, 34, 35, 36, 37, 39, 41, 45, 46, 47, 48, 49, 50, 51, 52, 53,
54, 56, and 58. Thirty-eight hexagrams out of the sixty-four have their
names found in their first lines. Those names of hexagrams which are
identical with the words of the second lines are found in the hexagrams 3, 4,
5, 6, 7, 8, 10, 12, 13, 15, 18, 19, 20, 21, 22, 23, 24, 27, 29, 30, 31, 35,
36, 39, 41, 42, 47, 48, 49, 50, 51, 52, 53, 55, 57, 58, 59, and 62. A total
of thirty-nine out of the sixty-four hexagrams find their names in the words
of the second lines. Those hexagrams which have their names found in the
words of the third lines are the hexagrams 1, 5, 7, 8, 10, 15, 16, 17, 18, 19,
20, 21, 22, 23, 24, 25, 27, 29, 30, 31, 32, 33, 34, 36, 37, 39, 41, 42, 43, 45,
46, 47, 48, 49, 50, 51, 52, 53, 54, 55, 56, 57, 58, 59, 60, and 62. Forty-
eight hexagrams out of the sixty-four have their names found in the words of
the third lines. This means only sixteen hexagrams do not have their names
in the third lines. The following hexagrams have their names found in the
words of the fourth lines: the hexagrams 4, 5, 6, 7, 8, 10, 15, 16, 17, 18, 19,
20, 21, 22, 23, 24, 27, 33, 34, 35, 36, 37, 38, 39, 40, 41, 47, 48, 50, 51,
52, 53, 54, 55, 56, 58, 59, 60, 62, and 63. A total of forty hexagrams have
their names found in the fourth lines. Again about two-thirds of their names
have some relation to the fourth lines. The names of hexagrams which are
found in the words of the fifth lines are as follows: the hexagrams 3, 4, 5,
6, 7, 8, 10, 12, 13, 18, 19, 20, 21, 22, 24, 25, 29, 31, 32, 33, 36, 37, 39,
40, 43, 45, 46, 47, 48, 50, 51, 52, 53, 54, 59, and 60. Thirty-six hexagrams
out of the sixty-four have their names found in the fifth lines. Finally,
those hexagrams which have their names found in the words of the last lines
are the hexagrams 4, 8, 10, 12, 13, 15, 16, 19, 20, 22, 23, 24, 25, 27, 31,

32, 33, 35, 36, 38, 39, 41, 42, 44, 46, 47, 48, 49, 50, 51, 52, 53, 55, 56, 57, 58, 59, 60, and 62. Thus the total number of hexagrams which have their names found in the top lines are forty out of the sixty-four hexagrams.

To summarize this analysis of the lines: the names of the hexagrams are as follows: 38 hexagrams have their names found in the first lines, 39 hexagrams in their second lines, 48 hexagrams in their third lines, 40 hexagrams in their fourth lines, 36 hexagrams in their fifth lines, and 40 hexagrams in their top lines. The 64 hexagrams have their names found in 241 different places of the lines. This means each hexagram has its name found in four lines out of a possible six. In other words almost two-thirds of the lines contain the name of the hexagram. Thus we can conclude that there is an immediate connection between the names of the hexagrams and the lines (or Hsiao tz'u). It is possible that the names of the hexagrams were derived from the lines if the former came after the latter. However, if we believe that the names of the hexagrams were already in existence before the composition of the lines by the Duke of Chou, it is certainly reasonable to believe that the lines were adopted from the names of the hexagrams. However, this hypothesis, that the composition of the lines is in accordance with the names of the hexagrams, seems more accurate and reliable.

It needs to be pointed out that there are few hexagrams which do not have their names contained in the lines. They are the hexagram 2, 9, 11, 14, 26, 28, 61, and 63. The names of these hexagrams do not have any relation to their lines. However, as we have already pointed out, both hexagram 14 and 61 might take their names from the first two words of the Judgments. The rest of them--the hexagram 2, 9, 11, 26, 28, and 63, do not have their names found in their lines. The lines of the hexagram 26, Ta Ch'u or the Great Power of

Taming, do not have the identical words of the name but they do have words which are identical in meaning. The third line of the hexagram deals with a good horse and the fourth line of it with the young bull. Both the horse and bull belong to Ta Ch'u, which literally means the great domestic animals.

Of the 64 hexagrams 48 have names which begin with a single letter or a Chinese character. The rest of them, the 16 hexagrams, have names with double letters or two Chinese characters. Among the 16 hexagrams half of the names are more or less the extension of one-letter names. The hexagram 9, Hsiao Ch'u or the Small Power of Taming, is an extension of Ch'u or domestic animal, that is, hsiao or the small. In other words, the name of this hexagram consists of the character of Ch'u, which means taming, and hsiao or the small. The hexagram 26, Ta Ch'u or the Great Power of Taming, is also the extension of Ch'u. This time the characteristic of Ch'u or the domestic animal is the great. Thus its name bears the great domestic animal of the Taming power. A similar example is found in the word "Kuo" or Excess, to which both "ta" or great and "hsiao" or the small are added. In hexagram 28, the word "ta" or the great is added to Kuo to form its name. Thus the name of this hexagram is Ta Kuo or the Great Excess. In hexagram 62, the word "hsiao" or the small is added to Kuo and makes the name Hsiao Kuo or the Small Excess. The name of hexagram 14 is an addition of ta or the great to yu or possession. Thus it is called Ta Yu or the Great Possession. The word "ta" is also added to chuang in hexagram 34. Thus the name of this hexagram is Ta Chuang or the Great Power. In hexagram 61, the word "chung" or the inward is added to fu or trust (or truth). That is why the hexagram is called Chung Fu or Inward Trust. Likewise, hexagram 21, Shih Ho or Chewing, may have received its name by adding the word "ho" to "shih." The rest of the names which have double letters or double Chinese characters are hexagram 13, Tung Jen or Fellowship; hexagram 25, Wu Wang or the Unexpected; hexagram 36, Ming I or Darkening of the Light; hexagram 37, Chia Jen or the Family; hexagram 54, Kuei Mei or the Marrying Maiden; hexagram 63, Chi Chi or After Completion; and hexagram 64, Wei Chi or Before Completion. It seems that hexagrams which bear names of two letters or two Chinese characters do not have any particular significance. In most cases two characters are necessary to express the idea fully.

It is safe to conclude that most hexagrams' names are well integrated with their Judgments and lines. There are a few exceptions which have been pointed out in our discussion. It is still questionable whether the names of hexagrams were based on the lines or the latter were based on the former. Nevertheless, since the names of the hexagrams are expressed directly or indirectly in most of the lines of the hexagrams, it seems clear that the composition of the lines was in accordance with the names of the hexagrams. However, the names of some hexagrams were clearly derived from their Judgments. Again, the question is whether King Wen, if he was responsible for the names and the Judgments of the hexagrams, formed the names of the hexagrams before their Judgments or the other way around. One thing which is certain is that the names of the hexagrams express what the hexagrams are saying in their Judgments and their lines. Thus the names of the hexagrams are to be understood as the re-symbolization of all the other symbols in the I Ching in their simplest form.

3. The Divination Texts

We have dealt with the names of hexagrams which precede the Judgments. Let us now focus our attention on the general characteristics of the Judgments and the lines. There are generally two types of sayings in both the Judgments and the lines. One has to do with the judgments or decisions on the matter of fate and direction, such as success or failure. These deal with the notion of divination. This type of saying can be called divination texts. Another has to do with the common form of literature, dealing with early proverbs, songs and omen sayings, which deal with non-divination elements. We may call this type of literature in the I Ching non-divination texts to distinguish them from the divination texts. Let us begin our examination by looking at the divination texts in the Judgments and the lines.

a. The Four Cardinal Virtues

The most common divination terms used to express the Judgments are described in hexagram 1, Ch'ien or Creativity. The Judgment of this hexagram consists of four words which also appear frequently in the Judgments of the other hexagrams in the I Ching. When we look at Legge's translation of this Judgment, we see the four distinctive terms: "what is great and originating," "penetrating," "advantageous," "Correct and firm." What is great and originating corresponds to yüan 元, what is penetrating to heng 亨, what is advantageous to li 利, and what is correct and firm to chen 貞. These four words represent the four creative powers and virtues in the early Chinese civilization. Yüan or originating signifies the original power of jen 仁,

which very closely resembles the meaning of Agape, or love, in the West. Heng or penetrating implies the li 禮, propriety of ceremony. Li or advantageous is the armor of i 義, the righteous. Chen or correctness is the uprightness of chih 質, the natural disposition. There is no doubt that these four virtues signify the archetypal forms which the Creative power of Ch'ien can fulfill. The original quality of jen, that is yüan, is one of the greatest virtues in man: "Great indeed is the generating power of the Creative; all beings owe their beginning to it. This power permeates all heaven."[1] Thus the yüan is the basis of all other qualities of good. Heng is the second creative virtue which works through the ceremonial attributes of early day. It is the creative power of propriety which is the way of doing all things. The power of propriety is to regulate all the behaviors and attitudes of man through the observance of true rites. It is then the principle of harmony, for the penetration of the divine will to human society is possible through the rituals. Li is the third virtue, which is associated with i or righteousness. The word "li" 利 may have its origin in the form of a sharp sickle, because it is the combination of a knife (刀) and crops (禾). The economic advantage was based on the harvest of crops through the sickle. Li is to be compared with the cutting edge of righteousness. Finally, Chen or the correct is associated with the quest of i or righteousness. The word "chen" 貞 is the combination of the two: pu 卜, which means divination, and pei 貝, which means shells. Thus chen may have its origin in the quest of righteousness through divination by means of tortoise-shells. Thus it was the search for knowledge and the beginning of the righteousness. These four

---

[1] See T'uan Chuan on Ch'ien in R. Wilhelm, op. cit., p. 370.

words, yüan or originating, heng or penetrating, li or advantageous, and chen or correctness, summarizes the four cardinal virtues in humanity. Yüan is the foundation of all moral and ethical principles, for it is the root of jen or love. The quality of heng is associated with the mores and propriety which regulate and control human behavior and social orders. The characteristic of li is correlated with economic righteousness which sustains all men to live in harmony and concord. Finally, the concept of chen is related to the quest of future and righteous knowledge, which is answered through the method of divination.

If these four words, which appear in the Judgment of the first hexagram, are important, it is important to see the application of these words in various places of the I Ching. Let us take each word separately and see how it is applied to the Judgments and lines of the hexagrams. The first two words, "yüan heng", which are translated by Wilhelm as "sublime success," are applied to various hexagrams. The concept of yüan heng or sublime success, which appears in the first hexagram, is applied to the second hexagram, K'un or Responsivity as well. The Judgment on this hexagram says, "The K'un will bring great (or sublime) success, advantageous (or furtherance) through the correctness (or firmness) of a mare." The same formula is repeated again in the third hexagram, Chun. The Judgment says, "Chun will have great success." In this hexagram the Judgment begins with the identical formula of the first hexagram. In the hexagram 14, Ta Yu or Great Possession, the Judgment says, Ta Yu has supreme success." Perhaps this is the shortest Judgment, along with hexagram 34, Ta Chuang or the Great Power, which has the last two words of the cardinal virtues, li chen or Correctness furthers. Hexagram 17, Sui or Following, also has the Judgment: "Sui will have great success. It is advantageous to be correct. No mistake." The Judgment of hexagram 19, Lin or Approach again has the identical formula: "Lin will have supreme success. It is advantageous to be correct." The same formula is found again in the hexagram 25, Wu Wang. The Judgment of this hexagram says, "Wu Wang will have supreme success. It is advantageous to be correct." In hexagram 46, Shen, the Judgment begins with Yüan heng or supreme success, but hexagram 49, Ko, ends with it. To summarize: those Judgments which contain yüan heng or suprme success are the hexagrams 1, 2, 3, 14, 17, 18, 19, 25, 46, and 49. In all these hexagrams the meaning of yüan heng does not vary.

The word "yüan" is also used in the I Ching along with the word "chi" 吉 , which means "good fortune" or luck. The combination of these two words, yüan and chi, is translated into English as "supreme good fortune." Yüan chi or supreme (or great) good fortune is found in both hexagram 41 and 50. In hexagram 41, Sun or Loss, the Judgment says, "Loss. Sincerity will bring supreme good fortune without mistake." In the hexagram 50, Ting or the Caldron, which is a human made object, the Judgment says, "The Ting will bring supreme good fortune and success." In both cases, the meaning of yüan chi is identical. There are about a dozen lines which contain yüan chi. To list those lines which contain it, they are the fifth line of the hexagram 2, K'un or the Receptive; fifth line of the hexagram 6, Sung or Conflict; the top line of the hexagram 10, Lü or Treading; the fifth line of the hexagram 11, T'ai or Peace; the first line of the hexagram 24, Fu or Return; the fourth line of the hexagram 26, Ta Ch'u or the Great Power of Taming; the second line of the hexagram 30, Li or the Flaming; the fifth line of the hexagram 41, Sun or Loss; the first and fifth lines of the hexagram 42, I or Gain; the fifth

line of the hexagram 45, Ts'ui or Gathering Together; the first line of the
hexagram 50, Ting or the Caldron, and the fourth line of the hexagram 59,
Huan or Disintegration. In all these lines the meaning of yüan chi is identical with that in the Judgments. Finally, the word "yüan" is used with fu
夫 or a man. The yüan fu appears in the fourth line of hexagram 38, K'uei
or Estragement. The line comments: "The estranged in loneliness meets a
great man." Here "a great man" corresponds to the term "yüan fu," which is
almost identical with ta fu 大夫 , which also means a great man. Here, the
word "yüan" means the greatness in terms of jen or magnanimous love. Yüan,
whether it is used by itself or with other words, means more than the supreme.
It is not only the supreme in the finest sense but the root of greatness.
It is unfortunate that there is no way to render the original meaning of
this word "yüan" in a Western language. The translation of this word in
English as the supreme may not do it justice.

The second word "heng", in itself, is used in both the Judgments and
the lines of hexagrams. In hexagram 4, Meng or Immature Youth, the Judgment
says, "Meng will bring success." Here heng is interpreted as "success."
Hexagram 5, Hsü or Waiting, uses heng in its Judgment. Hexagram 9, Hsiao Ch'u
or the Small Power of Taming is a good example. The Judgment literally says,
"Success. There are dense clouds, but no rain from the western sky." Besides
these examples those Judgments which begin with the word "heng" are: hexagram 15, Ch'ien or Modesty; hexagram 21, Shih Ho or Chewing; hexagram 22,
Pi or Adornment; hexagram 24, Fu or Return; hexagram 31, Hsien or Influence;
hexagram 32, Heng or Enduring; hexagram 33, Tun or Withdrawal; hexagram 45,
Ts'ui or Gathering Together; hexagram 47, K'un or Annoyance; hexagram 55,
Feng or Abundance; hexagram 58, Tui or Joy; hexagram 59, Huan or Disintegration;

hexagram 6, Chieh or Regulation; hexagram 62, Hsia Kuo or the Small Excess; hexagram 63, Chi Chi or After Completion, and hexagram 64, Wei Chi or Before Completion. Some judgments do not begin with the word "heng". For example, in hexagram 10, Lü or Treading, the Judgment ends with heng: "One treads upon the tail of the tiger, which does not bite him.It is a success." Here heng or success becomes the concluding remark of the Judgment. The same illustration is found in the hexagram 11, T'ai or Peace. However, in hexagram 13, T'ung Jen or Fellowship, heng is placed between the sentences. The Judgment reads, "Fellowship is possible in the open. Success. It is advantageous to cross the great river." Here the word "heng" or "success" is autonomous but is placed between the two sentences. In hexagram 28, Ta Kuo or the Great Excess, heng comes at the end of the Judgment, but in hexagram 29, K'an or the Abyss, it is situated between the sentences. Heng is also found in the first line of the hexagram 12, P'i or Stagnation. In all cases heng is translated by Wilhelm as "success." However, the meaning of this word should not be misunderstood. If we translate heng as success, we should not mean by success the accumulation of merits or the attainment of individual goals. It must be understood as heng t'ung 亨通, which means one's will or desire is in accord with or in communion with the principle of the Great Harmony. Success here means one's conformity to the principle of changes. In harmony with this principle everything goes well and is successful. Therefore, heng or "success" can be expressed as the idea of being on the right track. To be on the right track with heaven (or to be successful), the Chinese people thought that one must make a ceremonial rite which is the instrument for harmony of man with the divine. This is why the word "heng" is used in referring to the sacrificial rites. The second

line of hexagram 47, K'un or Annoyance, says, "It is advantageous to offer
sacrifice." Again the same idea is expressed in the third line of hexagram 14,
Ta Yu or Great Possession: "A ruler offers sacrifice to the son of Heaven.
A small man cannot do this." Since it is the propriety or li which makes
man right with the divine, heng also implies the offering of sacrifice to
the divine. Furthermore, we observe that the use of heng is much more frequent
in the Judgments than in the lines.

The third word "li" 利 is often translated into English as "furtherance"
or "advantageousness" in the I Ching. Those hexagrams which contain the word
"li" in their Judgments are as follows: the hexagram 1, Ch'ien or Creativity; hexagram 2, K'un or Responsivity ; hexagram 3, Chun or Difficulty; hexagram 4,
Meng or Immature Youth; hexagram 5, Hsü or Waiting; hexagram 6, Sung or
Conflict; hexagram 13, T'ung Jen or Fellowship; hexagram 16, Yü or Eagerness;
hexagram 18, Ku or Decaying; hexagram 21, Shih Ho or Chewing; hexagram 22,
Pi or Adornment; hexagram 23, Po or Breaking Apart; hexagram 24, Fu or
Return; hexagram 25, Wu Wang or the Unexpected; hexagram 26, Ta Ch'u or
the Great Power of Taming; hexagram 28, Ta Kuo or the Great Excess; hexagram
32, Heng or Enduring; hexagram 39, Chien or the Trouble; hexagram 41, Sun or
Loss; hexagram 42, I or Gain; hexagram 43, Kuai or Resolution; hexagram 45,
Ts'ui or Gathering Together; hexagram 46, Sheng or Moving Upward; hexagram 45,
57, Sun or Gentleness; and hexagram 61, Chung Fu or Inward Trust. The meaning
of li in these Judgments signifies that which is advantageousness over
against that which is disadvantageous, the direction of movement rather than
the hindrance to the goal. The direction of advancement to which the li
points is related to righteousness and justice. Movement toward unright-

enousness or injustice is the opposite of li. The negation of the advantageous is expressed in the I Ching as wu yu li 无攸利, which is the counterpole of li. Especially in both hexagram 54 and 64 we find the use of this term to negate li. In the hexagram 54, Kei Mei or the Marrying Maiden, the Judgment says, "The Kei Mei will bring misfortune. Nothing that would be advantageous (wu yu li)." In the hexagram 64, Wei Chi or Before Completion, the Judgment also reads, "Success. After nearly completing the crossing the river, the little fox gets his tail in the water. There is nothing that would be advantageous (wu yu li)." In both Judgments it signifies the counterpole of the advantageous or the furtherance. The use of this term is also found in the following lines of the hexagrams: the third line of hexagram 4, Meng or Immature Youth; the third line of the hexagram 19, Lin or Approach; the top line of hexagram 25, Wu Wang or the Unexpected; the third line of hexagram 32, Heng or Enduring; the top line of hexagram 34, Ta Chuan or the Great Power; the third line of hexagram 45, Ts'ui or Gathering Together; and the top line of hexagram 54, Kei Mei or the Marrying Maiden. In all the lines the term wu yu li is used to deny li. In translating this term. Wilhelm, for example, uses few varying phrases, such as, "nothing furthers,""nothing serves to further," "nothing would further," or "nothing that acts to further." Even though the translation of the term is varied in relation to the circumstances, it basically means the same, that is, the denial of the li. There is the negation of this negation in the I Ching. In other words the concept of li is double negated. This double negation of li is used to signify by the term "wu pu li" 无不利. This term is not found in the Judgment at all but only in the lines of the hexagrams. In the second line of hexagram 2, K'un or Responsivity, the term is interpreted as "nothing is not advantageous."

Here the double negation is the intensified affirmation of li. The fourth line of the hexagram 3, Chun or Difficulty, says, "Everything is advantageous (wu pu li)." The same term is translated in the top line of the hexagram 14, Ta Yu or Great Possession, as "nothing that does not advance." The term also appears in the following lines of hexagrams: the fourth and fifth lines of the hexagram 15, Chien or Modesty; the second line of the hexagram 19, Lin or Approach; the fifth line of the hexagram 23, Po or Breaking Apart; the second line of the hexagram 28, Ta Kuo or the Great Excess; the top line of the hexagram 33, Tun or Withdrawal; the fifth line of the hexagram 35, Chin or Progress; the top line of the hexagram 40, Hsieh or Liberation; the top line of the hexagram 50, Ting or the Caldron; and the fifth line of the hexagram Sun or Gentleness. There are a total of thirteen lines where the term "wu pu li" appears. Even though the translations can be varried according to circumstances, there must be a tendency to stress the intensive affirmation of li in various ways. The application of this term is, interestingly enough , found in the lines only. Finally, we observe that the word "li" is accompanied with "chen," which belongs to the last words of the four virtues we have described. The term "li chen" 利貞 is trnslated by Wilhelm as "perseverance furthers" or "furthering through perseverance" in the I Ching. It can be improved to translate it as "It is advantageous to be correct." To list the Judgments of those hexagrams which make use of this term , they are as follows: the hexagrams 1, 3, 4, 17, 19, 25, 26, 30, 31, 32, 33, 34, 45, 49, 53, 59, 61, and 63. There are only three lines which contain the term: the fifth line of hexagram 36, the second line of hexagram 41, and the fifth line of hexagram 50. The term appears twenty-three times altogether both in the Judgments and the lines. In some cases the two words "li" and "chen" appear separately and not as a term. For example in hexagram 2, K'un or Responsivity, the words for a mare come between these two words: "Advantage comes through the correctness of a mare (利牝馬之貞)." In the first line of the hexagram 52, <u>Ken</u> or Stillness, the word "<u>yung</u>" 永 : "Continued correctness will be advantageous (利永貞)." In the Judgments of both hexagram 12 and 13, the term "<u>chun tzu</u>" is placed between the words.[1] Whether the two words, <u>li</u> and <u>chen</u>, are used together or separately the meaning does not change. To interpret it as "furthering through perseverance" is a little bit too vague. It is closer to the idea to say that the advantageous comes from being correct. A correct choice will bring the advantageous or furtherance. To be correct means to be right with the principle of harmony through the help of divination. The advantageous or the furtherance can be attained, because of one's being in the right place and time. The furtherance is possible when one is directed to the righteous and justice.

Finally, the last of the four cardinal virtues in the <u>I Ching</u> is the concept of <u>chen</u> 貞 , which is related to the question of divination. Besides the term <u>li chen</u>, which we have already discussed, the word "<u>chen</u>" is used primarily with the word "<u>chi</u>" 吉 , which means "good fortune" or "luck." The term <u>chen chi</u> is often translated as "correctness brings good fortune" or "perseverance brings good fortune." Good fortune through perseverance and correctness is used to express ordinary life experiences as well as other experiences. Again, let us examine the application of this term in both the Judgments and the lines of the hexagrams. Those Judgments which express the

---

[1] In the hexagram 12, <u>P'i</u> or Stagnation, the Judgment, according to the translation of Wilhelm, says, "Standstill. Evil people do not further the perseverance of the superior man" (否之匪人不利君子貞). This translation is a little bit confusing. A better translation can be: "The evil people do not advance. There is no advantage for the superior man to be correct."

term clearly are hexagrams 5, 27, and 39. In all these hexagrams chen chi is
an independent phrase or a complete sentence by itself. Those lines which
contain the term "chen chi" are as follows: the fifth line of hexagram 5,
the second of 8, the first of 12, the second of 15, the second of 16, the
first of 17, the first of 19, the fourth of 31, the fifth of 35, the second
and fourth of 34, the first and second of 35, the second and fourth of
34, the first and second of 35, the second of 37, the second of 40, the top
of 41, the first of 44, the fifth of 46, the second of 56, the fifth of 57,
the second, fourth and fifth of 64. Chen chi is applied to tweinty-four
lines and three Judgments all together. Thus chen chi or "Correctness
brings good fortune" appears in the I Ching a total of twenty-seven times.
Sometimes a special word is added to it to modify the meaning. For example,
the word "hsiao" 小 is added to it in the first line of hexagram 3, where it
is said, "A little correctness will bring good fortune" (小 貞 吉).
In the fourth line of the hexagram 6, Sung or Conflict, the word "an" 安 is
added: "Peace in correctness is good fortune" (安貞吉). The same term is
used in the Judgment of hexagram 2, K'un or Responsivity: "Peace in correctness brings good fortune" (安 貞 吉). Also the word "chu" 居 is added
in the lines of both hexagram 27 and 49. In the fifth line of 27, it is
said: "To remain in correctness (or perseverance) will bring good fortune"
(居 貞 吉), which also appears in the top line of hexagram 49, Ko
or Revolution. Since the word "chu" means the place to stay or to live, chu
chen implies the place where divination was performed. As we have indicated
before, chen is the virtue which is linked with divination. There are also
a few places where some words come between the chen and chi. For example,
in the Judgment of hexagram 7, Shih or the Army, a strong man (丈 人) comes
between them: "The correctness of a strong man brings good fortune. No

mistake" (貞丈人吉无咎).[1] In the fifth line of hexagram 32, Heng or Enduring, the woman comes between these two words: "The correctness of woman brings good fortune" (貞婦人吉).[2] In all cases the meaning of chen chi, good fortune through correctness, seems to remain unchanged. Correctness brings good fortune when the situation demands it. When the situation does not demand perseverance or correctness it brings misfortune.

In some situations perseverance or correctness brings misfortune. The word "chen" is accompanied with "hsiung" 凶 to signify misfortune. The fifth line of hexagram 7, Shih or the Army, says, "Let the eldest lead the army, and the younger transports corpses. Then, correctness will bring misfortune." The situation of this hexagram demands that the continuation of this kind of war does not bring victory but rather misfortune. The fourth line of hexagram 17, Sui or Following, presents a similar situation: "Sui will be successful. Correctness will bring misfortune." In the third line of hexagram 27, I or the Jaws, the same term is used: "Correctness will bring misfortune." Besides these examples, the term "chen hsiung" is contained in the first lines of hexagram 32, the top line of hexagram 57, the top line of hexagram 60, and the top line of hexagram 61. Sometimes an adjective is added to them to delimit the meaning. In the fifth line of hexagram 3, Chun or Difficulty, a word "ta" as well as "hsiao" is added to chen hsiung to signify either great correctness or a little correctness in relation to misfortune. Thus the line says, "Difficulty in blessing. A little correct-

---

[1]It is translated by Wilhelm (and Baynes) as follows: "The army needs perseverance and a strong man. Good fortune without blame."

[2]Again, Wilhelm translates it: "This is good fortune for a woman."

ness brings good fortune. Great firmness will bring misfortune." In the first and second lines of hexagram 23, Po or Breaking Apart, the word mieh 烕 is added to chen hsiung. Both lines say that there will be destruction of the firmness which brings misfortune (烕貞凶).[1] Some of these examples cleary show that correctness or firmness does not always bring good fortune. According to the demands of the situation it can also bring misfortune. The demands of the situation correlate to the time, the opportune time, which often controls the outcome of good fortune and misfortune.

Chen is often used also with lin 吝 or li 厲 . The phrase chen lin appears in the top line of hexagram 11, T'ai or Peace: "Correctness will bring humiliation" (貞吝). It appears again in the third line of hexagram 32, Heng or Enduring, in the top line of hexagram 35, Chin or Progress, and the third line of hexagram 40, Hsieh or Liberation. The appearance of this term is rare in the I Ching. The term "chen li" appears in the third line of hexagram 6, Sung or Conflict: "Ancient virtue is nourished, but correctness is in danger. Nevertheless, the end will bring good fortune" (食舊德貞厲絡吉).[2] Chen li is contained also in the fifth line of hexagram 10, in the third line of hexagram 34, in the fourth line of hexagram 35, in the third line of hexagram 49, and in the third line of hexagram 56. Both chen lin and chen li express the negative aspects of chen. They are implicit in chen hsiung, the counterpole of chen or firmness.

To summarize, we have observed the application of the four cardinal

---

[1]Wilhelm's translation stresses different aspects: "Those who persevere are destroyed. Misfortune."

[2]Wilhelm's translation is as follows: "To nourish oneself on ancient virtue induces perseverance. Danger. In the end, good fortune comes."

virtues, yüan, heng, li and chen, which appear in the Judgment of the first hexagram. These four words have been used in the I Ching along with some other words in both the Judgments and the lines of the hexagrams. However, the central meaning of these words does not change. They have been used in more than one hundred and eighty different situations with reference to both the Judgments and the lines of the hexagrams. The first two words, yüan and heng, are most frequently used in the Judgments and less frequently in the lines of the hexagrams. On the other hand, the last two words, li and chen, appear most frequently in the lines and less frequently in the Judgments of the hexagrams. These four cardinal virtues which constitute the fundamental divination texts of the I Ching are important to an understanding of the meaning of the various words used in the hexagrams. They are the framework within which human decisions are made and human destinies decided.

b. Other Frequently Appearing Words

Besides these four cardinal virtues, there are six more words which appear frequently as a part of the divination texts in the I Ching. Most of them have already been discussed along with the four cardinal virtues. These six words which appear frequently are chi 吉 , hsiung 凶 , lin 吝, li 厲, hui 悔, and ch'u 咎 . Chi is often translated into English as "good fortune," as we have already mentioned. It is widely used in the divination texts in the I Ching. Chi or "good fortune" appears at the end of the lines of hexagram 1, Ch'ien or the Creative: "There is a flight of dragon without head. It is good fortune" (When all the lines are nines). In hexagram 4, Meng or Immature Youth, for example, chi appears in both the second and fifth lines.

In the second line, it is said: "To bear Meng will bring good fortune." The fifth line said, "Immature youth will bring good fortune." There is no point in looking at all the examples illustrating the use of the word "chi" in the I Ching. In almost all cases the word is used in the lines of the hexagrams. It appears more than seventy times. Those hexagrams which do not contain the word in both the Judgments and the lines are the hexagrams 2, 6, 10, 17, 18, 20, 22, 23, 29, 32, 42, 44, 48, 56, 62, 63, and 64. The word is also used with the movement of time. It is, for example, used with ch'u 初, which means the beginning. Thus ch'u chi means good fortune in the beginning. It appears in the Judgment of hexagram 63, Chi Chi or After Completion: "It is good fortune at the beginning and disorder at the end." In the Judgment of hexagram 6, Sung or Conflict, the chi is accompanied by chung 中 or the middle way: "The middle way brings good fortune. The end brings misfortune." Finally, the chi is used with chung 絡, which means the end. The chung chi 絡吉, good fortune at the end, appears in the second line of hexagram 5, Hsü or Waiting: "The end will bring good fortune." It also appears in the first and third lines of hexagram 6, the fourth line of hexagram 10, the first line of hexagram 18, the fifth line of hexagram 22, the top line of hexagram 37, and the third line of hexagram 50. The chi is used along with other words but its meaning does not change at all.

The word "hsiung" 凶 is the opposite of chi. It literally means "bad" or "misfortune." We have already discussed the use of this word with chen or firmness (correctness). However, the hsiung alone appears frequently in various places of the Judgments and lines of the hexagrams. It appears about forty times in the I Ching. For example, the Judgment of hexagram 8, Pi or

Uniting Together, says, "He who comes too late meets misfortune." Also in
the top line of the same hexagram, we read, "No head is held together. It
is misfortune." The hsiung or misfortune is used neither with ch'u, the
beginning, nor with chung, the center, but is used only with chung, the end.
The chung hsiung or the misfortune at the end appears only in the Judgment
of hexagram 6, Sung or Conflict: "The end will bring misfortune." In almost
all situations hsiung is used as an anti-thesis of chi. Fortune or misfortune
indicates the result of the creative work of the cardinal virtues. To be
out of harmony with the cosmic principle of changes is to bring misfortune.
On the other hand, to be with this principle is to bring fortune. All other
value judgments fall within these poles of chi and hsiung. However, these
poles are not contrary to but complementary to each other.

The word "lin" 吝 is generally known as "stinginess." Perhaps the
closest meaning in English is "misery." Since the condition of misery can
humiliate people, it is often translated in the I Ching as humiliation. This
word as already been discussed along with chen or correctness. However, lin
is used in the I Ching by itself or along with some other words. Lin, for
example, appears in the third line of hexagram 3, Chun or Difficulty: "To
return brings humiliation." The fourth line of the hexagram 4 says, "The
aimless youth will bring humiliation." The same word also appears in the
fourth line of hexagram 18, the first line of hexagram 20, the fifth line
of hexagram 22, the fourth line of hexagram 28, the third line of hexagram
31, the top line of hexagram 44, the third line of hexagram 57, and the
first line of hexagram 64. Just like chi, lin is neither used with ch'u, the
beginning, nor used with chung, the middle, but is used with chung, the end.
The third line of hexagram 37, Chia Jen or the Family, says, "When woman and

child laught,   it eventually leads to humiliation." As in these illustrations lin deals with hardship, which certainly causes humiliation.

Another word which appears occasionally in the I Ching is li 厲 ,
which we have already discussed in relation to chen. Li literally means
danger. It does not appear in the Judgment at all except in hexagram 43,
Kuai or Resolution, where the word is used along with yu or possession. The
Judgment of this hexagram says, "A truthful report is dangerous. Notice
must go to one's own city" (孚號有厲告自邑). We do not notice in
this translation the use of li with yu unless we see the Chinese text. Yu
li, or possession of danger, is not only used in the former but in hexagram 26,
Ta Ch'u or the Great Power of Taming. In the first line of this hexagram,
it says, "Danger is near" (yu li). It is also found in the fifth line of
hexagram 58, Tui or Joy. "Sincerity that influences disintegration is
dangerous." Besides these, li or danger is used without any special relation
to other concepts. In the third line of hexagram 1, Ch'ien or the Creativity,
it says, "Danger. No mistake" (li wu chiu 厲无咎). The first line of
hexagram 18, Ku or Decaying, says, "Danger in the end brings good fortune."
The word "li" or danger appears more than fifteen times altogether in the I
Ching. However, in all cases the meaning of li is retained. There is no
real change in its meaning.

The word "hui" 悔 appears in the lines of the hexagrams only. It
means regret or remorse. In the third line of hexagram 37, Chia Jen or the
Family, it is said, "When the family are excited, great severity brings
remorse." Also in the third line of hexagram 50, Ting or the Caldron, it
says, "When rain falls, remorse is gone." It is used with the word "yu" 有
to signify the existence of remorse. In the top line of hexagram 1, Ch'ien

or Creativity, it is said: "Arrogant dragon repents." Since regret makes it possible to repent, here the word "hui" is translated as repent instead of remorse. Yu hui also appears in the third line of hexagram 18, Ku or Decaying, in the third line of hexagram 16, Yü or Eagerness, and in the top line of hexagram 47, K'un or Annoyance. The word "hui" is also used with the word "wang" or "disappearance." Hui wang 悔亡 or the disappeaance of remorse appears in the fourth line of hexagram 31, Hsien or Influence: "Remorse disappears" (hui wang). It again appears in the second line of hexagram 32, the fourth of 34, the third and fifth of 38, the fourth of 43, the fifth of 45, the fourth of 49, the fifth of 52, the fourth and fifth of 57, the second of 58, the second of 59, the top of 60, and the fourth of 64. In all these circumstances hui wang implies the disappearance of regret or remorse. It means a removal of regret. A stronger expression than the hui wang is wu hui 无悔, which means no remorse. Wu hui or no remorse appears in the top line of hexagram 14, Ta Yu or Great Possession: "Fellowship in the meadow brings no remorse." It has been used in the fifth line of hexagram 10, the fifth of 31, the fifth of 34, the third of 59, and the fifth of 64. As we have observed, it is more or less a coincidence that most of those lines in which the wu hui is contained are the fifth line of the hexagrams, which represents the fullest evolvement of situations. Even though the word "hui" is accompanied by many different words, its meaning is essentially the incompletion of hope and the missing of proper time. Thus it is properly interpreted as remorse or regret.

Finally, the word "chiu" 咎 is perhaps most often used in the lines of hexagrams. It means disaster or fault, which is quite similar to misfortune as well as to remorse. Chiu means neither misfortune nor remorse but some-

thing between them. It is not as bad as hsiung or misfortune but is worse
than hui or remorse. Remorse comes as a result of disaster and disaster
comes as a result of misfortune. In other words, misfortune is followed by
disaster and disaster is followed by remorse. Their sequence is in relation
to the degree of their negation. Chiu does not appear by itself but always
with some other words. In the first line of hexagram 9, Hsia Ch'u or the
Small Power of Taming, chiu is accompanied with ho 何 , which is an inter-
rogative word. The line says, "How can it be blamed?" The ho chiu 何咎
appears in the fourth line of hexagram 17 Sui or Following: "To be with
tao brings clarity. How can it be blamed?" The word chiu is also used with
fei 非 , which means denial. The first line of hexagram 14, Ta Yu or Great
Possession, says: "It keeps away from what is harmful. There is no blame
(or mistake)." Chiu is also used with wei 為 or achieving. The first line
of hexagram 43, Kuai or Resolution, says, "Departure does not bring the
victory. It is an act of mistake." Here chiu is translated as a mistake,
which seems a better translation than blame. In most cases chiu is accompanied by wu 無 to negate the mistake. For example, in the third line of
hexagram 1, Ch'ien or Creativity , it says, "No mistake (wu chiu)." It is
also found in the fourth line of the same hexagram and altogether 93 times
in both the Judgments and lines of the hexagrams. As we have already indicated,
it is better to translate it as "no mistake," rather than "no blame," in most
cases. In this respect Legge's translation can be more faithful than Wilhelm's
to the original meaning of the text.

As a result of our study concerning the words which frequently appear
as divination formulas in both the Judgments and lines of the hexagrams, we
have noticed that their meanings have not altered in spite of the differences

in their usages. We have examined the use of about ten different words.
Among them the four cardinal virtues lay down the foundation of the divination formulas which are very frequently described by the six words that we
have examined. These words range from chi, good fortune, to hsiung, misfortune. Between these two poles, the remaining four words, lin 吝 , li 厲 ,
hui 悔 , and chiu 咎 are included. Lin is often translated as humiliation
but could be translated as the concept of misery while the idea of li
expresses the uncertain outcome associated with danger. The word hui means
regret or remorse and is directly related to the idea of mistake, which is
chiu. What is worse than a mistake is misfortune or hsiung. Thus the implications of these four words are relative within the polarity of fortune and
misfortune. As Ta Chuan says, "They wrote judgments in order to distinguish
between good fortune and misfortune. Thus these were called the Judgments"
(Sec. I, Ch. 12).

4. The Non-divination Texts

Previously we have dealt with the words which frequently appear in the
divination formulas which are arbitrarily differentiated from non-divination
texts, the literary character of the I Ching. We have made an arbitrary distinction between divination and non-divination texts for our convenience.
With this in mind, when we discuss the non-divination texts or the literary
characters of the I Ching we are reminded of the literary sources of the Old
Testament, which are the combination of several documents such as J, E, D,
and P. Just like the literary forms of the Old Testament, various literary

forms have been brought together to form the writings of the I Ching. Divination and non-divination texts are amalgamated and often are hardly distinguish-
able. Let us look at hexagram 6, Sung or Conflict, to see the distinction
between the divination and non-divination sayings. The Judgment says:
"Conflict. Sincerity is obstructed. The middle way brings misfortune. The
end brings misfortune. It is advantageous to see the great man. It is not
advantageous to cross the great river." The first sentence, "Conflict.
Sincerity is obstruced," is a description of one's condition. Thus it does not
belong to the divination formula. The second sentence, "The middle way brings
misfortune," is definitely related to the divination formula. Also the third
sentence, "The end brings misfortune," is analogous to the former sentence.
Thus it is also a divination text. The last two sentences of the Judgment
are ambiguous and uncertain. They may be the amalgmation of both divination
and non-divination sayings. As we have seen, it is almost impossible to
differentiate one form of saying from the other. However, there are enough
materials which are clearly differentiated from the divination sayings. Let
us take some time to examine the characteristics of these non-divination
descriptions.

Descriptions other than divination sayings are in the form of odes,
which may include proverbs, songs, omen sayings and other poetic descriptions.
These odes are the contents from which the divination sayings are made. They
explain the situation as expressed in the hexagram, so that a divination formula is to be prescribed. Thus the odes and divination texts are intimately
related to each other. They complement each other. The odes in the I Ching
can be divided in three different ways: 1) those which deal with the affairs

of man, 2) those which deal with the inner aspects of man, 3) those which deal with the images of man and nature.

The odes which deal with human affairs are many. In hexagram 1, <u>Ch'ien</u> or Creativity , the third line indicates the decision in the form of a proverb: "The superior man is creative all day long, but he is youthful in the evening." This proverb describes the affairs of the superior man. A similar saying is found in the second line of hexagram 15, <u>Ch'ien</u> or Modesty: "With modesty and deligence the superior man carries out his work to the end." Here again the affairs of the superior man have been described in a proverbial form. In the first, third and fifth lines of hexagram 7, <u>Shih</u> or the Army, we see the affairs of the army. The first line describes the disciplines of the army: "An army must go forth in order." The third line depicts the unfortunate situation of the army: "The army may have to carry corpses in the wagon." The fifth line describes the functional distinction between the elder and younger soldiers: "Let the eldest lead the army, and the youngest transport corpses." The affairs with wrong people are described in the third line of hexagram 8, <u>Pi</u> or Uniting Together: "Uniting together with the bad people." There are many examples such as we have already indicated. Perhaps the description of human affairs is most common in the <u>I Ching</u>.

The odes which deal with the inner aspects of human nature are rather penetratingly expressed. They describe the emotional and spiritual aspects of human life. One of the hexagrams which deals with the manifestation of human feelings is hexagram 31, <u>Hsien</u> or Influence. Let us first look at the structure of this hexagram, which consists of both the trigram <u>Ken</u> or Stillness below and <u>Tui</u> or Joy above. The <u>Ken</u> is the youngest son, and the <u>Tui</u> is the youngest daughter. Thus the universal attraction of the sexes to each other is presented here as the generating source of stimulation and emotion. This is the hexagram of courtship and marriage, which becomes the foundation of the emotional life. That is why it is the image of influence and feeling. The beginning line of the hexagram says, "The influence (<u>hsien</u> 咸) affects the great toe." The third line means: "The influence (<u>hsien</u>) affects the thights." The top line syas, "The influence (<u>hsien</u>) affects the jaws, cheeks and tongue." From these lines of the hexagram we observe that the influence (<u>hsien</u> 咸) moves from the toe to the legs, from the legs to the thighs, from the thigs to the neck, and from the neck to the mouth. The influence (<u>hsien</u>) which affects these parts of man is identically used with <u>kan</u> 感 , the feelings or emotions. As we notice from the Chinese character of <u>kan</u> 感 , it is the combination of <u>hsien</u> 咸 and <u>hsin</u> 心 , the heart. Since the archaic form of Chinese wrings made little use of significatives, it is reasonable to believe that the <u>hsien</u> 咸 could be used for the meaning of <u>kan</u> 感 , feelings. Let us examine another hexagram which deals with the emotional life of the Chinese people. For example, the feelings and tempers of family life are described in hexagram 37, <u>Chia Jen</u> or the Family. The third line of this hexagram states: "When the family are excited (家人嗃嗃)... the great severity brings regret... When women and children triflingly laugh (婦子嘻嘻), it eventually leads to humiliation." Both "<u>chia jen ho ho</u>" (家人嗃嗃) and "<u>fu tzu hsi hsi</u>" (婦子嘻嘻) express the conditions of emotional uplift in the life of family. The rest of them are divination formulas. The hexagram which deals with inner concentration is hexagram 20, Kuan or Contemplation. The structure of the hexagram is similar to the shape of a watch

tower, which commands a view of the inner spirit and conforms to the appearance of steady faith. In both the third and fifth lines of the hexagram, they signify "Contemplation of my life," which means self-reflection. Some of these illustrations help us to understand the inner and subjective disposition of man, which affects the Judgment of a given situation in the hexagram.

The odes which deal with images or symbols are divided into two groups: those which deal with living things, such as animals, insects, and birds, and those which deal with nature, such as thunder, stars, wind, or mountains. Most of the odes in the I Ching belong to these two categories or descriptions. We may deal with these in detail. The image which deals with animals is to be examined first. The dragon is the first image of animals used in the I Ching. The dragon symbolizes the energetic and creative power which is associated with thunder and lightning. The picture of the dragon is found in hexagram 1, Ch'ien or Creativity. In the first line of the hexagram, the dragon is hidden. In the second line the dragon appears in the field. In the fifth line, the dragon flies in the heaven. At the top of the hexagram the dragon becomes arrogant. This evolving manifestation of the dragon is analogous to the evolvement of creative energy in heaven and earth. The top line of hexagram 2, K'un or Responsivity, introduces the dragon again. This time the dragon as the symbol of heaven struggles with the earth. The dragon is the primordial image of animals as well as that of nature. Its creative energy

affects the life of all living and non-living beings. The movement of the
animal image appears in hexagram 3, Chun or Difficulty. In the second,
fourth and top lines of this hexagram the image of the moving horse appears.
Let us, for example, look at the top line of this hexagram and examine it.
The top line says, "Horse and chariot are divided, and blood and tears flow."
This is an omen saying, dealing with the hardship and struggle of a new
bride arriving at her husband's house. It signifies the primitive institution of marriage in China. Moreover, the horse represents the image of
transportation. The image of the tiger appears in hexagram 10, Lü or
Treading. The Judgment of the hexagram says, "Treading upon the tail of the
tiger, which does not bite him." This is a description of a dangerous
situation yet it is also one of good humor. This kind of description is a
characteristic expression of the I Ching. Again the situation of treading
the tail of the tiger appears in the fourth line: "He treads on the tail
of the tiger. He becomes cautious and apprehensive." Since the tiger is one
of the most dangerous animals, much care and caution are needed. The image of
the hog occurs in several places. The hexagram 33, Tun or Withdrawal, might
possibly be read as t'un 豚, instead of tun 遯 . In Chinese characters
the word shih 豕 means hog, and chu 逐 implies motion, that is, to drive out.
Likewise, chu 逐 is to follow and tun 遯 to hide or withdraw. In hexagram 33 the word "tun" 遯 is used in all its lines. However, the top line,
"a fat withdrawal" (肥遯), does not make sense. It is better to be understood
as the fat pig withdrawing. It is probable, therefore, that the hexagram
should be called t'un 豚 or hog rather than tun 遯 or withdrawal. The
image of the hog also appears in other places. For example, in the fifth line
of hexagram 26, Ta Ch'u or the Great Power of Taming, the tusk of a gelded hog
(豶豕之牙) appears. In the same hexagram the image of the young

bull (童牛) is also described in the fourth line. The image of goats (羝羊) appears in the fourth and the fifth lines of hexagram 34, <u>Ta Chuang</u> or the Great Power. In hexagram 57, <u>Sun</u> or Gentleness, we see three kinds of game being caught (田獲三品) in the forth line. It perhaps means three kinds of animals which were used as offerings to the gods. The image of the fox also appears in the Judgment of hexagram 64, <u>Wei Chi</u> or Before Completion. In oriental countries the fox became the symbol of the alert and careful animal. However, in this case, the little fox, which is less experienced in crossing the water on the ice, fails to reach the other side. It is also a type of omen saying: "After nearly completing the corssing, the little fox gets his tail wet in the water. There is nothing whould be advantageous." The omen saying here is combined with a divination formula.

There are odes on the image of insects. Hexagram 5 is an interesting one with which to begin our examination. All the lines of the hexagram, except the top, begin with the word "<u>hsü</u>" 需 , which means waiting:

The first line: <u>Hsü</u> in the meadow (需于郊).

The second line: <u>Hsü</u> on the sand (需于沙).

The third line: <u>Hsü</u> in the mud (需于泥).

The fourth line: <u>Hsü</u> in the blood (需于血).

The fifth line: <u>Hsü</u> at meat and drink (需于酒食).

From the contexts in which the word "<u>hsü</u>" 需 is written, it makes sense to substitute it for the word "<u>juan</u>" 蠕 , which means a "crawling thing," that is, a form of insect or worm. We also observe a similar case in the use of the word "<u>fu</u>" 孚 , which appears in the <u>I Ching</u> more than twenty times. It means "trust," "sincere" or "truth" and is often used as a **part** of the divination

texts. If we analyze the word fu 孚 in the contexts of its uses we see that
it was originally associated with the notion of ant. An ant or i 蟻 is,
in Chinese, the combination of both ch'ung 虫 or insect and i 義 or righteousness, which implies sincerity. Some of the illustrations are helpful in
identifying fu 孚 as ant. The fourth line of hexagram 17, Sui or Following,
says, "There is fu on the path" (有孚在遒). The fifth line says, "there
is a fu on the shelf (孚于嘉架). In the fifth line of hexagram 14, Ta
Yu or Great Possession, "the fu are connected on another (厥孚交如).
The top line of hexagram 64, Wei Chi or Before Completion, reads, "There is
fu in the meal and drink"(有孚于飲酒). This corresponds to the
fifth line of hexagram 5 as noted ealier. From these illustrations we can
imagine that the word "fu" 孚 is used not only to designate the abstract
concept of "trust" or "truth," but also the concrete symbolism of the ant,
the trustful and sincere labor. Hexagram 18, Ku or Decaying, is to be examined
carefully. The word Ku 蠱 signifies the phenomenon of decay due to worms
or maggots. The first, third and fifth lines of the hexagram help us to
understand the meaning of ku more clearly. All these lines talk about
"stem-father's maggots" (幹父之蠱), while the second line talks
about "stem-mother's maggots" (幹母之蠱). In both cases the maggots
refer to the freshly prepared food of sacrifice given to the spirits of
dead parents. It becomes much clearer if we analyze the word in two parts:
Ch'ung 蟲 , which means worms, and ming 皿 or vessels,which mean con-
tainers holding food. The food was perhaps prepared for sacrifice to the
ancestral spirits. From the analysis of the word ku, it is quite obvious
that it implies worms or maggots in the sacrificial food.

The image of birds is often given in a literary form in the I Ching.

For example, hexagram 53, <u>Chien</u> or Advancement, gives the image of wild goose, <u>hung</u> 鴻 , which somewhat closely resembles <u>chien</u> 漸 . Let us observe the lines of this hexagram:

The first line says, "The wild goose gradually advances to the shore" (鴻漸于干).

The second line says, "The wild goose gradually advances to the cliff" (鴻漸于磐).

The third line says, "The wild goose gradually advances to the plateau" (鴻漸于陸).

The fourth line says, "The wild goose gradually advances to the tree" (鴻漸于木).

The fifth line says, "The wild goose gradually advances to the summit" (鴻漸于陵).

In all cases the word <u>hung</u> 鴻 is followed by <u>chien</u> 漸 , which as the same phonetic sound as <u>chien</u> 占 , divination. If we believe the word "<u>chien</u>" 漸 is used here to mean <u>chien</u> 占 , or divination, we presume that the wild goose moves according to the direction of the divination. In other words, the wild goose is the object of omen sayings. The relationship between the wild goose and divination is well illustrated in the Book of Odes: "When the wild goose flies toward the island, this means the lord has nowhere to go. When the wild goose flies toward the land, this means the lord will not return" (No. 159). In China the wild goose became the symbol of conjugal fidelity, because this bird never takes another mate after the death of the first. Thus it is true even today that the wild goose has a special place in Chinese literature as well as in Chinese oracles.

The favorite image of the tree is a willow, which is well depicted in hexagram 28, <u>Ta Kuo</u> or the Great Excess. The second and fifth lines of the

hexagram indicate the withered willow tree. The image of the willow comes
from the structure of the hexagram. The trigram for wood, the <u>Sun</u> (☴),
stands under the trigram for the lake, the <u>Tui</u> (☱). Thus it means the
willow tree which grows near the lake. The relationship of the willow to
the omen sayings is clear when we examine the second and fifth lines of this
hexagram in detail. The second line says, "If a withered willow produces
shoots, an older man takes a young wife" (枯楊生稊老夫得其女妻).
The fifth line says, "If a withered willow produces flowers, an older woman
takes a young husband" (枯楊生華老婦得士夫). Just like the wild
goose, the willow tree becomes the object of odes and omens in Chinese minds.
The relationship between the tree and human life is well illustrated in
these omen sayings of the willow tree. The image of sprouting willow suggests the renewing life process, which represents the older man who takes
a young girl as his wife just as the image of a blooming willow corresponds
to the older woman who takes a husband. Such natural phenomena as trees,
birds, and animals are related to a series of germinal situations of human
life.

One of the favorite images in nature is the moon, which is known by the
Chinese as the object of odes. The moon has also been well known as the
object of constant movement. The calendar was set according to the orbits
of the moon because it is constant. The idea of the moon as constant movement is well expressed in hexagram 32, <u>Heng</u> or Enduring. The word "<u>heng</u>"
恒 was also written as 恒 , which has the moon or <u>yüeh</u> 月 between the two

lines. If we analyze the latter, we have two parts: 卜 and 亙 . The ideogram " 卜 " was originally connected with <u>pu</u> 卜 , which means divination. The ideogram " 亙 " consists of two lines and <u>yüeh</u> 月 , the moon. Thus the word "<u>heng</u>" suggests that it was originally a rite performed at the first appearance of the new moon. The sacrifice was made in order that the moon may continue to make a favorable journey to the end of its orbit.

There are many other images of natural phenomena which convey various meanings corresponding to the realities of human experience. However, there are only two images which the hexagrams depict that are connected with man-made objects. Hexagram 46, which represents the well, becomes the symbol of social structure. The well is not only the symbol of the source of water, which meets the basic needs of all people, but the symbol of the meeting place. The well is the place where women in particular get together for social life. Another hexagram which depicts man-made objects is hexagram 50, <u>Ting</u> or the Caldron, which becomes the symbol of nourishing the civilization. The primary function of the caldron is the preparing and cooking of food for nourishment, while that of the well is to meet thirst and to provide social life. In the lines of the hexagrams we find also man-made images. For example, the image of clothes is found in the fourth line of hexagram 63, <u>Chi Chi</u> or After Completion. It says, "The fine clothes turn to rags. Guard all day long." The image of the wagon is in the second line of hexagram 14, <u>Ta Yu</u> or Great Possession. "A big wagon is fully loaded. It may go in any direction." However, the man-made images in the <u>I Ching</u> are rare. Most images which become the objects of odes and omen sayings are natural objects, both the living and non-living phenomena of the universe.

As we have observed, the hexagrams of the Judgments and the lines are the combination of various forms of literature. We have made an arbitrary distinction between divination and non-divination texts for the convenience of our examination. Except divination formulas, the hexagrams in words are types of odes, which may have originally been transmitted orally until they were written as the I Ching. The odes become the substance of the divination formula. If the Judgments and the lines were written by King Wen and the Duke of Chou, as the Chinese tradition claims, then the divination texts were certainly added to them. However, it is probable that the odes have their origins much earlier than the divination formulas. There is no way to verify the prior existence of the odes even though we can make such a hypothetical statement. Even if we can make a distinction between non-divination and divination texts in the I Ching, we must not separate them in any way. They are mutually complementary to each other.

CHAPTER V. A GUIDE TO INTERPRETATION

1. Understanding the Nature of Symbolism as the Background of Our Interpretation

The I Ching is primarily the book of hexagrams and secondarily the book of literary works. The hexagrams are primary symbols which represent the most primitive forms of human expression. The Judgments or hsi tz'u are secondary symbols which interpret the primary symbols or hexagrams. A clear distinction between the primary and secondary symbols is needed. The secondary symbols are always relative to the primitive (or primary) symbols, while the latter are the bases for the former. This distinction constitutes the hierarchy of symbolisms in the I Ching. To illustrate this hierarchical relationship between these symbolisms, let us consider the art student who takes notes on paintings in the museum of arts. The student looks at the paintings and interprets them in words. In this case, the paintings represent the primary symbols, while his notes on the paintings are the secondary symbols. Just as the written notes of this student interpret the paintings, the Judgments are interpretations of the hexagrams. The hexagrams are analogous with the paintings, which depict reality, but there is a difference between them. Paintings are not only the images but also the objects of the viewers. The hexagrams can never become objects in themselves but are always the symbols which point to those things which they symbolize. The distinction between the primary and secondary symbols is important here in understanding the hierarchy of authenticity in symbolism.

Just as the paintings are more authentic than the notes on the paintings,
the hexagrams are more authentic than the Judgments. In interpreting the
symbols in the I Ching it is important to keep this distinction in mind.

Within the secondary symbols, the Judgments, there is also a distinction. The Judgments on the hexagram or kua tz'u are differentiated from
the judgments on the lines or hsiao tz'u. We have already made a distinction
between them in the previous chapter. We have decided to call the former
Judgments and the latter lines, in order to distinguish them. The lines are
merely the reinterpretations of the Judgments. Thus lines are relative to
the Judgments, for the former show the process of evolvement. Since the
lines do not function independently of the Judgments, the former are not
known independently of the latter. The relationship between the Judgments
and the lines can be compared with the relationship between the descriptions
on the paintings as a whole and the analytical descriptions on the paintings.
The student is not only interested in his impressions of the painting as a
whole but in his analytical approach to it. In other words, an art student
might be interested in a comment on the painting as a whole, before he can
make other comments on the specific aspects of that painting. The comment
on the painting as a whole is analogous to the Judgment, and comments on the
different aspects of the painting are analogous to the lines of the hexagram.
Just as the comments on various aspects of the painting are relative to the
comments on the painting as a whole, the lines are relative to the Judgments.
Just as the lines are dependent on the Judgments, the Judgments are also
relative to the hexagrams. To bring all three different symbolizations
together, we may say that the I Ching contains triple strata of symbolizations;
the primary, the secondary and the supplementary symbolizations. The

correlation of these different symbolizations is necessary for the interpretation of the I Ching. However, their correlation must be in a hierarchical order, for their authenticity is relative to the nature of their symbolizations. For example, the secondary symbols must conform to the nature of primary symbols, and the supplementary symbols must conform to the secondary symbols. In this way the chains of symbolic authenticity are to be established in a proper order.

Let us take hexagram 46 to illustrate what we have said so far. Hexagram 46 is Sheng or Moving Upward, which is the combination of both the trigram Sun or Gentleness below and the trigram K'un or Responsivity above. The primary symbol of this hexagram is the hexagram itself, that is, six of either the broken or unbroken lines as follows:

This primary symbol is interpreted in the Judgment, the hexagram in words, which is the secondary symbol. The Judgment says, "Moving Upward has supreme success. It is necessary to see the great man. Fear not. Departure toward the south will bring good fortune." As we see, the Judgment or Kua tz'u is called the secondary symbol, because in Chinese kua or hexagram, the primary symbol, is symbolized again in tz'u or words. The supplementary symbols are the lines of te hexagram. The lines are always counted from the bottom up. The lowest is the beginning line, which says, "Moving upward is welcome." The second line means: "If it is sincere, it is advantageous to bring a small offering." The third says, "One moves upward into an empty city." The fourth says, "The king must offer sacrifice to Mount Ch'i (which is located

in the western China, the homeland of King Wen, the founder of Chou dynasty)."
The fifth means, "One moves upward by steps." The top line means "Moving upward
blindly." In all cases the lines indicate their movement toward gradual
evolvement to complete the Judgment, that is, "Moving upward has supreme success." Lines represent the supplementary symbols, because they are interpretations of the secondary symbol, the Judgment. In other words, the Judgment
can be compared with a thematic description of a given situation, while the
lines can be compared with the elucidation of it in a meaningful order. That
is why the lines must be seen in the context of the Judgment, just as the
Judgment must be seen in the context of the hexagram.

In addition to the understanding of the hierarchical symbolizations
in the I Ching, it is important for our interpretation to know the nature
and function of symbols themselves. We see the indiscriminate use of the
word between symbol and image. When we use the word "hsiang" 象 for
the hexagrams, they mean the symbols, which are different from the images.[1]
The hexagrams are symbols and not images. The symbol points to something
beyond itself, while the image points to itself. The symbol never becomes
its own object. It does not convey the reality in itself but is a means to
that which it represents. On the other hand, the image becomes the object
of its own. It does not transcend its intrinsic nature. The symbol,
however, is not real in itself but is real only in relation to that which
it signifies. In this respect, the symbol is quite different from the
image. Thus the hexagram cannot be the image, which becomes its own object.
The Chinese word "hsiang" can mean either symbol or image according to the
context of its use. When hsing is used for the hexagram, it always means

---

[1]The word "image" used in the I Ching must be differentiated from that
of common usage. It is identically used with the word "symbol" of ordinal sense.

the symbol. According to Ta Chuan, the symbols or the hexagrams are not the
object of the holy sages: "The holy sages could survey all the phenomena
under heaven. They observed forms and appearances, which represent things
and their attributes. These were called hsiang (or symbols)" (Sec. I, Ch.8).
Here the symbols are not the objects of their contemplation but are represen-
tations of the things and phenomena of the universe. In other words, the
hexagrams as symbols represent forms and phenomena rather than being the
forms and phenomena themselves. The hexagrams are the symbols which point
beyond the visible lines themselves. They point to the germinal situations
which are invisible. The primary symbols are then characterized as visible
pointers to the invisible realities of the universe. On the other hand, the
secondary symbols, the Judgments, are characterized as the translation of the
primary symbols into meaningful expressions of human experience. The Judgments
are in a strict sense the symbolizations of the primary symbols. The Judgments
are symbols, in so far as they point beyond themselves. They are also
interpretations, in so far as they make the hexagrams meaningful to the
common experience of man. Just like the Judgments, the lines are also the
symbols which point byond themselves. They point to something beyond the
lines thmselves. Both the Judgments and lines are the symbols which point
to another symbol, the hexagrams. Thus they are the symbolization of symbols.

To understand the symbolic nature of the I Ching is to understand
enough for us to interpret it. Since the symbols are not something which
can be arbitrarily created or destroyed, they grow out of the situations
which they signify. Thus, the symbols bear the characteristics of the

civilization in which they were formed. Because the symbols cannot be fully understood without the contexts in which they have grown, the characteristics of these symbols in the I Ching cannot be comprehended without their relation to the Chinese civilization in which they were created. The symbols are different from the poles which can be erected arbitrary. They are like the trees which must grow in a particular kind of soil. They are like the trees which adapt themselves to given circumstances. Therefore, the characteristics of the symbols in the I Ching are relative to early Chinese civilization. The civilization in which the symbols in the I Ching were formed marks the beginning of Chinese civilization. According to Chinese tradition, the origin of the symbols may go back as far as the period of king Fu Hsi, the symbol of beginning civilization. If we follow the traditional view, the origin of the symbols was also the origin of Chinese civilization. If Fu Hsi, who formed the symbols of the hexagrams, was also the initiator of Chinese civilization, the beginnings of Chinese civilization and of the hexagrams is inseparable. The mutual relationship between them is not unbelievable. The civilization was based on symbols, which were, at the same time, the sources of the civilization. Ta Chuan stresses the civilization as the product of the symbols rather than the other way around. If we take the idealist's point of view, we have no trouble in saying that the idea is the basis for civilization. For him it is not the civilization which produces the idea, but the idea which produces civilization. The symbols in the I Ching or the hexagrams can be compared with the reproduction of ideas which become the foundations for civilization. The most primitive form of civilization which has to do with hunting and

fishing is attributed to the hexagram of the Li: "Knotted cords were used
for nets and baskets in hunting and fishing. They were perhaps taken from
the hexagram of the Li" (Ta Chuan, Sec. II, Ch. 2). What it tries to say
is that an invention of this kind such as fishing and hunting tools comes
first as an idea, which is symbolized in the hexagram, before it becomes
real in civilization. As we see from the structure of this hexagram, Li or

the Flaming, it appears to be a form of nets which become the basic idea
for the invention of nets and baskets for fishing and hunting. The idea of
agriculture developed from hexagram 42, I or Gain: "He split wood to form
a plowshare and bent it to make the plow handle, and taught the whole world
the advantage of ploughing and weeding. This idea was probably taken from
the hexagram of I" (Ta Chuan, Sec. II, Ch. 2). As we see from the structure

of constituent trigrams, this hexagram gives the idea of plowing the earth.
The constituent trigrams are Sun and Chen, wood and movement. The nuclear
trigrams, K'un and Ken, are associated with the earth. Thus the primary
and nuclear trigrams together give the idea of cultivating the land for
planting. In a like manner the author of Ta Chuan attempts to show that all
other invenstions for the development of Chinese civilization have been

primarily based on the archetypal ideas which are symbolized in the hexagrams. The growth of commerce and market was based on hexagram 21, Shih Ho or Chewing, that of upper and lower garments from both hexagram 1, Ch'ien or Creativity , and hexagram 2, K'un or Responsivity, that of marine life from hexagram 59, Huan or Disintegration, that of transportation from hexagram 17, Sui or Following, that of defense from hexagram 16, Yü or Eagerness, that of mill from hexagram 62, Hsia Ku or the Small Excess, that of weapons from hexagram 38, K'uei or Estrangement, that of city and buildings from hexagram 34, Ta Chuang or the Great Power, that of burials from hexagram 28, Ta Kuo or the Great Excess, and that of writings from hexagram 43, Kuai or Resolution. The main idea is that every civilization is preceded by ideas which are embodied in the hexagrams. Just as the invention of something new is based on the idea of the inventor, the development of civilization through various inventions in China was thought to be based on the archetypal ideas in the hexagrams. The hexagrams, which symbolize the primordial ideas of all inventions, are not mere products of civilization but the basis for it. The hexagrams are thus the symbols of all other symbols. Here we notice that the hexagrams, the primordial forms of all other symbols, are not relative to any certain form of civilization. They transcend the expressions of cultural difference because they become the bases for the origin of all civilizations. Therefore, the hexagrams are the universal symbols, which can be applied to all people. However, the Judgments are always relative to civilization, for they grow out of it. The relationship between the hexagrams, or primary symbols, and the Judgments, or secondary symbols, can be compared with the relationship between cause and effect.

The hexagrams are the causes for civilization, while the Judgments are the effects of civilization, which the hexagrams created. This is not intended to mean that the hexagrams are the causes for the Judgments. Rather the Judgments take their symbolisms from that which is caused by the hexagrams. We see a similar relationship between the Word of God and the Bible in Christianity. The Word of God is the cause for the development of the Church, while the Bible is the book of the Church. The Bible takes its symbolic expressions from what is said by the Word of God. Likewise, the Judgments were written later, perhaps during the early Chou dynasty, to explain the hexagrams through the use of word symbols which grew out of civilization. That is why the secondary symbols in the I Ching are to be understood in relation to the Chinese civilization in which they were formed while the hexagrams or the primary symbols transcend every form of civilization.

Since the secondary symbols, mainly the Judgments, are traditionally attributed to King Wen and the supplementary symbols, or the lines, to the Duke of Chou, they must be understood in relation to the civilization of the early Chou dynasty about three thousand years ago. The civilization of the early Chou dynasty is clearly reflected in the Judgments and lines. There is not sufficient material to secure in detail an accurate picture of that period in which the Judgments were written. The Book of Songs or Odes somewhat reflects the mood of that time but does not give enough evidence to see the real picture of civilization prior to the Ch'un Ch'iu period (722-481 B.C.). The literary character of the appended Judgments expresses the primitive forms of lyrics, proverbs, omen sayings and oracles. The early Chou dynasty was ruled by a feudal aristocracy.

In each feudal state all members of the ruling houses held their offices
in hereditary perpetuity and the common people were completely denied any
share in political power. The government of the feudal states was not only
held by hereditary offices but there was an elaborately graded hierarchy of
offices. The hierarchical system of feudal government is well expressed in
the Judgments of hexagram 7, Shih or the Army, which describes the hierarchical
order from the masses of people at the bottom to the great prince at the top.
We see that there are only two Judgments which express man-made objects
at that period. They are the caldron in the Judgment on hexagram 50, and
the well in the Judgment on hexagram 48. These objects represent the most
primitive symbols of civilization as well as the fundamentals of any form
of civilization. Hexagram 48, which gives the idea of the well, consists of

the trigram Sun or wood and the trigram K'an or water. This image derives
from the pole-and-bucket well of early Chou period. The handle of the bucket
is still a wooden pole which is connected by rope. The Judgment of this
hexagram describes the types of well and bucket symbols in the early Chou
dynasty: "The well changes the town, but the well cannot be changed. It
neither decays nor grows. They come and go and draw the water from the
well. When the drawing is almost accomplished and the rope does not go
all the way, the bucket is broken. Thus it brings misfortune." The Judgment
gives us not only the type of bucket and well but the function of the well
for civilization. It functions not only to supply water but to provide people with

social intercourse. It is still true in many villages of the Orient that the well serves, particularly for women, as a social gathering place. Another man-made object, the Caldron, is drawn from hexagram 50. The concept of caldron may be drawn from

the trigram Sun below and the trigram Li above. Sun represents wood and wind, and Li the flame and fire. Both Sun and Li together bring out the image of the caldron which is used for cooking the food. The shape of the caldron is rather well described in the lines of the hexagram. The caldron possesses legs to stand by itself (the first line), and handles (in the third line). Moreover, the handles were yellow with golden carrying rings (the fifth line). We can depict from these lines the elaborated form of the caldron which is still found in many places in China, Korea and Japan. Anyone who spent most of his life in Asia may not be totally unfamiliar with these symbols of civilization which were already in existence as early as the beginning of the Chou dynasty. These evidences give some comfort for those of us who are interested in the study of these symbols in relation to their civilization. The civilization in which these secondary symbols were formed is not totally strange to the traditional culture of China. The continuity of Chinese civilization until the rise of Communism helps us to get a fairly good picture of the time when the secondary symbols of the I Ching were born. However, for those who do not share Oriental civilization it is difficult to interpret the secondary symbols in the I Ching. The I Ching is not only the basis for the development of Chinese civilization

but also a product of it. Thus the I Ching cannot be understood and
properly interpreted without some knowledge of Chinese civilization.   There
are many peculiar expressions in the Judgments and Lines of the hexagrams,
which are not familiar to the West. Some of these weird expressions such
as the flying dragon, sagging the ridgepole, or treading upon the tail of the
tiger, cannot be meaningfully interpreted without some background in
Chinese history and civilization.

Another problem in the interpretation of the secondary symbols has
to do with the language in which they are expressed. Since the secondary
symbols, including the supplementary symbols, are nothing but the hexagrams
in Chinese words, we cannot understand these symbols unless we know some
characteristics of the Chinese language. To summarize the characteristics
of the Chinese language, we may include the following aspects: picto-graphic
symbolism, simplicity and intuitiveness. First of all, the Chinese uses
the picto-graphic symbols. Every Chinese character is an integrated visual
symbol of lines or strokes which expresses a single concept or idea. We
can see this quite clearly if we study the origin of some characters. The
picto-graphic characters can be classified into three groups: simple,
complex and compound characters. Let us look at the origin of simple
characters. For example, the word "person" 人 may be described in the
beginning as 大 , which evolved to the present form of picto-graphic
symbol. The word for water in Chinese is 水 , which was originally
written as 川 , the form of flowing water. The origin of complex characters
is similar to the preceding. For example, the word for stand in Chinese
is 立 , which may come from 立 , the combination of a person 大 and

the place __. The word for fruit in Chinese is 果 , which is the combination of 木 and 田 . Originally, 田 was shaped like a fruit ⊗ . Since the fruit comes from trees, the combination of both makes the meaning clear. The compound characters are more complicated than the preceding ones. For example, the word "trees" 木 , which may be written originally as 朩 , is combined with another word:"tree" 木, and makes forest 林 When one more word "tree" 木 is added to the forest, it becomes a jungle 森 . The structure of Chinese characters evolved from one stage to another in history. Perhaps the earliest form of character is found during the Shang dynasty, about 1300 B.C. through archaeological evidence. The Shang inscriptions were originally written in oracle bones and shells, which proceeded the I Ching. Since they were written on bones, they were called Chia ku wen 甲骨文 . The evidence of Shang inscription was discovered at Anyang in Honan province in China. The second stage in the evolvement of Chinese characters came during the Chou dynasty (1115-403 B.C.). The Chou inscriptions are known as Chung ting wen 鐘鼎文 , for they were written on bronze caldron. The original copy of the I Ching was undoubtedly written in the Chou inscriptions or Chung ting wen. The Chou inscriptions are quite different from the current inscription of Chinese characters since they are not easily identifiable. After the Chou inscriptions there came the so-called Hsiao Chuan 小篆 , which was written in the Ch'in dynasty (221-207 B.C.). During the Han dynasty (202 B.C. - 220 A.D.) Ni shu 隸書 style came into being. This style is very similar to current form, which is called K'ai shu 楷書 . K'ai shu has been used in China since the Chin dynasty (280-420 A.D.). In almost two thousand years the Chinese characters have not changed. From the evolvement of Chinese characters, we see the problems in interpreting the I Ching, which was written originally in Chou inscriptions.

Another characteristic feature of the Chinese language, which we must
be aware of when we approach to Judgments, is the simplicity in its structure.
In comparison to English or German, Chinese is almost without grammar. Chinese does not have any inflection. That is why it is often called the language
of isolation. There is no tense, no case, no genders and no numbers. Let us
take the Judgment of hexagram 1, Ch'ien, in Chinese and then try to interpret
it in English. The Judgment in Chinese is 乾元亨利貞 . Ch'ien 乾
means the dry or creative, yüan 元 origin or sublime, heng 亨 penetration
or success, li 利 advantageous or furtherance, and chen 貞 correctness or
perseverance. Let us now look at the translations of both Wilhelm and Legge.
According to Wilhelm's translation, the Judgment says, "The Creative works
sublime success, furthering through perseverance." Legge translates it as
follows: "Khien (represents) what is great and originating, penetrating, advantageous, correct and firm." Both translations come from the same text of
the Chinese but have different meanings. As we compare both of them, we see
that Legge's translation is much closer to the original text, even though
Wilhelm's makes sense to English-speaking people. Neither of them is a translation in a strict sense but interpretation. There is no way to translate
strictly from Chinese to English. Let us take a phrase from the fifth line
of hexagram 12, P'i or Stagnation. The original text of it in Chinese is
"其亡其亡," which is translated by Wilhelm "What if it should fail, what
if it should fail?" On the other hand, Legge translates it, "We may perish!
We may perish!" Even though both of them are the translations of the same
text, their meanings are varied. The word "ch'i" 其 is a demonstrative and
possessive pronoun, and "wan" 亡 means perish. Again, we notice Legge's

translation is a much more literal interpretation than Wilhelm's. From these illustrations we notice that the translations of the I Ching are more or less interpretations of the original texts. In this respect the problem of interpretation becomes much more complex. What we have to do is to interpret from what is interpreted. We must bear this in mind as we approach the I Ching.

Finally, the characteristic feature of the Chinese language is aesthetic and intuitive. The Chinese language is more congenial to expressing imagination and intuitive insights than many other languages. That is why it is a language of excellence for poetry and art. The lack of grammatical features is a hindrance to a precise expression of particular circumstances. It cannot be effective in describing logical and mathematical relationships. The simplicity of sentence structure and the possibility of using many metaphors help the Chinese people to be more poetic and aesthetic. Chinese is an excellent medium for poetry, art and creative thinking. Thus when we use the translation of the I Ching, we fail to comprehend the richness of these aesthetic and emotive expressions which is found in the original texts of Chinese. For those of us who will never learn to read and speak Chinese, it is only a reminder of how limited we are as to the interpretation of the I Ching.

2. Practical Suggestions for an Interpretation

We have so far discussed some of the problems and issues as the background for a guide to interpretation of the I Ching. With this background let us discuss practical steps for an interpretation. Several steps are to be followed for the understanding of the I Ching. The first step is to deal with the hexagrams alone without reference to the secondary symbols. Since the hexagrams transcend the cultural and linguistic differences, they are accessible directly to English speaking people as well as the Chinese people. Wang Pi, one of the great commentators on the I Ching, found much insight by contemplating the hexagrams alone without any reference to the written words in the Judgments. Let us illustrate this with an analogy of painting as we did previously. The student of painting is asked to go and see the painting directly to find out the various combinations of colors and contractions of shades, etc. He is not going to read the notes on the painting to find out what the painting means to him. Likewise, in the study of the I Ching, we must take up the primary symbols first before consulting the secondary and supplementary symbols. In approaching the primary symbols, we need to be aware of some general guide-lines for an interpretation. We may take three different hexagrams to illustrate some of the practical steps for an inter-pretation. Let us arbitrarily choose hexagram 11, hexagram 21, and hexagram 31 as models for illustration in this chapter. Hexagram 11 is T'ai or Peace, which consists of the trigram Ch'ien below and K'un above. Since the attri-

bute of Ch'ien is creative and active energy, it seeks to unite with the other pole, K'un, which is receptive and passive. Thus the combination of both trigrams brings harmony and unity, which results in good fortune. The unity of the sexes is fundamental to prosperity and reproduction. Thus it is related with the Spring season and the beginning of new life. Some of these ideas are suggested in the structure of hexagram 11. Hexagram 21,

Shih Ho or Chewing, has a strange shape, the shape of an open mouth.
However, instead of looking at it externally, we can analyze the attributes
of the constituting trigrams. The trigram Chen is below and Li is above.
Since Chen signifies arousing like thunder, it tends to move upward. The Li
means fire and flaming, which also move upward. Since both trigrams move
upward, they neither meet together nor are in conflict with each other. Since
thunder is accompanied by lightning, which is fire, there is co-existence of
the two trigrams without interference. This time we can look at the structure
of this hexagram from the constituting nuclear trigrams: Ken below and K'an
above. The trigram Ken means mountain or stillness, while K'an the abyss or
water. Both nuclear trigrams move downward and co-exist with each other.
Mountain and water are conspiring each other, as we see in Chinese landscapes.
The combination of mountain and water or lake is favorable. The upward movement of two primary trigrams and the downward movement of two nuclear trigrams
are well balanced. It, therefore, suggests the concept of justice and equilibrium. Hexagram 31, Hsien or Influence, appears to be that its center is
closely knitted together. The concentration of yang lines in the center sig-

nifies firm unity and togetherness. The constituting primary trigrams are
Ken below and Tui above. Ken is, as we said, the symbol of mountain and
stillness, while Tui the symbol of lake and joy. As we have already pointed
out, the lake and mountain go together. They are mutually attractive.
Furthermore, Ken represents the youngest son and Tui the youngest daughter.
Both of them are the youth in the opposite sexes. This suggests a union of

vitality and joy. The nuclear trigrams which constitute the hexagram are
Sun below and Ch'ien above. Sun is penetrating, while Ch'ien is creative.
Both the penetrating and creative are qualities of achievement. Thus it
suggests the penetrating creativity which can influence every possible situation. As a whole hexagram 31 is very favorable and good. The observation
of these hexagrams alone without reference to the written words gives us some
clues to understanding the situations. Since the primary symbols or the hexagrams are not conditioned by civilization and language as is in the case of
the secondary symbols, they are directly accessible to the discernment of our
own.

The second step for an effective interpretation of symbols in the I
Ching deals with the words or the Judgments alone without any reference to
the structure of the hexagrams. In other words, the secondary symbols are
to be taken into consideration without the primary symbols. Wang Pi also
found a great wisdom by reading words in the I Ching without reference to the
shape of the hexagrams. A difficulty in this case is clearly to those who
are not capable of reading Chinese. The advantage of reading the Judgments
alone without reference to the hexagrams is that it provides an opportunity
to think deeply about the meaning of the words. It helps us to concentrate
on the implications behind these words. Just like our reading of notes on
the painting, we may be able to get some ideas which we can never get from
the primary symbols. The individual characters and creative insights provide
an extra dimension of rich cultural heritage through the study of the Judgments alone. Let us take the same hexagrams and read only the written words
without any reference to the structure of hexagrams themselves. The Judgment

of hexagram 11 says, "Peace. The small departs, and the great approaches. It is good fortune and success." We presume that the translation of this Judgment is identical with the meaning of the original text in Chinese. There are many shades of meaning on the concept of peace, as we reflect upon the Judgment. We can inject some of our personal conjectures when we read the written words. For example, we can concentrate on certain words like "the small departs, and the great approaches." Is the small the small fortune or advantage? Does it imply wealth or knowledge? What does the word "depart" signify? Many questions are to be asked from the statement on the Judgment. Many of the writings in the I Ching are cryptical sayings and not descriptive statements. For example, the expression of "the small departs, and the great approaches" is a metaphor which contains deep implications. Without reading the words, we do not understand the profound metaphor which the author of the Judgments implies. The written words in the I Ching can be compared with the Book of Revelation in the New Testament. There is no way to interpret them directly. We must search for the meaning behind the words or between the lines when we attempt to interpret the Judgments in the I Ching. Just as the Book of Revelation cannot be understood without a creative insight to project our imagination beyond the written words, we cannot get the real meaning of the Judgment without reading into the depth of every word in the I Ching. Let us now look at the Judgment of hexagram 21, which says, "Chewing brings success. It is advantageous to use the power of justice." Here, the concept of chewing is a metaphor which points to the inner meaning of the actual implication of these words. We can conjecture many ideas of our own when we attempt to interpret it without a hexagram. The Judgment of hexagram 31 says, "Influence brings success.

It is advantageous to be correct. To take a maiden will bring good fortune." What does the word "influence" mean to us? What do we have to do
to be correct? What does it imply to take a maiden? As we ponder some of
these questions, we may be able to project our unconscious feelings in searching for the deeper meaning of the words in the Judgments. Perhaps that is
why Ta Chuan says: "First take up the tz'u (Judgments), and see the principles
to which they point. Then the rules reveal themselves" (Sec. II, Ch. 8).

The third step is the correlation of the first and second steps together in a meaningful way. It is to see both the primary and secondary
symbols together at the same time. The interpretation of the Judgment must
be seen in the light of the hexagrams themselves. This is the time to integrate both interpretations of the hexagrams and the Judgments. The correlation of these two independent interpretations makes the deeper understanding
of the meaning of the hexagrams possible. Let us take the same hexagrams
again to relate our interpretations of the hexagrams with those of the Judgments. Hexagram 11, T'ai or Peace, consists of the trigram Ch'ien below and

the trigram K'un above. The Judgment says, "Peace. The small departs, and
the great approaches. It is good fortune and success." If we observe both
the structure of the hexagram and the Judgment together, we can get much more
reliable interpretations of this hexagram. In other words, the combined approach
is much more reliable than the independent approach. Since both the trigrams,
in spite of their opposite character, move towards each other, we see from the
structure of the hexagram that it is a sign of harmony and unity. The concept of peace in the Judgment may come from the idea of harmony and unity as

expressed in the structure of the hexagram. We have also observed from the structure of the hexagram that the union of two opposite sexes signifies the beginning of new life, that is, the Spring. "The small departs, and the great approaches" in the Judgment might imply that the force of the cold Winter is ready to depart and the force of the Spring begins to appear. The cold Winter is dominated by yin forces, which are less active. Thus it represents the small. On the other hand, the Spring is known by the domination of yang forces, which are active and strong. Thus it represents the great. The light, or yang, is powerful and great in its brightness, while the darkness, or yin, is submissive and weak. Thus the Judgment says: "Peace. The small departs, and the great approaches. It is good fortune." Let us now look at hexagram 21, Shih Ho or Chewing, and its Judgment together. The Judgment says,

"Chewing up brings success. It is advantageous to use the power of justice." The name of the hexagram probably came from its external appearance. It certainly resembles the open mouth, which is the shape of hexagram 27. However,

when we compare hexagram 21 with hexagram 27, the former has the undivided line on the fourth place. Thus the open mouth is obstructed because of the fourth line. This obstructing line must be bitten through or chewed up, for it comes between the teeth. Perhaps this is why this hexagram is named as "Chewing." What is the meaning of "chewing" from the point of view of justice? Since the word "justice" appears in the Judgment, it might be related to the law and order. This hexagram is meaningful to our generation because of the

youth revolt and obstruction. The trigram <u>Chen</u> or the awakening is below
and the trigram <u>Li</u> or the flaming above. The awakening thounder and the
flaming fire can be compared to the violent cities and the revolt of the
youth in the campus. The obstructing revolt of the youth is represented
by the <u>yang</u> line on the fourth place. It is a powerful and energetic one,
which stops the functioing of the bureaucratic machine. According to the
Judgment, the government must use the legal constraints or penitentiaries
(狱). The law should not yield to the demands of the revolting youth
who obstruct the institution. Thus the Judgment says: "It is advantageous
to use the power of justice." Finally, let us look at hexagram 31, <u>Hsien</u> or

Influence. The Judgment says, "Influence brings success. It is advantageous
to be correct. To take a maiden brings good fortune." The concept of influence might be derived from the attributes of the constituting trigrams.
The trigram <u>Ken</u> or Stillness is below and the trigram <u>Tui</u> or Joy is above.
The mountain with the lake and the steady with the joyous are mutually attractive. Moreover, the nuclear trigrams, <u>Sun</u> below and <u>Ch'ien</u> above, actively
influence others. The trigram <u>Sun</u> means to penetrate like the wind, while
<u>Ch'ien</u> means an active energy similar to a dragon. Combining the attributes
of both penetration and active energy, we receive the idea of influence. The
compatibility of the mountain with the lake and the penetration with the active
engery makes the success possible. The idea of taking a maiden to wife may
be derived from the two primary trigram: <u>Ken</u>, the youngest and most youthful
son and <u>Tui</u>, the youngest and most youthful daughter. Thus the union of the
most youthful sexes produces the image of the marriage. Of course, this results

in good fortune. Some of these illustrations have been made to correlate the approaches of both the structure of the hexagrams and the meaning of the Judgments in the process of interpretation. One of the advantages of bringing them together in a coherent system is to understand them as a unity.

The fourth step in the interpretation of the I Ching is to relate the meaning of lines to the Judgment. This time we need to observe each line of the hexagram rather than to observe the hexagram as a whole. What we can do here is to correlate each line of the hexagram with the hexagram as a whole. If we look at both the individual lines of the hexagram and the Judgment together, they are somehow coherent, just as the structure of the hexagram is coherent with the Judgment. However, it is important to understand the hierarchical structure of symbols. The lines, which are supplementary symbols, are always relative to the Judgments. The lines thus must be interpreted within the signification of the Judgments. With this in mind let us again take up the same hexagrams which we have already discussed. Hexagram 11 described in its Judgment is as we have already mentioned: "Peace. The small departs, and the great approaches. It is good fortune and success." The lines of the haxagram move from bottom up. Let us look at the moving line at the beginning. It says, "When ribbon grass is pulled up, it brings the sod with it. Advance will bring good fortune." What is said here is relative to the Judgment. It has to do with the peace time, for the Judgment deals with peace. Since the first line represents the mass of people who are led by officials, it deals with the common people, who are roots of social structure. It is also an indication that there are certain kinds of people but they act together in the community of a peaceful living. There is no way to single out

one particular person among the group, for the concord and harmony of
community prevail in peace. This kind of situation is the sure foundation
of leadership in a peace time. The second line says, "One who is uncultured
can cross the river without a boat. He does not neglect for those who are
distant because of his friendship. Thus he may manage to walk in the middle."
The second place of the hexagram is an official's position. It indicates the
carefulness of officials in time of peace. Their ability to practice their
ability to practice their leadership in the middle way in respect to action
is their nobility and wisdom. This line is also relative to peace as is
in the Judgment. The third line says, "There is not peace which is not liable
to be disturbed. There is no going that is not followed by a return. It is
difficult to maintain righteousness without mistake. Do not complain about
this truth; enjoy the blessings which you still possess." The third place of
the hexagram is a transitory position, for it meets with the upper trigram.
Thus it deals with the transitoriness of all things in peace. Everything
is subject to change. Even peace and prosperity change to the uneasiness and
poor. This line certainly depicts the mood of transition taking place from
the time of peace to the time of turblence. The fourth line means: "He flutters
down and does not boast his wealth. He calls his neighbors in sincerity."
The fourth place is also the position where two trigrams meet each other. It
belongs to the upper trigram, occupying a higher rank than the third place.
But the characteristic feature of peaceful society is that the people of higher
rank come closer to the lowly people. The correspondence between the wealthy
and the poor is the sound basis for a mutual trust and confidence which maintain
peace. The fifth line means, "The king I gives his daughter in marriage. By
doing this there will be blessing and supreme good fortune." Since the fifth
place is the position of ruler, it has to do with the sovereign ruler, I, who

who may mean here the first ruler of the Shang dynasty. Moreover, the marriage is the symbol of supreme harmony and unity, which is the foundation of peace and prosperity. It is the crowning event of the situation symbolized in this hexagram. The top line means: "The wall returns into the moat. Don't use army. Announce your orders to the people of your own city. Correctness will bring regret and humiliation." The height of peace and prosperity which is expressed in the fifth place begins to decline on the top place. The top place represents the transitory situation, just as the third place does. The transition of peace to turbulence is already alluded on the third place and is actually taking place on the top place. Thus the lines evolve from the inner to the outer, from the least to the most and from the bottom to the top within the delimitation of the Judgment. All lines are relative to the Judgments, for their movements confine themselves to the significations of the Judgments. That is why the lines are supplementary symbols to the Judgment, just as the Judgments are secondary to the hexagrams.

Let us look at hexagram 21, Shih Ho or Chewing. The Judgment of this hexagram says, "Shih Ho brings success. It is advantageous to use the power of justice." Again let us examine each line in relation to the Judgment. The moving line at the beginning means: "His feet are in the stocks, so that his toes are deprived. It is no mistake." Since the Judgment deals with the time of unrest and disturbance, the individual lines must be seen in the light of this unfortunate circumstance. The beginning line, as we see from the structure of the hexagram, corresponds to the top line.

The beginning line deals with the foundation of the situation represented by the hexagram, while the top line deals with the head of a hierarchical structure. The beginning line is fixed at the bottom, that is, the feet. On the other hand, the top line is fixed at the top, the neck. At the bottom the toes diappear, while at the top the ears disappear. Both represent the yang lines which are obstructed by the presence of the fourth. Thus they are fixed and do not move. The rest of the lines of the hexagram deal with the punishment for crimes. In the second line it bites or chews up the tender meat, while in the third line it chews on old dried meat. The evolvement of the greater punishment for crimes is expressed in these cryptical sayings in the time of turbulence. The tender meat means the light punishment, for the tender meat is easier to chew. The old dried meat is harder to chew, so that it represents the heavy punishment for a greater crime. In the fourth place it is the most difficult to bite through, for it "chew on dried gristly meat." From the structure of the hexagram, the fourth place is represented by the strong obstacle. Thus it is the most difficult to bite through. It further indicates, "He receives metal arrows. It is advantageous to be firm at the time of difficulties." The yang line of the fourth place is analogous with the metal arrows which are almost impossible to chew up. This is the most difficult one to overcome by the law and order. The fifth place is less difficult to chew up. It says, "He chews on dried lean meat. He receives the yellow gold." The lean meat is less hard than the gristly meat. Also the yellow gold is much more tender than the metal arrows. As we see from the structure of this hexagram, the most intensive trouble has been caused by the fourth line, the yang line, which obstructs the peace. Thus the fifth line represents the overcoming of the most difficult time.

Lines are certainly relative to the Judgment. They support the Judgment in detail and express the movement of each position within the structure and condition delimited by the Judgment of the hexagram. In this way they act as supplementary symbols to the Judgment, which is the secondary symbol of the hexagram.

Finally, let us observe the lines of hexagram 31, Hsien or Influence, in the light of the Judgment. The Judgment says: "Influence brings success. It is advantageous to be correct. To take a maiden brings good fortune." Since the lines show the movement of changes within the given situation of hexagram, we can observe how the power of influence moves from the bottom to the top. The moving line at the bottom says, "The influence affects his great toe." The great toe is a metaphor which expresses the lower end of the body. Since the position of the line is at the bottom of the hexagram, it corresponds to the lower end of the body. It moves upward and comes to the second place. The second line says, "The influence affects the calves of his legs." The calves of his legs belong to the upper parts of the body rather than the toes in the first place. The third line says, "The influence affects his thighs." Here the movement of influence reaches a higher part of his body. The influence then moves from the thighs to the heart in the fourth place. The fourth line thus says, "One's correctness brings good fortune and prevents remorse. If his thoughts are not settled, his friends will follow his thoughts." Here, there is no explicit word about the heart being influenced. However, the content of this line suggests that the influence affects his heart. It is the heart where his conscious thoughts are fixed. From the heart the influence reaches up to the back of his neck in the fifth place: "The influence affects the back of his neck." Since the neck is located at the upper portion of his body rather than the heart, the influence moves upward. Finally, at the top line the influence reaches its height, but at the same time it begins to decline. It says, "The influence affects his jaws, cheeks and tongue." Those parts of the body which are located at the upper portions rather than the heart are the jaws, cheeks and tongue, as mentioned in the top line. Here the influence reaches at the highest place. However, they represent the influence through the talk that has nothing real by itself. Thus it is the beginning of falling downward. In other words, the influence is at its maximum, and therefore it is the verge of decline. The process of this movement accords with the principle of changes. As we have seen from these illustrations, the lines themselves show the movements of changes within the delimitation of the Judgment. They are not autonomous in a sense, because they are supplementary to the Judgment on the hexagram as a whole. They, therefore, must be correlated with the meaning of the total situation as depicted in the Judgment. by doing this we come to know in detail the significance of the situation which the hexagram symbolizes.

The fifth step for the interpretation of symbols in the I Ching has to do with the consultation of the Ten Wings. The Ten Wings, which were added later, should not be used in the interpretation side by side with the main texts. Among the Ten Wings the most reliable and helpful materials are Ta Chuan or the Great Commentary and Shuo Kua or Discussion of the Trigrams. Both of them deal with general philosophy of the I Ching and the principle of changes. These commentaires can serve as our background knowledge for an interpretation of the hexagrams. The rest of the Ten Wings is to be used

for some illuminations for our interpretations of the main texts themselves.
The function these commentaries is supplementary to our own interpretations.
They cannot be the basis for our interpretations. They can add an enrichment
to our understanding. Some commentaries ocasionally confuse us rather than
clarify the meanings we seek in our interpretations. Thus we must not
rely on the commentaries too much. T'uan Chuan or Commentary on the
Judgments and Hsiang Chuan or Commentary on the Symbols are also important.
Let us now see how these commentaries enlighten our interpretations of the
hexagram. The Commentary on the Judgment of hexagram 11, T'ai or Peace says:

> "The small departs, and the great approaches. It is good for-
> tune and success." Therefore, heaven and earth unite, and all
> things come into harmony. The unity of above and below makes one
> will. The yang (light principle) is within, and the yin (dark
> principle) is without. Strength is within, and devotion is with-
> out. The superior man is within, and the inferior man is without.
> The way of the suprior man is growing, while the way of inferior
> man is decaying.

This is a good commentary, which illuminates our understanding of this hexagram. Various attributes of both the trigram Ch'ien and K'un help us to see
the rich meanings of this hexagram. The trigram Ch'ien represents the inner
nature of the hexagram, because it is located below. On the other hand, the
trigram K'un represents the outward or external aspect of the hexagram, because it is elevated above the Ch'ien. The concept of "within" or "without"
is relative to the position of the constituting trigrams. However, the
attributes of both Ch'ien and K'un are opposite: the light versus the shadow
(or yang to yin), strength versus devotion, and the superior versus the inferior. The commentary specifically points out that the small represents the
inferior man and the great represents the superior man. In this way the
commentary enriches our understanding of the hexagram. Let us see what the
Hsiang Chuan or Commentary on the Symbols tries to say on hexagram 11. The

Commentary of the Symbols is divided into two parts: Commentary on the Great Symbols and on the Small Symbols. The Great Symbols or Ta Hsiang deal with the individual hexagrams as a whole, while the Small Symbols or Hsiao Hsiang deal with the each individual line of the hexagram. The former symbols correspond to the Judgments, and the latter symbols to the lines. The Commentary of the Great Symbols on hexagram 11 says: "The unity of heaven and earth signifies peace. Thus the ruler fashions and completes the course of heaven and earth. He advances and regulates the wills of heaven and earth. Thereby he aids the people." Here, this commentary is less comprehensive than the commentary on the Judgments. It certainly suggests the idea that Spring comes from the unity of both heaven and earth. However, it does not add any extra dimension of knowledge to what we have already seen in the Commentary on the Judgments. When we come to the Commentary of the Small Symbols, we find its exposition very concise and suggestive. At the beginning line it is said: "When ribbon grass is pulled up... Advancement brings good fortune. His will is external to himself." The will that is directed outward can be understood as the direction of the movement of energy from the inward, the bottom line, to the outward, the upper lines. Since the lower trigram represents the inner nature of the hexagram, the movement from the bottom line is directed to the outward, the upper trigram. Here the commentary stresses something that is not important. What this commentary says is rather insignificant. Thus it is only a supplement to our knowledge. The second line of the hexagram the Hsiang Chuan says, "He who is uncultured... thus he can walk in the middle, because the light is great." The brightness or the light in the second line is clear, for it is yang line occupying the middle of the trigram Ch'ien. The importance of this line cannot be denied. The greatness of the ruling position is shown in the way of walking in the middle axiom. This commentary is suggestive but incomprehensive. In the third line of the hexagram the commentary says, "There is no going that is not followed by coming, because it is boundary of heaven and earth." The reason why there is no going or not followed by coming is that it stands on the boundary between the trigram Ch'ien or heaven and the trigram K'un or earth. The third line is a boundary line between the two grigrams. However, the commentary fails to explain further the implication of the boundary line. In the fourth line the commentary says, "He flutters down and does not boast his wealth, because he and his friends lost what is real. There is no warning, because he desires it in the depths of his heart." This is not a clear commentary. "He and his friends have lost what is real" could be understood as the renounciation of the material wealth for the spiritual wealth. However, it is still vague. In the fifth place, the commentary says: "This brings blessings and supreme good fortune, because he is central in carrying out his wishes." He is central, for he is in the middle of the trigram K'un. He is in the ruling position, and therefore he can carry out his works and his wishes. In the top place, the commentary remarks: "'The city wall returned back into the moat' shows how the (governmental) orders have (long) been in disorder."[1] The cause for the fall of city is attributed to the disorder of community, which is followed by prosperity and peace. Even peace and prosperity are subject to the principle of changes. Thus the hexagram ends with the decline of wealth and peace which have prevailed for a long period. From what we have observed, these commentaries are helpful and

---

[1]See Legge's translation.

suggestive in many ways. However, they are inadequate and insufficient to
deal comprehensively with the basic questions involved in the exposition of
the lines and the Judgments of hexagrams.

Again let us take hexagram 21, Shih Ho or Chewing. T'uan Chuan or the
Commentary on the Judgments is quite helpful. It explains first why it is
called Chewing. The reason for this is "There is something between the jaws."
From the structure of the hexagram the fourth line represents "something between the jaws." The jaws are based on the formation of hexagram 27,
where the top and bottom line represents the jaws. The hexagram of Chewing

is successful, because firm and yielding lines are distinct from each other.
In other words, its success is based on the distinctiveness of both yin and
yang lines. That is to say that the judge, for example, can easily notice
the yang line, the fourth line, from the rest of the second, third, and fith
which are yin lines. It is easily noticeable that the yang line occupies the
wrong place. Just like the long beared youth sitting on the hallway of an
administration building for demonstration, he is not only easily noticeable
but is in the wrong place. Thus he becomes an obstacle for others. The
last part of the commentary remarks: "Thunder and lightning are united together and make lines. The yin lines receive the place of honor and advance."
The trigram Chen, which is below, signifies the thunder, and the trigram Li,
which is above, signifies the lightning and fire. Thus the combination of
these two trigrams forms the lines of hexagram. The yin lines receive the
honor, because the yang line, which occupies the fourth place, is to be chewed
up. They advance, for both Chen and Li are light and move up. The result of

advancement is the successive outcome of the enforcement of the law and order, which is stressed in this hexagram. Thus the Commentary on the Judgments is most helpful to our understanding of the Judgment. The Commentary on the Symbols or Hsian Chuan is also helpful to understand the firm enforcement of the law by the government: "Thus the former kings made effective the laws through clearly defined penalties." The turbulent society can be successively governed through the firmness of laws and a clearly defined penal system. Both commentaries provide us helpful insights for our discernment of the Judgment. The Commentary on the Small Symbols deals with the lines of the hexagram. In the first line, the commentary remarks: "His feet are in the stocks and his toes are deprived. Thus he cannot walk (to do evil)." It is self-evident that he cannot walk, because his feet in the stocks. On the top place it remarks: "His neck is fastened... so that his ears are deprived. Thus he does not hear clearly." It is also self-evident that he cannot hear clearly when his ears are cut off. In both cases the commentary stresses the wrong aspects of the lines. The stress in both cases should be on fastened feet and neck. The commentary on the second line says, "He chews up the tender meat, so that his nose is deprived. Thus he rides on a hard line." From the structure of the hexagram, we notice that the second line, the yin line, is rested on the yang line or a hard line, which is also the beginning line. In the third place, the commentary remarks: "He meets something poisonous. The place is not the right one." The place is not right, because the third line is the yang position rather than the yin. In the fourth place the commentary says, "It is advantageous to realize the difficulties of his work and to be firm. It is good fortune. His light is not yet manifested." This is an ambiguous statement. It seems to suggest that the light is not yet given, because the trigram Li or the light begins with this line. The stress on the fourth line should be the dried gristly meat, which represents the obstacle between the jews of mouth. In the fifth place the commentary states: "Be aware of danger. There is no mistake. It has found an appropriate place." This is also an ambiguous statement. From what we have observed on hexagram 21, we can conclude that the most helpful commentaries are both T'uan Chuan and Hsiang Chuan on the great symbols. The Hsiang Chuan on the small symbols is less valuable.

Hexagram 31, Hsien or Influence, is clearly expounded in the Commentary on the Judgments: "Influence brings stimulation. The weak is above, and the strong is below. The two forces stimulate and respond to each other." The weak means the trigram Tui, the youngest daughter, while the strong is the trigram Ken, the youngest son. The female represents the weak and the male the strong. Thus the combination of both sexes makes the stimulation and attraction possible. The commentary further stresses the relationship between these two primary trigrams: "Ken and Tui. The male subordinates himself to the female. Hence it brings success. It is advantageous to be firm. To take a maiden brings good fortune." The attribute of the trigram Ken is stillness, and that of Tui is joy. The male, the trigram Ken, is subordinated to the female, the trigram Tui. However, the commentary does not explain further why this kind of relationship produces good fortune. The rest of its exposition inclines to be exaggerative. It describes that the relationship between Tui and Ken has a universal significance, identifying Tui with earth and Ken with heaven. The relationship between Tui and Ken, thus, is identical with the union of both earth and heaven: "Heaven and earth stimulate each other and produce all things. The holy sages stimulate the hearts of people to attain the peace of the world. If the place of Influence is known, the attributes of all things are to be understood." The commentary makes the relationship between the male and female, that is, the relationship between yin and yang the basis of all phenomena of the universe. This kind of exposition provides us a philosophical foundation to the interpretation of the hexagrams. As to the Commentary on the Symbols, it is not as comprehensive as the proceding one. The commentary on the great symbols says on this hexagram: "A lake on the mountain is influence. Thus the superior man make ready to receive people." The mountain, Ken, takes the initiation, for it is a male. However, the statement is not comprehensive to indicate real significance to the understanding of the hexagram as a whole. The commentary on the small symbols stresses the will as the power to move the influence. In the first line the commentary says, "Influence in his great toe; his will is external to himself." Here the will is directed from inside out. We have already explained the reason why it is directed outward. The commentary says on the third line that the will is firmly founded toward the greater influence. It says, "When the will is external to things that one's friends desire, it is very low." In the fifth line the will reaches to its final destination. The commentary thus says, "The influence affects the back of his neck. The will is going to reach to the end." The second and fourth lines are too insignificant to be examined. The commentary does not say too much on these lines. On the top line the commentary remarks, "The influence(finally) affects his jaws, cheeks and tongue. He opens his mouth and talks." Tui here signifies the mouth, and the jaws, cheeks and tongue which have to do with talking. Thus it is connected with a talkative girl. The divided line on the top is analogous with the open mouth. As we have already experienced, the commentary on the small symbols often stresses something less important. Moreover, it often misleads or even confuses us in our attemp to understand the meaning of the hexagrams. Therefore, our appraoch to the commentaries must be selective. It is not a wise practice to read the commentaries side by side with the main texts of the I Ching. The commentaries are not the basis for our interpretation, rather our interpretation is assisted and enlightened by the use of these commentaries. The commentaries are to be referred always after the main texts are fully studied. In this way, as we have already indicated, we can avoid some of the mistakes which have been committed by the commentators. On the other hand, we need also to check our own interpretations in view of these commentaries so that our inter- pretations may be improved and enriched accordingly.

The sixth and final step is to adopt the meaning of the hexagram to our particular circumstance. Unless the interpretation of the hexagram meets our personal needs, it loses its significance. The interpretation of symbols in the I Ching is complete when it meets our needs. How can we then make the interpretation meaningful to our existential situation? The questions which have occupied my mind have to do with my intention of writing this book and the future predicament of it. "Why am I writing this book?" "What is the future predicament of this book?" These two questions must be answered to meet the needs of my existential situation. It is more or less coincidental that hexagrams 11 and 21 are selected for the first question and hexagrams 21 and 31 for the second through the manipulation of stalks. Hexagrams 11 and 21 correspond to the first question, and hexagram 21 and 31 correspond to the second question.

The first question deals with both hexagram 11 and 21. The question then begins with hexagram 11 and ends with hexagram 21. If we look at the structure of hexagram 11 in relation to hexagram 21, it is easy to notice that the second and third lines of hexagram 11 are transformed from <u>yang</u> to

<u>yin</u> in hexagram 21, and the fourth and sixth lines of hexagram 11 are changed from <u>yin</u> to <u>yang</u> lines in hexagram 21. Thus the changing lines of hexagram 11 are the second, third, fourth and top places. We need to pay attention to the Judgment and the changing lines of hexagram 11 as well as the Judgment of hexagram 21.

Hexagram 11 is <u>T'ai</u> or Peace, which is the symbol of concord and unity between heaven and earth, between the positive and negative, or between the primordial polarities which produce all things. The writing of this book must be based on the harmonious union between the positive and the negative. The <u>I Ching</u> is full with active energy, while the writings about the <u>I Ching</u> result from the passive receptivity. If my intention is to introduce the <u>I Ching</u>, I must be receptive and the <u>I Ching</u> must be active. The harmony and correlation of the positive and negative of the <u>I Ching</u> and I make the book possible. The second line of this hexagram is a moving line. Thus Nine in the second place

is a mediator who mediates the essence of the I Ching. This book attempts
to introduce the I Ching to the people of the West who represent the beginning line. The nine in the third place is a transitory position, where the
lower trigram meets the uper trigram. When I encountered many problems in
comprehending the I Ching, I questioned my ability to be an effective mediator to introduce the I Ching to the poeple in the West. But when I came to
the fourth line, I am convinced that I have a message to tell to the West. My
conviction that the West needs to be acquainted with the I Ching gives me a
strong will to finish the manuscript. However, when I reach the top place,
my conviction and enthusiasm are beginning to decline and I begin to question as to the future predicament of this book. I begin to feel a sense of
inadequacy on my part to deal adequately on the subject of this book. I then
come to hexagram 21, Shih Ho or Chewing. Just as the hexagram symbolizes
the chewing up the fourth line which obstructs the jaws of mouth, I have
to overcome the feeling of inadequacy which obstructs the future predicament of this book. However, it will be overcome through the self-discipline.
Finally, it will be sent to the publisher for publication.

The second question is correlated with both hexagram 21 and 31. From
the structure of both hexagrams, hexagram 21 is transferable to hexagram 31

through the transformation of the first, third, fifth and top lines. The
scope of our examination includes these four moving lines and the Judgments of
these two hexagrams. Since the question has to do with the future predicament
of this book, the hexagram 21 will act as a layout for hexagram 31. According

to the hexagram 21, there will be a difficulty to initiate the readers at
first, but success is followed by the overcoming of this difficulty. At
the beginning there is no break-through, just as the feet are in the stocks.
However, when the book starts to be circulated, it may face a serious hardship and humiliation because of slanderous reviews and irresponsible criticisms. Thus six in the third place says, "Chews on the old dried meat and
meets something poisonous. Slight humiliation will come. No mistake." At
both the fifth and the top lines the difficulty still persists, even though
the most difficulty is over. However, when the book comes to hexagram 31,
the difficulty is completely overcome and it is not only widely accepted
by the readers but influencial all over the world. They are attracted by
the readers, just as the youthful girl or Tui is attracted by the youthful
body or Ken. Thus the Judgment says, "Influence brings success. It is
advantageous to be firm. To take a maiden brings good fortune."

To sum up, the six steps are suggested for a meaningful interpretation
of the symbols in the I Ching. The sixfold appraoch is in harmony with the
structure of the hexagram. Each line of the hexagram is correlated with each
step of the sixfold approach to the interpretation. Just as there is a definite direction of movement within the hexagram, there is a definite step to be
taken as we interpret the hexagram. The first step corresponds to the beginning line of the hexagram. Just as the beginning line deals with the most
inner structure of the hexagram, the first step has to do with the most inner
symbol of the I Ching, that is, the lineal structure of the hexagram. At this
stage a careful observation is made on the structure of hexagram without
any reference to the written words. This, of course, presupposes some basic
knowledge on the nature and characteristics of the lines and trigrams which

constitute the hexagrams. The means by which the hexagrams are interpreted
is not a logical system but an intuitive perception. This is one of the most
effective ways to conjecture our hidden thoughts and unconscious minds. The
second step is the concentration of our minds on the written words, especially
on the Judgments, without any reference to the structure of the hexagrams.
Since the written words on the hexagrams bear rich cultural heritages and
meaningful suggestions of Chinese civilization, we receive much wisdom through
lines. The third step is to bring the first and the second step together and
to integrate them in a meaningful way. The correlation of the primary symbols
or the hexagrams with the secondary symbols or the Judgments is indispensable
in the process of interpretation. The fourth step is to relate the lines of
the hexagram to the Judgment. Since the lines are relative to the hexagram
as a whole, they must be interpreted within the delimitation of the Judgment
or Kua tz'u, which deals with the hexagrams as a whole. The fifth step is to
consult the commentaries to the I Ching or the Ten Wings. The commentaries
cannot be the basis for our interpretation. Rather our interpretation is
assisted by them. They are secondary sources and are not to be confused with
the primary sources of the I Ching. Finally, the sixth step is to apply the
implications of the hexagrams to the existential needs of the given situation.
Unless the hexagrams are made to be relevant to the practical needs, our
interpretation is not complete. The hexagrams for which we interpret are
acquired through the application of the I Ching to divination. For this let
us turn to the next chapter.

CHAPTER VI. THE APPLICATION OF THE I CHING TO DIVINATION

1. The Nature of Divination

The I Ching is most of all the book of divination. It has its origin in divination, and it has continued its existence as a divination book. The word "divination" is often misunderstood by our time. Divination is not superstitious. It does not deal with something irrational or unreal. On the other hand, it deals with things that are real and profound. It concerns itself with what is not commonly available to an empirical research. It attempts to get into the deep realm of unconscious and cosmic conscious strata, which are beyond the control of scientific knowledge. Thus divination is simply a means whereby the unconscious strata are meaningfully correlated with the realm of consciousness. Divination is not in any way inferior to technical science. The former deals with intuition, while the latter with reason. An intuitive approach to reality does not conflict with the rational approach. Rather, both divination and technical science are complementary to each other. They are different in character but mutually inclusive. Just as yang and yin are opposite yet complementary, intuition and reason or divination and science are opposite in their characters but complementary in their mutual satisfaction.

Since divination deals with the unconscious and spiritual realms of the universe, it is often accused of being heretical and ungodly. This negative attitude comes from the misunderstanding of the nature of divination. We must not be ashamed of ourselves for consulting the I Ching. Divination is not a religion. It cannot be heretical, because of its non-religious nature. The rejection of divination by Christianity in the West is based on the false idea of its meaning. Divination is a counterpart of empirical science, but is not a counterpart of religion. Both divination and empirical science belong to the realm of human investigations, but religion includes the realm of the transcendent. Divination is the method whereby the spiritual and invisible principles are known to us. It is man's tool for the investigation of unrevealed reality, just as scientific technology is interested in the investigation of the revealed reality of the world. Christianity, for example, does neither deal with unrevealed reality alone nor with revealed reality alone. It deals with both of them at the same time. Religion concerns itself with both the revealed and unrevealed truth of the world. In other words, religion deals with both divination and science. Divination according to the I Ching is not a religious knowledge but a human wisdom. Established religions, like Christianity, prohibited the practice of divination, for they thought the spiritual realm exclusively belongs to religion. They delimited the human investigation into the empirical realm only. If man has a right to investigate the visible world, he also has the same right to investigate the invisible world in which he is also a part. If religion is concerned with what is invisible only, then it is less than the true religion. Religion, if it is real, is concerned with the world as a whole, that is, both the invisible and the visible world. If divination in the I Ching attempts to correlate the invisible with the visible, the unconscious with the conscious, and the inner experience with the outer experience, it cannot be the enemy of religion but the means for the enrichment of religious life. Let not Christians and Hindus be ashamed of their consulting the I Ching for guidance in the time of trouble and confusion. As we have already indicated, the I Ching is not the fatalistic teacher but the indicator of supreme wisdom of the sages. When do we then need the I Ching for divination? Why do we turn to the I Ching for guidance?

2. Our Preparation for Divination

No one should consult the I Ching in order to test the validity of its divination. The idea of divination is much more subjective than objective. Its authenticity cannot be tested or validated, for the effectiveness of divination is possible only when the mental condition of those who consult it is pure and genuine. It is not the textbook of science or mathematics. It is hidden by itself. It is like the electric circuit which has only the potentiality of lighting. It does not give light by itself. When its contact with a definite situation is established, that is, when its contact with those who are genuinely and sincerely asking the guidance of the I Ching is established, it is activated and illuminated. That is why the proper contact between the I Ching and the questioner is necessary to make divination effective and sound. Approaching the I Ching to test its validity does not provide a proper contact. Thus it remains hidden without revealing its truth.

The mental attitude of a man who consults the I Ching must be sincere and genuine. Unless we honestly feel the guidance of the I Ching, we must not consult it. When we are sincere and genuine in the search for reality, the I Ching and we are properly contacted. The proper contact is established when those who consult the I Ching become one with its inner spirit. Those who are arrogant and proud of their wisdom are unable to establish the proper contact. Just as an improper contact of electric circuit with codes leading to light bulb does not illuminate the room, unless the mental attitude of those who consult the I Ching is   properly tuned with it, divination does not make effective at all. The proper attitude which connects between the I Ching and those who consult it is much similar **to** the Christian notion of faith or **to** the scientific idea of reason. Many believe that we cannot become Christians without faith (or the proper attitude) in God through Christ. Likewise, we cannot ask the I Ching to help us without sincere heart and pure mind. We cannot be good scientists without the capacity of reasoning (or the proper attitude of mind) on the world phenomena. The proper mentality or attitude of those who consult the I Ching can be compared with the Taoist painter who paints only when he is one with the object of painting. The unity between the painter and the object of his painting is attained when he is sincere and pure in his intention to be guided by the spirit of that object. Likewise, we can become one with the I Ching when we are sincere and pure in our intention to be guided by the spirit of the I Ching. When is it possible for us to have the genuine and pure intention? It is usually possible when we face the most devastating moment in our decision. When we fail to decide what to do with the problems and issues at hand, we need help from something which transcends our own wisdom. As an illustration of the most desperate moment for decision, let me narrate a story of a young man who has to decide whether he should go to join with the beautiful girl to whom he has just married or to become a monk under the great teacher whom he respects the most. The final choice he has to make is to take either "love" or "success." He has to make a choice either to give up his wife or to give up his ambition to become a monk. In this devastating moment, he writes the following poem:

Love or success, the two separate ways.
Shall I go to this or that way?
I have to make a choice but I cannot.
If I take the way of love, the success will cry.
If I take the way of success, the love will cry.

When we face this kind of circumstance, we cannot decide it by ourselves. We need the assistance of the I Ching. When we have to take one from the equally valuable item of choice, we have to rely on a chance in most cases. We throw the coin in the air and let the head or tail of the coin decide it for us. That is why "The mental attitude which leads a person to consult an oracle, is, after all, not foreign to our own culture either. We too, are familiar with symbols, prophets, and places from which prophetic sayings emanate ."[1] The mental condition of those who consult the I Ching does not always deal with the desperate moment for decision. It is also called to clarify that which is not yet known. It becomes a means to gain advance information in the course of events, in so doing we can either avoid misfortune or pursue fortune. Even though our proper attitude toward the I Ching can be readily created at the moment of our devastating circumstance, it can be created at any time whenever we approach the I Ching with humiliation and sincerity. We must not approach it with fear, for it is not an idol or god. Our attitude toward it must be pure and sincere in our search for truth. When we are right with the spirit of the I Ching, we are ready to consult it for divination.

---

[1] H. Wilhelm, Change, p. 8.

3. The Method of Divination

The philosophy and method of divination are well described in the
Ta Chuan. The process of manipulating the yarrow stalks in the I Ching is
not based on an arbitrary device, but on the profound philosophical understanding. In order to understand the philosophy of divination method through
the manipulation of stalks, we must go back to the diagram known as Ho T'u,
the Yellow River Map, which became, according to tradition, the basis of
the formation of the hexagrams.[1] There is a clear description in the Ta
Chuan that this map served for the formation of the hexagrams:

> Therefore: Heaven produced spiritual things, which were perceived
> by the holy sages. The transformation of heaven and earth was imi-
> tated by them. They put images in heaven to indicate good fortune
> and misfortune. They reproduced these images. The Ho (Yellow River)
> brought forth the T'u (map), and the Lo (Lo River) brought forth a
> Shu (writing). The holy sages modelled after them (Sec. I, Ch. 11).

The writing from the Lo River has been often questioned as to whether it
was anything to do with the formation of the trigrams. However, the map from
the Yellow River is extremely important to understand the rationale not only
for the formation of the trigrams and the hexagrams but for the method of
consulting the I Ching for divination. From the map the light circles
represent the heavenly or yang numbers, while the dark circles represent the
earthly or yin numbers. Thus "Heaven belongs to one, earth belongs to two;
heaven belongs to three, earth four; heaven belongs to five, earth to six;
heaven belongs to seven, earth to eight; heaven belongs to nine, earth to ten"
(Ta Chuan, Sec. I, Ch. 9).   All the odd numbers represent the heavenly
numbers, while the even numbers the earthly numbers. There are five odd numbers

---

[1]See the map in the first chapter of this book, p. 19.

and five even numbers. Thus, "The heavenly numbers are five. The earthly numbers are also five. When they are received each other in their places, each finds its complement" (Ibid.). As we see from the map the five of odd circles are distributed to five different places. The center represents earth, the south the fire, the east the wood, the north the water, and the west the metal. Thus both heavenly and earthly numbers are complementary in all these five places. From the map four elements representing the directions of east, south, west and north are relative to the earth, the center. Water, wood, fire and metal are the substances of earth. Earth has sprung from the five of heaven. The five of heaven is complemented by the ten of earth. This five of heaven is the core of the map. That is why the process of divination has a direct connection with this core, which is brought into relationship with cosmic processes. This core is called the "great overflow" ta yen 大衍 . The number of this great expansion or overflow is fifty. The number fifty derived from the ten of earthly number, which is complemented by five of heavenly number. Since ten is complemented by five, the sum of all possible combination is ten times five. Thus we get the number fifty as the total number of the great expansion. This is why we have to begin the process of divination with fifty yarrow stalks. The number of stalks represents the number of the great expansion. "Among them, forty-nine are used for manipulation" (Ibid.). The reason why one is taken out of the total number fifty is clearly based on a philosophical one. The one which is taken out represents the great ultimate which symbolizes the absolute or unchangeable reality, the background of all possible numbers. Thus it is not counted as a number, since all numbers come from it. A practical reason why one is taken out from the fifty is, as Legge has pointed out, when fifty are divided into two, it gives either two odd numbers or two even.[1] Therefore, these forty-nine out of fifty are used in divination. "They are divided into two portions, which represent the the two great powers" (Ibid.). Here, we see the process of divination is brought into relationship with the cosmic process. The two great poles of powers represent the powers of heaven and earth, which are the prototypes of yin and yang forces. "Then one is set apart to represent the three principles" (Ibid.). The one which is set apart from the the two heaps represents man, who occupies the center between heaven and earth. It is the trinity of world principles that man together with heaven and earth forms the complete and autonomous union which symbolizes the wholeness of the universe. The trigrams which represent the basic units of germinal situations consist of three lines of either broken or unbroken lines. When the one is taken from the heavenly numbers, it becomes the yang force. On the other hand, when it is taken from the earthly numbers, it becomes the yin force. To summarize thus far, a couple of steps are taken to form the trigrams. Before we start to manipulate the stalks, we eliminate the one which represents the absolute, for it does not represent the changing number. Thus, among the fifty, forty-nine are used for the process of divination. The first step is to divide them into two groups, for everything is ultimately categorized into both heavenly and earthly realms or yang and yin forces. The second step is to take one stalk from the left-hand heap, which represents heavenly numbers and makes the trigram.[2] The undifferentiated continuum of cosmic principles

---

[1] Legge, tr., op. cit., p. 368.

[2] There are different views as to the division of the earthly with the heavenly numbers. Some commentators believe that the left-handed heap represents the earthly number and the right-handed heap the heavenly numbers.

first comes to be differentiated into <u>yang</u> and <u>yin</u> forces, and gain forms

the trigram which is the complete unit in itself. It follows precisely the

process of cosmic evolution which is well described in the 42nd chapter of

<u>Tao Te Ching</u>: "The Way begot one, and the one two; then the two begot three

and three all else." The one here is identical with the undifferentiated

whole, consisting of 49 stalks. The division of the undifferentiated whole

into two primary forces results in the process of begetting two from the one.

The two again beget three by taking one from the one of the two heaps. Three

means the trigram, which is the basis of all other existences in the world.

The third step is to count through by fours, because of the four seasons of

year. They are counted through by fours, because the number four represent

the four seasons (<u>Ibid</u>.). The trigrams are now arranged according to seasonal

changes. The correlation of the trigrams with four seasons shows the directions

of changes. This correlation is found in the writing of the Lo River or <u>Lo</u>

<u>Shu</u>, which is, along with <u>Ho T'u</u>, understood as the basis for the formation

of the trigrams. Following is believed to be the <u>Lo Shu</u>:

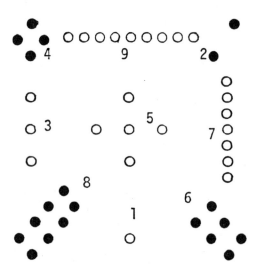

The arrangement of trigrams according to seasons as in the <u>Lo Shu</u> corresponds to the "inner-world arrangement" or "sequence of later heaven" which is believed to be arranged by King Wen.[1]   The correlation of the trigrams to the seasonal changes makes a change complete. A complete change then consists of four operations: 1) the random division of forty-nine stalks into two heaps, 2) among stalks of left-hand heap, the heavenly numbers, one is taken out to represent man, 3) the remaining stalks of left-hand heap are counted through by fours, and the remainder (four or less) is retained, and 4) the stalks of right-hand heap, the earthly numbers, are to be counted through by fours, and the remainder (four or less) is to be retained. "Therefore four operations are needed to produce a change" (<u>Ta Chuan</u>, Sec. I, Ch. 9). For the sake of convenience a stalk from the second operation is inserted between the ring finger and the little finger. The remainder of the third operation is to be inserted between ring finger and the middle finger, and that of the fourth between the forefinger and the middle finger. Now the sum of stalks held in one's hand is either five or nine. The possible variables are 1+4+4, 1+3+1, 1+2+2, or 1+1+3. Thus the number five is much easier to obtain than the number nine. "The remainder is put aside to represent the intercalary month. There are two intercalary months in five years. Therefore, the putting aside is repeated, in order to make the whole possible"(<u>Ibid</u>.). According to a Chinese calendar, the days of year correspond to 360, and a month corresponds to about 29 days. Since there are twelve months in a year, when 29 days are multiplied by 12 months, it results in 348 days. Thus twelve days a

---

[1]There is also another arrangement of the trigrams which seems to be older than the inner-world arrangement. It is often called primal arrangement, which is believed to be arranged by Fu Hsi himself.

year are short. Twelve days are multiplied by five and get 60 days, which correspond approximately to two intercalary months in five years. Because of these two intercalary months, the same process for a change is to be repeated twice. Thus all together three changes are necessary to get the value of one line of the hexagrams. The remainder of the second and third changes are either four or eight. The possible combinations are 1+4+3, 1+3+4, 1+1+2, 1+2+1. Thus changes of obtaining number 8 and 4 are equal. The five stalks of the first process and the four of each of the succeeding processes are regarded to have the numerical value three. The nine stalks of the first process and the eight of the succeeding processes have the numberical value two. The nine stalks of the first process are similar to one plus eight, which is a double unit, having the numerical value two. The five stalks of the first are identical with one and four, which are a complete unit and have the numerical value three. The total numerical value of the three processes can be 9, 8, 7, or 6. There is only one possible change of obtaining the numerical value nine: the sum of five (value three) + four (value three) + four (value three). Numerical value six can be obtained also once when the sum of the composite remainders is nine (value two) + eight (value two) + eight (value two). On the other hand, there are three possible variables for each numerical value seven and eight. If the sum is 9 (value 2) + 8 (value 2) + 4 (value 3), 5 (value 3) + 8 (value 2) + 8 (value 2), or 9 (value 2) + 4 (value 3) + 8 (value 2), the numerical value is seven. If the sum is 9 (value 2) + 4 (value 3) + 4 (value 3), 5 (value 3) + 4 (value 3) + 8 (value 2), or 5 (value 3) + 8 (value 2) + 4 (value 3), the numerical value is eight. The characteristics of these numerical values are decided by the structure of the Ho T'u or the River Map. From the map the outer sides of circles correspond to the similar circles of insides:

●●●●●● opposite to ●●; ooooooo opposite to o; ●●●●●●●● opposite to ●●●●; ooooooooo opposite to ooo. Hence the numerical value six is assigned to the old yin (‾‾ ‾‾), the yin line that changes; seven to the young yang (‾‾‾‾), the yang line that does not change; eight to the young yin (‾‾ ‾‾), the yin line that does not change; and nine to the old yang (‾‾‾‾), the yang line that changes.

When the first line of the hexagram has been obtained in this process of three changes, all the forty-nine stalks are again gathered together and the same procedure is repeated to obtain the second line. The rest lines of the hexagram are to be obtained in the same manner. There are altogether 18 changes, for each line of hexagram comes from three changes. Thus it is said in the Ta Chuan: "eighteen mutations give a hexagram" (Ibid.). It is important to make the changing lines, the old yin or old yang lines, to distinguish them from the rest of unchanging lines. These changing lines will create a new hexagram. For example, suppose we have obtained hexagram 1, Ch'ien, through the maipulation of the stalks. Among the six lines of the hexagram 1, if the beginning line is the old yang or changing line, hexagram 44, Kou or Intercourse (Ccntact), is to be created. This hexagram 44 is byproduct of the changing

line. Thus it is called Chih kua 之卦, which is distinguished from the original hexagram or Yüan kua 原卦. Here the original situation or Yüan kua, is expressed in hexagram 1 or the Positive, and it changes to a new situation or Chih Kua, which is expressed in hexagram 44 or Intercourse. As a rule we consult only the words of the changing lines and the Judgments on both hexagrams. The Judgment of the hexagram 1 says: "The Ch'ien is originating, success, advantageous and corret." The beginning line, which is a changing line, says: "Dragon is hidden. It is not the time to act." The Judgment of the hexagram 44, the situation changed, says: "The maiden is strong. It is not good to marry such a maiden." The situation of hexagram 44,, that is Chih kua, is a result of change being taken place from the original situation of Yüan kua, hexagram 1. In interpreting these situations it is helpful to follow the practical suggestions in the preceding chapter.

Use the coins developed later for a similar method of divination. In early China the coins were made of bronze with a hole in the middle, inscribed on one side with a blank on the other. Since these Chinese coins are not available to us, it is practical to use any coins which we have. Three coins are to be used to toss together and each toss gives a line. The inscribed side counts as yin, value 2, and the reverse side counts as yang, value 3. If we decide to use nickels or dimes for tossing, the head of coins should be yin and the tail of them be yang. Adding these numerical values we get a line. If all three coins are yang, the line is a nine; if all three are yin, it is a six. Both of them are changing lines. Two yin and one yang produce a seven, and two yang and one yin produce an eight. Both the seven and eight are resting lines. We notice here that each coin represents the process of change. Three coins thus form three changes which make a line of the hexagram possible. Since 18 changes are needed for all the six lines of the hexagram, three coins which represent three changes are to be multiplied by the six to make the hexagram complete. This is a shorter method for divination, but the accuracy of this method is much lower than the use of the yarrow stalks. In tossing the coins the greater concentration is needed at the moment of divination for an accurate result. We have already indicated the importance of our mental attitude at the moment of the divining process.

4. Corrleation as a Basis of Divination

We have attempted so far to relate the process of divination in terms of cosmic principles. The certain ways of manipulating the divining stalks or coins are illustrated according to the cosmic changes and transformations. The correlation of the process of divination with the cosmic principles is significant, because both of them are interrelated to each other. This inter-relation between divination and cosmic principles makes the process of diviation effective. We can see the similarity of this correlation with the correlation between the day and time. The day is correlated by our time, so that we can know when the sun will rise and set by watching our clock. We don't have to go outside to tell whether the sun is still there. We know it because our time is correlated with the movement of the sun and earth. Just as we can tell the morning from the evening by looking at the clock, we can also tell the principle of changes in the cosmos by looking at the result of divining process, for the process of divination is correlated with the principle of cosmic changes. Here we presuppose the relationship between the microcosm, the process of divination, and the macrocosm, the process of cosmic changes. The hexagram which is obtained through the process of divination is the microcosm of the cosmic situation. Thus to know the ger-minal situation expressed in the hexagram is to know the cosmic situation.

However, the question is whether our question for divination is correlated with the process of divination or not. In other words, we have discussed the correlation of divining process with the cosmic principles, but we have not pointed out the relationship between the process of divination and that of our thinking. Without correlation between the process of divination and the process of our thinking or our contemplation at that moment, the situation which is obtained through the divining process does not correspond to the question. We see the correlation among three dimensions: the process of our thinking at the moment of divination, the process of divination itself, and the process of cosmic principles. These three processes must be interrelated to make the result of divination meaningful and effective. Since we have already dealt with the relationship between the process of divination and that of cosmic principles, let us examine the correlation between the process of questioning mind and that of divination.

The correlation between our mental activity and the process of divination is complicated. Man's mental condition is relative to both time and space. The hexagram which is the product of divination is also the germinal situation in which both the space and time are undifferentiated. To correlate the mental activity of the questioner with the process of divination means to bring them together in this undifferentiated continuum of time and space. Since the questioner is also the diviner at the same time, the process of thinking on the question and that of performing divination must be one and coherent. Perhaps it is well illustrated in the process of meditation which aims at the oneness with the object of our mediation. At the moment of divination, the questioner who is also the performer must be in the state of deep mediation, so that he is one with the process of divination. If he is one with the process of divination, his question also corresponds with

the divining process. In deep and intensive concentration of mind and thinking on the question he is in the midst of the undifferentiated continuum of
space and time. In this undifferentiated situation the past, present and
future are united. The past is present, and the present is also future at
the same time. Moreover, in this kind of germinal situation what is here is
also there and what is there is also here at the same time. In this undifferentiated continuum alone,our consciousness is correlated with our unconsciousness. The correlation of our conscious and unconscious thinking
processes is possible only when we are one with the process of divination.
In other words, the unconscious is correlated with the conscious when the
process of thinking (intuitive) is one with the process of divination.
Because of this correlation, it is enabled to reach all depths and to grasp
the seeds of all things (Ta Chuan,Sec. I, Ch. 10). Being united with the
process of divination our mentality reaches down into the regions of the
unconscious where both space and time are undifferentiated. The space which
is the principle of diversity and confusion is overcome by the deep concentration, which comes as a result of the simple. The time which is the
principle of uncertainty and anxiety is overcome by the easy. That is why
the process of divination is easy and simple. It is easy to overcome the
hurried life in time, and is simple to overcome the complexity of mode by
space. The principle of both easy and simple in the I Ching is the way of
eliminating the distinction between time and space as well as overcoming the
separation between the conscious and the unconscious. When the process of
our thinking and that of divination are one, the hexagrams that we have
obtained will correspond to the undifferentiated continuum of time and space
as well as of the conscious and the unconscious strata. The hexagram

represents the symbol of our germinal situation in which what is separating and diversifying is overcome. When the process of thought, the process of divination, and the process of cosmic changes are united in harmony, as Ta Chuan says, it is "like an echo which is neither far nor near, neither dark nor deep. Thus he knows the things that are coming" (Sec. I, Ch. 10).

In this undifferentiated continuum both the individual mind and the universal mind are correlated. It is quite similar with the Hegelian notion of the coincidence of Absolute Mind with the relative mind. The mutual influence and interplay between the cosmic and individual minds are inevitable, for the I Ching views the cosmos as an organism. The correlation between the universal spirit or mind with the individual spirit or mind is possible, because the principle of cosmic changes is in harmony with the principle of divining process which is united with the individual mind of diviner. The multidimensional correlatedness in the process of divination is possible, because of the organic view of cosmos. The correlations between the conscious and unconscious, between the time and space, between the cosmic and individual mind, and all other connotations are reduable to the sixty-four germinal situations in the I Ching. To obtain the sixty-four hexagrams through the process of divination is to obtain the whole of the universe, including both spiritual and physical entities. That is why through the I Ching we know all things.

5. The Laws of Causality and Chance

How do we get a certain form of the hexagram out of the sixty-four? It must be dependent upon how to manipulate the divining stalks or coins. How

we divide the stalks at the time of divination may affect what kind of
hexagram we get. If we use the coins for divination, the result of it is
conditioned by the way we toss them in the air. We know that we cannot control it through the mathematical calculation or logical syllogism. When we
divide the stalks or toss the coins in the air, we do them at random. In
other words, there is no way to control the result of the divining process
through the use of logics or mathematics. It is a mere chance in many ways.
It is not dependent on the principle of cause and effect. That is why it does
not belong to the realm of empirical and rational investigations. It is the
chance which is a means for our understanding of the future. The chance is a
key to understanding the way in which the selection of the hexagrams has
taken place. Carl Jung rightly points out in his preface to Richard Wilhelm's
translation of the I Ching that the Chinese have traditionally been inclined
not to think in terms of cause and effect relationship. If all things are
governed by the law of the cause and effect, there is no room for the I Ching
at all. The I Ching employs the chance as a means for governing the reality
of the world. In view of this issue there are two questions which are vital
to the process of divination. One deals with the existence of chance other
than the principle of causality, and another with the probability of chance
happenings. Let us deal with the first issue which concerns itself with the
question of chance and causality.

If every happening can be traced according to the causality principle,
there is no room for divination. The process of divination uses the law of
chance rather than the law of causality. The former deals with the intuitive
and immediate insight, while the latter with the logical and rational
approach. If everything is based on the law of causality, the scientific

technology can answer almost all natural phenomena of the universe. Especially in the West, technical reason is stressed as a means to know reality. However, as our scientific knowledge evolves further and further, we come to recognize the limitation of causality principle. In our time scientists come to recognize that it is not only the causality but the chance as the means to know the reality of world phenomena. It is commonly believed that both chance and causality are interdependent. It is no longer enough to say either causality or chance but <u>both</u> causality <u>and</u> chance are ways to know truth. Max Born gives us better insight on this than I can do. He said:

> In fact, all primitive polytheistic religions seem to be based on such a conception of nature: things happening in haphazard way, except where some spirit interferes with a purpose. We reject to-day this demonological philosophy, but admit chance into the realm of exact science. Our philosophy is dualistic in this respect; nature is ruled by the laws of cause and laws of chance in a certain mixture.[1]

As Mr. Born said, it is not either the laws of cause or the laws of chance but both of them are interdependent in governing the phenomena of the universe. Even in the realm of exact science there is a room for chance. Many new discoveries are made merely by chance. This means even an exact science comes to rely on chances. The world is governed by the polarity of laws; the laws of causality and chances. Just as the world is subject to both necessity and accident, both causality and chance are inevitable for the government of the universe. If the world is ruled strictly by the laws of causality alone, it is more or less like a mechanical world in which we are only little cogwheels. This means materialistic determinism. If the world is, on the other

---

[1] Max Born, <u>Natural Philosophy of Cause and Chance</u> (New York: Dover Publications, 1964), p. 3.

had, governed strictly by the law of chance, the world becomes chaos. Since
the world is neither chaotic nor deterministic, both causality and chance
play important roles in the governing of the universe. Since the world
phenomena are subject to both the laws of causality and of chance, the divination which makes use of chance can be a means to understand the reality of
the world. The difference of divination from scientific technology is primarily in the use of means to know reality. Divination uses the law of
chance, while scientific technology makes use of the law of causality in
most cases. Since both of them are interdependent and complementary in
governing the principle of the world, both scientific technology and divination claim their unique characters. We cannot say one is better than the
other, for both of them are instruments for the understanding of reality.

The second question which we have asked deals with the random principle
within the laws of chance. If chance is a means to know reality, how much
is it reliable? Is the chance operation in the process of divination based
on the principle of probability or on something else? Is it a sheer chance
to obtain a certain form of the hexagram through the manipulation of stalks
or coins? If it is based on a sheer chance, why is it necessary to consult
the I Ching for divination? If we believe in the reliability of divination
through the use of the I Ching, it must be more than a mere chance. We take
chances in many ways. We take a chance to pass the car in front of us. We
take a chance to draw lottery for a military draft. Games are based on chances.
Many stores and business firms put up prize contests which are purely based
on the laws of chance. We know that the public believes in the chance
opterations but does not take them seriously. Is the divination of the I
Ching more reliable than all other chance opterstions? Unless it is more

reliable than others, we don't need to go through the painful process of manipulating the stalks. We don't have to consult the I Ching. Thus the reliability of chance happenings in the I Ching is perhaps one of the most crucial issues which we must consider here.

6. Synchronicity as a Key to the Reliability of Divination

The chance operation in the I Ching is much more reliable than a sheer chance, which is based on the principle of random distribution. It is based on meaningful correlation of the conscious with the unconscious and time with space. It is more than a mere chance in a strict sense. Because of the correlation between the visible and invisible or between the microcosm and the macrocosm, the chance operation in the I Ching is reliable and meaningful. The chance which the I Ching speaks of is not something that is independent of time and space. Rather it is dependent on the order of the universe and the principle of changes. In other words, the chance with which the divination of the I Ching is operated is relative to the correlation of different strata in which we are part. Everything, whether it is conscious or unconscious, spiritual or material, past or future, and far or near, is interdependent and correlated together as a part of organism. Thus "there is no such a thing as a sheer chance," as Paul Veide indicated. Because of the meaningful correlation between the known and the unknown, it is more than sheer chance. This principle which is more than a mere chance is called by Carl Jung "synchronicity." Synchronicity means "the

---

[1]Paul Veide, "Poor Man's Computer" in Commonwealth, March 8, 1968, p. 693.

coincidence of events in space and time as meaning something more than mere chance."[1] This synchronicity is an acausal connecting principle, which is diametrically opposed to the principle of causality. Synchronicity is more than a principle of mere chance. It is neither mere causality nor mere chance. Because of synchronicity, divination is different from mere chance operations. The principle of synchronicity gives the power to divination and makes the I Ching a living book. Because the principle of sychronicity is applied in the I Ching, the meaningful correlation of two different orders, whether they are conscious or unconscious strata, and empirical or theoretical continuum, is possible. As Carl Jung said, "The I Ching presupposes that there is a synchronistic correspondence between the psychic state of the questioner and the answering hexagram."[2] The principle of synchronicity is also applied to the astrological zodiac as well. Its significance is illustrated through one study of horoscopes of married people. The one of summaries of Jung's study is as follows:

> Together with my co-worker, Mrs. Lilliane Frey-Rohn, I first proceeded to collect 180 marriages, that is to say, 360 horo-scopes, and compared the 50 most important aspects that might possibly be characteristic of marriage, namely the conjunctions and oppositions of ☉ ☾ ♂ (Mars) ♀ (Venus) Asc (Ascendent) and Desc (Descendent). This resulted in a maximum of 10 per cent for ☉ ☌ ☾ . As Professor Markus Fierz, of Basel, who kindly went to the trouble of computing the probability of my result, informed me, my figure has a probability of 1: 10,000.[3]

The evaluation of his second group of 220 marriages yielded a maximum figure of 10.9 per cent for ☾ ☌ ☾ . The probability of this figure is about

---

[1]C. Jung, "Foreword," p. XXIV.

[2]C. Jung, "On Synchronicity" in Man and Time, p. 207.

[3]Ibid., p. 208.

1:10,000 again. Some of these experiments suggest that the correlation of the positions of the horoscope in marriage is more than a mere chance. Thus Jung concludes that "Their concurrence, however, is so improbable that one cannot help assuming the existence of an impelling factor that produced this result."[1] If we make a statistical study on the reliability of the I Ching concerning individual cases, we may find a surprising result of coincidence of the psychic condition of the questioner with the answering hexagram. The meaningful correspondence exists not only in the psychic structures of man and universe but in all other structures of world phenomena. One of the great commentators of the I Ching, Wang Fu-chih (1619-92), illustrates well the synchronicity of two basic strata of existence. He correlates the immediately experienced reality with the invisible order of existence which is not immediately accessible. His idea of invisible order is similar to Kantian notion of "noumenon", theoretical continuum, which is differentiated from "phenomenon", the immediately accessible experience. These two different orders, experienced order and theoretical order, are brought together in the process of divination. Thus the synchronicity which is disclosed by the process of divination is the experience of having these two different strata at the same time. This correlation of empirical and theoretical strata makes the divination reliable.

The synchronicity of the question with the answering hexagram is possible because of interrelatedness of all things in a manner of organic structure. If the world is understood in terms of mechanical structure,

---

[1] C. Jung, "On Synchronicity," p. 209.

there is no synchronicity possible. Because the world is seen in terms of
organism, it is possible to have the law of synchronicity. It gives the
meaningful correlation between the known and unknown, between the seen and
unseen, between the present and the future, between the conscious and the
unconscious, between the empirical and theoretical, and between all other
counterpoles of existence in the world. However, the relation between them
is not contradictory but complementary. All the dimensions of existence are
correlated in terms of this mutually complementary relationship. As Tung
Chung-shu, one of the Early Han writers, said:

> In all things there must be correlations. Thus there are such
> correlations as upper and lower, left and right, external and
> internal, beauty and ugliness, obedience and disobedience, joy
> and anger, cold and heat, day and night. These are all corre-
> ates. The yin is the correlate of the yang, the wife of hus-
> band, the son of the father, the subject of the ruler. There
> is nothing that does not have such correlations, and in each
> such correlation there is the yin and yang.

Just as the correlation of our body, flesh and blood, thinking and feeling,
pain and joy, seeing and hearing are correlated to one another in such a
manner that one affects the whole and the whole affects the one. Martin
Buber, one of the outstanding Jewish philosophers, indicates that the "I-
Thou" relationship, the personal relationship, can be established not only
between persons but between personal and impersonal objects as well. Nature
can be the subject of our relationship, just as our neighbour becomes the
subject of ourselves. To the oriental mind the tree, for example, becomes
the subject of our relationship. The tree can relate to us, just as we
relate ourselves to the tree. The tree talks to us, and we can also talk
to the tree. There is a mutual communication of our feelings. The principle

---

[1]Tung Chung-shu, Ch'un-ch'ui Fan'lu, 12:8; also found in Fung Yu-lan,
A History of Chinese Philosophy, II, p. 42.

of synchronicity presupposes this kind of personal relationship existing in the organic view of the universe. Since everything in the world consists of two forces of <u>yin</u> and <u>yang</u>, it can be reduced to these two fundamental relationships. Nothing can be separated from this complementary relationship. Thus the mutual interconnection and interdependence make the concept of synchronicity possible.

Let us apply the concept of synchronicity directly to the process of divination. Our mental attitude is correlated with our physical activity at the moment of casting the coins or dividing the stalks. If our mental attitude, which is conscious, is affected by the unconscious, our activity is certainly controlled by this unconsciousness. Just as the physical activity is affected by the spiritual force, the movement of our hands at the process of divination is influenced by the unconsciousness. We see many examples of this kind. In Christianity, we read the event of Pentecost in the Acts of Apostles. When the Holy Spirit came, the people spoke in tongues. Here the spirit, which is of cosmic consciousness, controls the movement of their tongues. The idea of a spiritual healing is also related to the concept of synchronicity. For example, Christian Scientists believe that the healing of the physical body can be brought through spiritual exercise. The spirit or psychic power can restore the physical disorder. We also see the primitive shamanist dancer who moves his hands, arms and legs according to the directions of the spirit. There are countless examples that the unseen is influenced by the seen and vice versa. Thus it is not totally strange for us to believe that our unconscious mind, which is a part of the cosmic spirit, can influence the movement of our hands in the process of divination. Because the process of divination is correlated with the cosmic order, our mental activity

at the time of divination coincides with the cosmic spirit. This coincidence
makes a meaningful correlation between the conscious activity of the questioner
and the unconscious situation of the answering hexagram possible. Thus the
reliability of divination is possible because of synchronicity.

7. The Uniqueness of the I Ching as a Divination Book

The divining method of the I Ching is not unique because of synchronicity.
All other divination processes make use of the principle of synchronicity.
Astrology, for example, operates on the basis of the same idea of acausal
principle. What does then the divination of the I Ching make unique from
all other divinations? Why is the I Ching a great book of divination? The
uniqueness of the I Ching as a divination book lies in the following aspects:
1) the elimination of a middle man or a professional diviner, 2) the sufficient freedom of man to decide his own fate, 3) the possibility of moral and
ethical responsibility, and 4) the capacity of projecting one's own unconscious feelings through the help of the hexagrams. Let us examine each in
detail.

First of all, the I Ching is unique from other divination books,
because it is accessible directly to all the people who want to consult it.
It does not necessitate the middle man or the professional diviner who per-
forms and interprets the process of divination to the questioners. In most
cases the professional diviner mediates the questioners. The diviner acts
as though he is a priest who mediates the will of heaven to the people. The
I Ching, in this sense, is based on the Protestant principle of Christianity,
that is, the priesthood of all believers. All those who believe in the

reliability of the I Ching can be the diviners by themselves. They can directly go to the I Ching and perform divination without the assistance of the professional diviner. Thus the questioners are not only the performers but also the interpreters of divination at the same time. Thus one person can act in three different ways to make the divination effective. His sincerity toward the question he asks will affect his performance, and his proper performance will affect the accuracy of answer in the given hexagram. His interpretation of the answer expressed in the hexagram cannot be separated from either performance or his question. These three functions are united to make the undifferentiated whole. One cannot be separated from the rest of them. Thus the uniqueness of the I Ching is in this threeness or the trinity of divining functions. The reliability of divination is dependent on the coherence of these three functional principles. The same intention which has controlled the question must be expressed at the time of performance and interpretation.

Even though the I Ching is accessible directly to all of us, its efficacy is not the same. Just as the use of the Bible in Christianity is possible to all but its effectiveness is limited to those who are sincere, the efficacy of divination is relative to the degree of their proper attitude and sensitivity to spiritual reality. Thus Ta Chuan stresses the right attitude: "If you are not a kind of person, the meaning does not real itself to you" (Sec. II, Ch. 8). The kind of person does not mean the one who is professionally trained for divination but the man who has the right attitude and sensitivity to the spiritual things. The right approach is not rational but intuitive. Thus the I Ching is accessible to all, but its reliability is not applied to all. It demands more on our part, for its privilege is given to all of us.

Secondly, the I Ching as a divination book is unique from all others, because it allows us a sufficient freedom to decide our own fate. Other forms of divination do not provide any freedom for us to make decisions by ourselves for our own destiny. They usually foretell our fate which is inescapable. Their approaches are somewhat deterministic and fatalistic. Unlike these approaches, the I Ching approaches the idea of divination instructionally. It teaches us what to do to avoid misfortune as well as to attain good fortune. It helps us to control our destiny, rather than being controlled by fate. It provides us freedom to decide for action, even though this freedom is limited within the given situation. The I Ching views that our freedom is limited because of our relation to time and space. Freedom is often misunderstood in the West. Man often believes that he has the unlimited freedom to make his own decision. The idea of the unlimited freedom of man is not only unrealistic but contrary to the very limitation of human existence in time and space. As long as man is in time and space, he is relative to them. We know that we cannot get away from our predicament in which we are placed. However, what the I Ching tries to say is that our freedom is relative to our existence. Thus the limited freedom which the I Ching presents is the denial of the absolute freedom. Man does not have the absolute freedom to control his destiny. The freedom which we have is a relative freedom, because our existence is also relative to time and space. Our freedom is relative, because we are free insofar as we are within the given. We are free because of this givenness, but our freedom is limited because of it at the same time. This givenness is expressed in the hexagram, the germinal situation, in which our particular existence is found. Our freedom is to actualize that given potentiality, which is symbolized in the hexagram. It has all the ingredients for the possible future predicaments, just as the egg contains all the possible ingredients for becoming a chicken. What is obtained from the process of divination is this potential situation which is to be actualized by the action of our free decision. Our freedom cannot exceed beyond this potentially given situation. The idea of relative freedom is very akin to the very nature of human existence, which is relative to the givenness. However, it does not delimit the essential freedom of man, that is the freedom of actualization. The assertion of this relative freedom is the denial of both the absolute freedom, which is unrealistic, and the mechanical determinism, which is fatalistic.

To illustrate this limited freedom in the I Ching, let us look at hexagram 6, Sung or Conflict. The Judgment of this hexagram says: "Conflict. Sincerity is being obstructed. The middle way will bring good fortune. The end will bring misfortune. It is advantageous to see the great man. It is not advantageous to cross the great river." It depicts the situation of conflict, that is, the situation of being obstructed. The Judgment indicates further how to avoid misfortune and to obtain good fortune. The actualization of this situation toward good fortune is to be cautious. On the other hand, our impetuous action will lead the situation to unfortunate circumstance. On the basis of this instruction, we have freedom to decide either to be caustious or to be impetuous. Here our freedom for decision is limited, for it is ralative to the situation which is symbolized in hexagram 6. If the fourth place is the changing line, it means: "One cannot overcome the conflict. He turns back and submits to fate. He changes his attitude and finds peace. His firmness brings good fortune." Here again we receive the instruction what to do to obtain peace and good fortune. We have freedom to decide in the

situation of conflict either to be persistent or to change our attitude. As
we have noticed, our freedom for decision in regard to action is limited
within the given situation in which we are confronted. This freedom within
the givenness is meaningful to those who consult the I Ching for guidance.
Because of this freedom of choice, it gives a sense of responsibility,
which is not found in other forms of divination.

We are responsible for something which we have chosen freely. Responsibility marks the third characteristic, which constitutes the uniqueness of the
I Ching as a divination book. Responsibility is inherent within the poss-
bility of choice. However, our responsibility is also limited because of our
limited freedom. We are not responsible any further than to fulfill the
decision we have made in relation to the situation presented in the hexagram.
For example, if we look at hexagram 31, Hsien or Influence, the Judgment says,
"Influence brings success. It is advantageous to be correct. To take a maiden
brings good fortune." If we confront this kind of situation, we may decide
to take a maiden to be a wife, for it will bring good fortune. In this case
our responsibility is to act for what is chosen, that is, to make the marriage
actual. We are not responsible for the outcome of this marriage. Even though
the marriage may turn out to be an unfortunate one, it is not our responsibility
at all. We can attribute the unsuccessful result to the failure of divining
process or our improper attitude at the time of divination. Thus in a final
analysis our responsibility lies within the realization of the decision we
have made according to the instruction of the I Ching. We see throughout the
appended Judgments that there are substantial amount of teachings dealing with
moral and ethical responsibility. For example, in hexagram 1, Ch'ien or Creativity, the Judgment conveys four cardinal virtues, which appear in almost

all other Judgments. They are: originating, success, advantageousness, and correctness. These four virtues, as we have already pointed out, parallel to four cardinal values in humanity. The concept of originating is the fundamental principle for all other attributes of love. The concept of success is the principle to embrace the attributes of the mores, which regulate and control the expression of love in community. The concept of advantageousness is the principle to embrace the attributes of justice, which is the foundation of good individual and society. The concept of correctness is correlated with the attributes of wisdom, which discerns the law of changes in all aspects of life. These four cardinal virtues are fundamental to moral and ethical principles of good life. There are various accounts of the moral and ethical teachings in the I Ching. For example, hexagram 15, Ch'ien or Modesty, the Judgment gives a moral teaching: "The superior man humbles himself when he is exalted, and increases where there is any short-coming, in order to bring about an equality in all manners of his contact with others."[1] This is a profound statement on moral and ethical teachings. In hexagram 3, Chun or Difficulty, the T'uan Chuan comments on the beginning line: "When a superior man subordinates himself to his subjects, he will win the hearts of all mankind." This is much similar to the moral and ethical teachings of Jesus in Christianity. Jesus said, "Whoever exalts himself will be humbled, and whoever humbles himself will be exalted" (Matt. 23:12). Since most teachings in the I Ching are related with the moral and ethical virtues, to be responsible for the fulfillment of the decision we make on the hexagrams is to follow the life of moral and ethical responsibility. The I Ching, unlike other divination books, does not encourage us to take the fate unconditionally.

---

[1] See the T'uan Chuan on the Judgment of hexagram 15.

It provides us enough freedom and responsibility which deny the fatalistic
determinism.

Finally, the I Ching as a divination book is unique from all other
books, because it provides the means by which we can project our unconscious
feelings. Its function is much similar to the Rorschach test, where the series
of ink-blot designs of various shapes are provided. The hexagrams can serve
as much more effective mediums of revealing our unconscious feelings than the
ink-blot designs, even though their function is much identical with the Rorschach test. We can effectively project our subjective feelings to the hexagrams,
because they convey much more suggestive ideas and implications than the series
of ink-blot designs. As Carl Jung remarked, "The Chinese sage would smilingly
tell me: 'Don't you see how useful the I Ching is in making you project your
hitherto unrealized thoughts into its abstruse symbolism.'"[1] No other forms of
divination can do this kind of service. The absurdity of symbolism in the I
Ching provides considerable latitude in interpretation. Moreover, the hexagrams
are structured in a binary system of yin and yang elements according to mental
processes, so as to become effective means of creative thinking. Thus the I
Ching can be regarded as a work of psychological genius. As we concentrate our
thoughts on the hexagrams which we have obtained through the process of divination, we are able to express all the possible imaginations which can be expressed
in no other ways. Perhaps it is easier for us to understand the psychological
implications of the I Ching if we take an example for an illustration. Suppose
a young man who does not believe in the war which his country is engaged in
has to face the draft into the army. He cannot go to fight in the war but he

---

[1]See his "Foreword," p. xxxix.

must not avoid his duty as a citizen of his country. He cannot resolve this
question by himself. Thus he decides to consult the I Ching for guidance.
Through a careful manipulation of the stalks, he has obtained hexagram 36,
which is Ming I or Darkening of the Light. The hexagram consists of two

primary trigrams: the earth above and the fire below. It is the symbol of
the light hidden under the earth. As he contemplates on this hexagram, he
is able to think so many things that he had never been able to think through.
It may imply to him the suppression of his conscience if he had to obey
the draft law. He may think that he can no longer escape the draft, because
the light that is hidden will soon come out from the earth. The hexagram
may suggest to him that he needs perseverance until his will prevails,
in spite of difficulty at the present moment. There are all kinds of suggestive ideas and implications possible as one meditates on the hexagram.
Without the hexagram some of the ideas were never possibly brought out. Because it helps us to project our unconscious feelings and thoughts, it not
only helps us to understand ourselves but also serves us to release our psychic
melancholy. In other words, the I Ching is more than a mere divination book.
It is a book of psychotherapy. It assists us to release our emotional troubles,
because it becomes an effective medium to project our unconscious desires which
are associated with guilty feelings. If we consider all these possible measures
of this book, we are convinced to say that it is superior to many other
divination books being used in the West.

8. Some Practical Suggestions for Divination

To conclude this chapter, I would like to suggest a few precautionary measures for those who like to consult the I Ching for divination. First of all, we must make sure that the process of divination for the same question cannot be repeated. If it is done once, it is sufficient. To repeat it is to show the lack of our sincerity and genuineness. It is the negation of our own trust in the I Ching and the betrayal of our own confidence. Moreover, what is done once is done and cannot be repeated. Everything changes continuously and nothing can be reversed.

Secondly, we must not consult the I Ching unless what we are going to ask is right and acceptable to the community at large. We should not ask the I Ching to guide us in anything that has to do with the immoral and unethical nature. To ask such a question is derogatory. Since the purity of heart and the concentration of mind are the necessary parts of performing the process of divination, such an unacceptable question must not be asked at first place. It is contrary to the spirit of our understanding of the I Ching.

Thirdly, we should not ask the question which we can answer by ourselves. When our wisdom is exhausted, we can come to the I Ching for guidance. We must not come to it if the answer could be found in some other places than the I Ching itself. The I Ching must be the final appeal for help. That is why it is necessary for us to renounce our pride in our own wisdom before the wisdom of the I Ching. When we know that we cannot deal with the question by ourselves, we can fully trust in that which we ask for help. Thus, the I Ching demands the unconditional surrender of our own wisdom when it is contrary to the wisdom of the <u>I Ching</u>.

Fourthly, in the formulation of the question we must be careful not to make it absurd and ambiguous. The question must be specific in nature. We should not ask the question which involves so many different answers. For example, do not ask the question like this: "What shall I do in the future?" This kind of question is inadequate to divination. It is too absurd and abstract. Rather the question must be like this: "Shall I take a trip to Japan this summer?" Unless the question must be specific and simple, it cannot get a reliable answer. The question must be formed as concrete and simple as possible. As the question is simpler and more concrete, the answer will be more reliable.

Fifthly, in the process of divination our mental and emotional attitudes must be calm and genuine. Unless we can calm down our feelings and thinkings, we cannot proceed with divination. The concentration of our thought through the question we ask is required at the moment of divination process. The oneness of ourselves with the act of divination can make the answer most reliable. We should select a quiet place for divination. Our mental process must not be detracted by the surroundings. We must be alone when we do it, in order to avoid anything that detracts from our undivided concentration.

Finally, we shouldn't feel guilty to consult the <u>I Ching</u> for assistance. It is not disgraceful to ask a guidance from the <u>I Ching</u>. Divination belongs to the depth of human wisdom and the counterpart of scientific technology. We must not think that we are betraying our loyalty to our own religious beliefs, because of our reliance on the wisdom of the <u>I Ching</u>. We rely on so many other wisdoms of man. Our reliance on scientific knowledge and logical systems of thinking does not give us a feeling of guilt. We must give a new look to occult study as the counterpart of empirical science. The former deals with the spiritual and psychic realms, while the latter with the sensual and conscious realms. They must be complementary to each other. Thus we must not be ashamed of practicing divination, if we are allowed to practice the scientific way of doing things in our life. Just as science is not contrary to religion, divination cannot be an enemy of religion either. It must be understood as the creation of human ingenuity rather than the practice of religious belief. Religion deals with what is the ultimate, which includes bot the spiritual and material, unconscious and conscious, or natural and supernatural. Divination is a gift of God for us, so that through it we may avoid grievous mistakes in the future.

CHAPTER VII. THE SIGNIFICANCE OF THE I CHING IN OUR TIME

What does this archaic book of China have to do with the twentieth century civilization of our time? Is it relevant to modern man? Is it compatible with the scientific technology of our time? Unless it is compatible with the scientific world view of our time, it cannot be relevant to our time. Since the I Ching has been understood as the microcosm of the universe, we may begin our investigation with the relevance of the world view which the I Ching describes to that which contemporary physics attempts to say. However, the comparison of the world view between the I Ching and modern science is impossible in principle, because in principle everything is changing. Moreover, the relationship between metaphysics and empirical science cannot be tested with the same category of expression. The I Ching is not written as a textbook for science. It is a wisdom book which indirectly deals with the world view of that time. In this respect there is no way, in a strict sense, to compare between them. What we could do here, then, cannot be a comparison but the compatibility between them. Thus the aim of our investigation here is to find out some   common denominators between the I Ching and modern physics in their understanding of the universe.

1. The I Ching and Modern World View

It was Wilfred C. Smith, the director of the Center for the Study of World Religions at Harvard University, who said, "Some observers hold that twentieth-century science in the West is moving closer to a fundamental yin-yang type of interpretation of the natural universe than traditional

Western views."[1] The traditional Western view of the world, to which we are still accustomed, is materialistic, mechanistic and deterministic. This world view consists of impenetrable particles of material moving in time and space in accordance with fixed laws. Space and time are independent, so that the particles can move by themselves within these fixed space and time. It deals simply with the common-sense notion of the three-dimensional Euclidian space. Everything in the world is related mechanically and ruled by the inexorable laws, so that the future state of the world could be predicted in principle. All existence can conform to the law of nature and the principle of cause and effect. This kind of world view prevailed until the beginning of the twentieth century. For example, the Newtonian physics did not make any radical break with the Euclidian concept of space and time. For him the category of space and time is absolute and a priori to all other existence in the universe. However, the radical break with the traditional Western view of the world came by the great scientist, Albert Einstein, who brought us the new understanding of the world. This new understanding of the world is radically different from the traditional Western view of the world but much closer to the world view of the I Ching. Just as the new idea of the world since Einstein is radically different from the traditional Western view, the world view of the I Ching is also radically different from it. Just as Galileo brought a new understanding of the earth in relation to the sun and other stars, Einstein introduced the theory of relativity, which brought us a radically new idea about the world.

---

[1]Wilfred Cantwell Smith, The Faith of Other Men (New York: The New American Library, 1963), p. 67.

The traditional Western idea of the world no longer holds truth. The idea of the absolute space and absolute time is gone. Space and time are no longer independent realities and a priori categories of all other existence in the universe. They are not used as stationary reference points to understand others in relation to them. According to the theory of relativity nothing can be stationary. Everything moves and changes according to the principle of changes and transformations. Einstein's theory of relativity means to me the denial of absolute in all existence of the universe. Nothing is absolute in itself, for everything changes and transforms. Nothing is independent from others. Everything is a part of the whole and the whole is also a part of the one. "The theory of relativity acknowledges that frames of reference are relative, and that one is as good as another."[1] Since time and space are not stationary, nothing acts as the steady frame of reference. Everything is relative to each other. As Coleman said:

> There is no heavenly body in our universe that we can use as a stationary reference point. The earth rotates on its axis ; it travels in its orbit around the sun; the sun and the solar system are moving about within our galaxy, the Milky Way, which is itself rotating. And our galaxy is also moving relative to the other galaxies. The whole universe is filled with movement. And in all this seemingly haphazard turmoil, no one can say what is moving and what is stationary. We can only say that all the heavenly bodies are moving relative to one another and no one of these is different in this respect.[2]

---

[1] William Bonnor, The Mystery of the Expanding Universe (New York: The Macmillan Co., 1964), p. 90.

[2] James A. Coleman, Relativity for the Layman (New York: William-Frederick Press, 1958), p. 41.

Everything moves and changes constantly. The galaxies recede from one another, and new ones are formed by condensation out of the newly created matter, which takes the place of the old ones which have moved away. The whole universe is in the process of constant movement and change. The good illustration for this is the running water, which flows constantly without stationary references. Here we see clearly that the concept of Einstein's relativity and the principle of changes in the I Ching are intimately related to each other. However, the concept of changes is not based on the concept of relativity. Rather the latter is based on the former. In other words, the theory of relativity is relative to the principle of changes in the I Ching, just as the concept of relativity is conditioned by the idea of changes. We can say then that the principle of changes in the I Ching is the ground of Einstein's theory of relativity, even though he was not aware of the existence of this book. Because of this relationship between them, we can say that the contemporary world view in the West is moving closer to the world view of the I Ching. It is not the world view of the I Ching moves closer to the contemporary Western world view, but the other way around. In other words, we must reverse the question we have asked in the beginning. The question is then: "Does the contemporary world view of the West move closer to the ancient world view of the I Ching?" This question becomes the focus of our discussion.

We have already indicated that the concept of relativity presupposes the principle of changes. We cannot say that the latter presupposes the former. The contemporary world view which is based on the theory of relativity is moving closer to the idea of the world which is expressed in the principle of changes. According to the principle of changes all things in the world are mutually interrelated as if they are organic. The new view of the world in the West also presupposes the mutual interdependence. However, Wilhelm makes a sharp distinction between the Eastern and Western view of the world: "For according to Western ideas, sequent change would be the realm in which causality operates mechanically, but the Book of Changes takes sequent change to be the succession of the generations, that is, still something organic."[1] He is right when he said that the I Ching describes the world in terms of organism. However, it is questionable whether he is right to say that the West is oriented toward the mechanical world view. He was perhaps thinking of the traditional Western view of the world. The mechanical world view is questioned by the contemporary scientific view of the world. The mechanical view of the world must be given up as long as there are freedom and chance in the happenings of the world. Thus Max Born radically denounces the mechanical view of the world:

> An unrestricted belief in causality leads necessarily to the idea that the world is an automaton of which we ourselves are only little cogwheels. This means materialistic determinism. It resembles very much that religious determinism accepted by different creeds, where the actions of men are believed to be determined from the beginning by a ruling of God. I cannot enlarge on the difficulties to which this idea leads if considered from the standpoint of ethical responsibility. The notion of divine predestination clashes with the notion of free will, in the same way as the assumption of an endless chain of natural causes.[2]

If we believe that nature as well as human affairs seems to be subject to both necessity and accident, we cannot regard the world as a machine. The mechanical world view is deterministic and based on the law of cause and

---

[1] R. Wilhelm, tr., op. cit., p. 285.

[2] Max Born, op. cit., p. 3.

effect. As long as the law of chance is operating in the world, the world cannot be viewed in terms of materialistic determinism. Moreover, from the special theory of relativity we come to explain that the mass is equivalent to energy. The energy-mass equivalence formula, $E = mc^2$, says that the energy, E, and mass, m, are not independent. Both of them are one and inseparable. The continuity between energy and mass makes mutual interaction possible. In this mutual interaction one is the manifestation of the other. Thus this kind of relationship makes the world more than a mere machine. It is closer to the organic world view which the I Ching seems to present. In other words, the world which is depicted by the contemporary scientists is neither mechanic nor organic. As Birch said, "If physics and biology one day meet, and one of the two is swallowed up, that one will not be biology."[1] Certainly, physics and biology can come close together in the continuity between energy and mass. Whitehead's view is appealing in view of contemporary scientific development, because he seems to present the balanced world view between biology and physics. His world view can be said as "organic-mechanism," which recognizes the validity of both organic and mechanic world views. Whitehead conceives that the microcosmic structures of the world are characterized by mechanisms in which molecules may run in accordance with the general laws which can be discovered by physics and chemistry. But the total structure of the world is organic, because its inner aim is to actualize itself in the process of changes. That is why he said, "Biology is the study of the larger organisms, whereas physics is the study of the smaller organisms."[2] The world view which is neither organic nor mechanic is quite

---

[1]L.C. Birch, Nature and God (London: SCM, 1965), p. 69.

[2]A.N. Whitehead, Science and the Modern World (New York: Macmillan, 1925), p. 105.

similar with the world view of the <u>I Ching</u>. According to the <u>I Ching</u> the world consists of two primary categories of existence, <u>yin</u> and <u>yang</u> forces, which are both organic and inorganic at the same time. For example, the <u>yin</u> and <u>yang</u> not only signify the female and male but stand for the dark and light at the same time. Because of this mutual relationship, it is not totally correct to say that the world which the <u>I Ching</u> describes is organic only. It is both organic and mechanic at the same time. In this regard, it is strikingly similar with the contemporary world view which the theory of relativity subscribes. Both the contemporary world view in the West and the ancient world view of the <u>I Ching</u> are to be described in terms of the category of "both/and" rather than "either/or." The world is both organic and mechanic, and is not either organic or mechanic.

The principle of changes in the <u>I Ching</u> is based on the idea that the world is a finite and self-contained with which is both expanding and contracting. The process of changes operates according to the principle of expansion and contraction or growth and decay. This kind of process presupposes the self-contained universe which is limited but infinitely unbounded. The self-contained flux of world phenomena constantly changes and reproduces according to the principle of expansion and contraction. As <u>Ta Chuan</u> says, "Contraction and expansion act upon each other to produce that which increases" (Sec. II, Ch. 5). The contemporary view of the universe also comes closer to the universe which the <u>I Ching</u> presents. It is commonly accepted that the space is full of hydrogen which is constantly changing into helium. The process of conversion of hydrogen into helium is going on all over the space of the universe.[1] The ever-changing phenomena of the universe are

---

[1]Bonner, <u>op</u>. <u>cit</u>., p. 13.

the background of the concept of relativity. According to the "steady state" hypothesis of the universe, there is a continuous creation of new matter (hydrogen atoms) throughout the space. The newly created matters are condensed to form new stars and galaxies between the older galaxies. In this way the constant change is taking place in the universe. The old galaxies disappear and the new ones are formed, just as the old yang and yin are changed into the new yang and yin. The process of change according to the growth and decay, formation and destruction, or expansion and contraction is operative in this hypothesis. In this kind of changes constant spatial density with time is maintained. In the process of continuous procreation of the new stars from the old the universe has no beginning and no ending. Another hypothesis which is widely accepted is the "big bang" theory of the universe, which was first proposed in 1929 by Lemaitre. According to this hypothesis, the concentrated mass and energy exploded at the zero point of time from the primordial state. As a result of this primordial explosion, the fragments of that explosion--now galaxies--are continuously moving outward and away from each other forever, like the spots on the surface of the expanding balloon. The fact that all the distant objects are moving away from us at the definite rate is a clear indication that the whole universe is expanding. The "present rate of expansion is about 0.000,000,01 % per year, so that each second the radius of the universe increases by ten million miles. Our little universe grows comparatively much faster, gaining in its dimensions about 1 % per minute."[1] The evidence of expansion of the universe is based on the "red shift," which is the

---

[1]G. Gamow, Mr. Tompkings in Paperback (Cambridge: At the University Press, 1967), p. 52.

slight increase in the wave length of light observed in far-away stars, with more change the more distant (apparently) the star. This slight increase is observed from the far-away stars and galaxies withdrawing from us because of the receding motion of light, just as the pitch of a receding train whistle sounds lower than it would if the train and observer were not in the relative motion.[1] In light of these observations the old concept of static universe is overthrown. The universe is in constant motion and change. The question is "Will this expansion never stop?" If the curvature of interstellar space is negative, the expansion could be permanent. The universe will expand forever without an end. This idea of the open universe could be a possibility. However, the most possible form of the universe is to be understood as the opposite direction of the curve. That means the curvature of interstellar space is positive, which indicates that space is finite. If this is the case, the relativistic theory predicts that the expansion will come to a halt and then begins to contract again. Therefore, as Coleman said, "We can conclude that according to the general theory of relativity, the universe is finite and unbounded."[2] In this finite and unbounded universe the expansion stops when it reaches to its maximum and then contracts again to its minimum. At present the relativistic theory that the universe is infinite and unbounded is favorable, even though no decisive evidence makes this kind of decision conclusive. If this view is accepted, this process of the pulsating universe is based on the principle of changes, which operates according to the process

---

[1]David Dye, Faith and the Physical World: A Comprehensive View (Grand Rapids: Wm Eerdmans, 1966), pp. 129-30.

[2]Coleman, op. cit., p. 118.

of expansion and contraction. It is the principle of changes in the I Ching that when everything reaches its maximum it is destined to decline. The universe which is finite and unbounded and self-contained whole is expanding at this time but is also expected to contract again when it reaches its maximum. In this kind of cosmos the overarching principle seems to be the constant interplay of the yin and yang, which is the symbol of dynamic interdependence. In the ever-changing universe, space, time, matter and energy are not independent elements but are mutually interdependent on one another to make one complex continuum. This total system of the mutually interdependent whole is strikingly similar to the concept of the universe which the I Ching describes.

2. The I Ching and the Concept of Time

The curvature of space which is based on the general theory of relativity makes the contemporary view of time closer to the concept of time in the I Ching. The laws of Newton were predicated on the fact that light traveled in a straight line. The general theory of relativity showed that light rays are deflected by gravitational masses. If the universe is finite and unbounded, when we travel in a straight line on the surface, we will eventually come back to the same point where we have started. Because space itself is curved, all things including man move along the curve. Time is no exception to this. Time is not something which exists objectively by itself. It is a part of the process of changes in the universe. The process of changes is based on the movement, which is curved. Thus time also moves along the curvature of space. It is enormously suggestive to hear the

statement of Alexander, who said: "time is the mind of space."[1] If
time is the mind of space, time moves along the space which is curved.
Since space and time are one complex continuum which is undifferentiated, the
curvature of space is the curvature of time. If the curve is positive, time
moves cyclically, for the universe is finite and unbounded. The I Ching
and Eastern philosophy as a whole believe in the cyclic movement of time.
In view of the curvature of space, it is certainly difficult to assert the
linear concept of time as has been traditionally accepted in the West. The
general theory of relativity helps us to see that the contemporary view of
time moves closer to the cyclic movement of time which the I Ching describes.
Moreover, time is not a principle of abstract progression in the I Ching.
It is the situation of immediately experienced and perceived. Time in the
I Ching is not a prior principle which Newton prescribes, but is an event
in relation to what is right or wrong as well as favorable or unfavorable.
In the undifferentiated continuum of space and time we see that time is not
a priori principle but is concrete event in relation to the process of
changes. In the process of production and reproduction or of expansion and
contraction time never comes to an end or repeats itself. Every production
and reproduction has an element of the new, because of the constant changes
through the new relationship of yin and yang forces. As long as the universe
is in the process of changes, time never repeats itself. The cyclic movement of time is not the repetition of the same pattern but the movement of
the similar cyclic pattern without repetition. The birth of the new and the
decay of the old stars re-occur in the process of changes but they never

---

[1]Samuel Alexander, Space, Time and Deity (New York: Macmillan Co.,
1920), p. 44.

repeat the same way. Just as the son may follow the similar pattern of his father without repreating the same life of him, time never repreats itself. The movement of time is relative to the process of changes, which is the denial of repetition. Moreover, if the universe itself is rotating as being suggested by Gödel in 1949, time which is not independent from the universe must also rotate. If we consider some of these possibilities, we can come to see that the contemporary view of time in the West is quite similar to the Chinese notion of time as expressed in the I Ching.

3. The Hexagram and Atoms

Let us now move our discussion from the macrocosm to the microcosm of the universe. The I Ching is understood as the microcosm of the universe. It is the microcosmic reproduction of the cosmos. As Ta Chuan says, "The I is the book which contains the measure of heaven and earth. Thus it can help us to comprehend the tao of heaven and earth" (Sec. I, Ch. 4). The hexagrams in the I Ching are similar to the atoms and seeds of the universe. They are like the seeds which contain all the potential possibilities of growth and change. Again Ta Chuan says: "For he knows the seeds, which are the slight beginnings of movement and the initial indications of good fortune and misfortune. The superior man sees the seeds and acts immediately without a delay of a single day" (Sec. II, Ch. 5). These seeds are somewhat analogous with the atoms which are the microcosms of the universe. Just as the hexagram, the structure of atom is the microcosm of the universal structure. In 1916 Sommerfeld proposed that the electron paths were not circles but ellipses, and that the electrons revolved about the nucleus which was situated at one of the foci of the ellipse, in the same way that planets revolve around the sun.[1] The similarity between the structure of submicrocosmic world and the ordinal phenomena of the world is clearly evidenced by the brilliant piece of theoretical work by a Japanese scientist, Hideki Yukawa in 1935. His finding of the particle which is now called the pion was based on his assumption that the forces of nature which he observed in everyday life are intrinsically related even to the minutest pieces of the world. Just as the structure of submicroscopic world corresponds to the structure of the whole universe, the relationship between yin and yang, which constitutes the hexagrams, corresponds to the structural relationship of the universe. If we look at the hexagrams as the microcosms of the universal phenomena, the structure of the hexagrams may be compared with the structure of atoms, which are also the microcosms of the universal phenomena. Just as the hexagram consists of the six lines of either the yin or yang, an atom is made up of both the negative and positive charges. There is a rather striking similarity between their constituent elements. Here, the positive and negative charges are almost identical with the yang and yin forces. The differences between the structure of atom and that of hexagram are due to the varying combinations of positive and negative charges. To illustrate it, let me take the structure of hexagrams. Even hexagram consists of six lines but the difference of each hexagram is the different combination of yin and yang forces. Both hexagram 1, Ch'ien or Creativity, and hexagram 2, K'un or Responsivity, are the same, except

---

[1]Coleman, op. cit., pp. 70-71.

the destributions of <u>yin</u> and <u>yang</u> or negative and positive charges. A
similar phenomenon is also found in the structure of atom. If we look at
the nucleons which consist of protons and neutrons, even though they have
different names, "protons and neutrons are now considered simply as two different electronic states of the same elementary heavy article known as the
'nucleon'."[1]   In other words, the proton is nothing but a charged neutron, and
the neutron is nothing but an uncharged proton.[2]   What makes the structure of
atomic nuclei different is none other than **the** difference of electronic charges.
The electrons, which move around the nuclei, are also born in pairs, otherwise
it would contradict the law of conservation of electric change.[3] Then, the
basic structure of atom is nothing but the positive and negative charges, just
as the basic structure of hexagram is nothing but the <u>yang</u> and <u>yin</u> forces.
Since <u>yin</u> and <u>yang</u> forces are identical with negative and positive chargnes, we
are almost obliged to say that the structure of both atom and hexagram is not
different. Also the hexagram and an atom represent the germinal situations
which are complete units in themselves. If there are ninety-two germinal situations in physical science, there are sixty-four germinal situations in the <u>I</u>
<u>Ching</u>. Whether the germinal situations are ninety-two or sixty-four, they rep-
resent all the possible phenomena of the universe. When the delicate balance

[1]Gamow, <u>op</u>. <u>cit</u>., p. 136.

[2]Kenneth Ford, <u>The World of Elementary Particles</u> (London: Blaisdell,
1963), p. 168.

[3]Gamow, <u>op</u>. <u>cit</u>., p. 125.

in the atom between neutron and proton, which is maintained through the activity of pion, is upset, the new atomic structure or the new situation is to be created. The same principle can be applied to the hexagram as well. When one line of the hexagram changes from yin to yang or from yang to yin, the new situation or the new hexagram is to be produced. Just as the change of an electron in the atomic field of particles produces a new atom, the change of a line in the hexagram will produce an entirely new hexagram. The delicacy of structural balance within the germinal situation of both atom and hexagram is quite identical. As a result we can safely conclude that the contemporary development of physical science assists us to see the significant place of the I Ching in the twentieth century civilization of the West.

4. The I Ching and Computer

The I Ching is not only significant to the recent development of physical science but also to the growing application of mathematical science to a computer. Perhaps the most significant development in the field of mathematical science in our time is the application of the computer in many areas of our life. We are familiar with the decimal system, which is based on man's practice of counting things on his fingers. However, the number system need not employ base number 10. The most used number system in our time other than the decimal system is the binary system, which is commonly applied to the computer machine. This binary system is almost perfect for the telephone company, because they are interested in a two-value system, that is, a closed circuit and an open circuit. Here, we notice the yin and yang lines which have been applied to the hexagrams are quite synonymous to this binary system. The yang line always changes to the yin line and the yin line to the yang line, just as the closed circuit always changes to the open circuit and the open circuit to the closed circuit. An electronic computer, even when its output is translated into the decimal system, operates on the binary system. "It consists of a series of circuits, each of which is switched either on (1) or off (0) by means of a flip-flop."[1] Suppose that the circuit is already on (1), which is identical with the yang line in the I Ching, and we add 1 or the yang line to it, then it changes to 0 and carries over to the next circuit. We notice that the two yang lines make the old yang which is the changing line, so that the old yang line or 1 + 1 is to be changed to the yin line which is indicated by 0. The carry-over will effect the change of the next circuit in the same way. The sequence of the binary system would look as follows: 1, 10, 11, 100, 101, 110, 111, 1000, 1001, 1010, 1011, 1100, 1101, 1110, 1111, 10000, etc. This system was thought out by Leibniz, who attempts to systematize the spiritual truth in mathematical terms. Leibniz was rather surprised to realize that Shao Yung had already discovered the same binary system more than six hundred years before him. To Leibniz, the key to the system was a number, but to Shao Yung, it was the hexagram. Shao Yung used the hexagrams to form a binary system in order to validate the natural phenomena of the universe. His arrangement of the hexagrams is known as the natural order, which is different from the present order of the hexagrams in the I Ching. If we take the broken

[1]Harold E. Hatt, Cybernetics and the Image of Man (New York: Abingdon, 1968), p. 43.

line or the yin line for zero and the unbroken line or the yang line for one, we notice that this arrangement corresponds perfectly with the binary system of Leibniz. If we begin with hexagram 1, Ch'ien or Creativity, it can

be symbolized in the binary number 111111. Hexagram 44, Kou or Intercourse, is symbolized by the binary number 111110, where 1 or the yang line changes

to 0 or the yin line. Hexagram 13, T'ung Jen or Fellowship, is symbolized by the binary number 111101, where the yin line or 0 is again changed to the

yang line or 1. Thus the carry-over changes 1 or the yang line to 0 or the yin line. In this process of transformation the binary system works in the I Ching, just as in the computer. Consequently, we can say that the binary system which is widely applied to the electronic computers in our time is nothing but the application of the binary system of the I Ching. The real significance of the I Ching is the inputs of this binary system. What is fed in the system is not a mere information. It deals with the arche-types of cosmic phenomena. Thus the I Ching might be called the archetypal computer. The principle in which the I Ching operates is not really different from the electronic computer of our time. Only the difference of this is the manual operation. The manual operation of yarrow stalks or coins in the I

Ching takes greater patience than to operate the electronic computer. However, in spite of its slow method of operation, the I Ching is the most comprehensive form of computer because of its inputs. It contains the archetypal situations which can be applied to all the possible situations of world phenomena. The multidimensional use of the I Ching in human situations makes it unique from all other computers of our time. It gives the basis for all other possible answers. That is why Paul Veide calls the I Ching "poor man's computer."[1]

5. The I Ching and Our Life-Styles

The significance of the I Ching to our time lies more than in the field of scientific development. Its affect on our moral and ethical life cannot be underestimated. The so-called situation ethics in our time appeals to many people in our generation. The growing interest of people in this ethics is a sufficient evidence that the principle of changes in the I Ching influences even in the realm of our moral and ethical decisions. Situation ethics presupposes the principle of changes which we have already expounded. The ethical decision is relative, according to this ethics, to the context or situation in which the decision is made. Because the decision we make is relative to the situation, it is called situation ethics. Just as the principle of changes denies the absolute phenomenon other than the change itself,

---

[1] Veide, op. cit., p. 692.

situation ethics negates also any absolute law or principle other than the
Agape love. According to situation ethics all ethical values are relative
to situations, just as all phenomena are relative according to principle of
changes. What is good in a certain situation may not be good in another situation. Our value judgment changes according to situations. The I Ching
teaches precisely the same thing. The value judgment changes according to
the change of situation. For example, in hexagram 6, Sung or Conflict,
crossing the great river is not advantageous. But the same action, that is
the crossing the great river, is advantageous in another situation, hexagram
18, Ku or Decaying. Killing people in the war is perfectly acceptable but
in the peaceful community it is a criminal act. Wearing a miniskirt was not
acceptable in the seventeenth century but is perfectly accepted in our time.
No law is absolute. Everything, including the moral and ethical laws, is
constantly changing. Nothing can be the stationary reference point. The
value system which we prescribe in our time is certainly relative to the
principle of changes.

Besides in the ethical and moral life of our time, the I Ching occupies
an important place in almost all areas of our life. For example, as we confront the mounting problem of pollutions, we come to appreciate more the
world view which the I Ching presents to us. The world which the I Ching
views is the self-contained one, in which all things are mutually interdependent to one another. Because the world is self-contained and closed, what
we do eventually affects us one way or another. We have used DDT for insecti-
cides but it eventually reaches us. Our cars and factories exhale smoke in
the air which we have to breathe into our lungs. The world which the I Ching

views is so neatly structured that it is more like an organism. In this kind of structure, if one is out of balance, it immediately affects the others. Thus the world view which the I Ching describes becomes not only significant but real in view of the growing problems of our environment.

The I Ching also becomes a background of the contemporary movement of existentialism, which is easily understood in terms of "ex-is-tentialism." Since the "ex" signifies "outside" and "is" the essential being, we can define existentialism as the human experience without (ex) a being of essence (is). Existential situation means then the experience of estrangement from the essential being. It is the experience of frustration, uncertainty and threat, because of changes. Man experiences today more than any other time the realities of anxiety and despair, because he fails to accept the fact of changes. Man wants to stop the movement of changes. He wants to be young forever, but he cannot stop his aging. Changes are the enemy of those who don't want to accept the reality of changes. Because many people do not accept this, they cannot escape the existential threat, that is, the possibility of losing the meaningful existence in life. The I Ching teaches us in our time that nothing is absolute but the principle of changes itself. The axiom "the change that is changeless" provides us the background of our existence. Those who wish to be changeless are constantly threatened by changes, while those who are in the stream of changes experience the reality of changelessness. To know yourselves is to know the reality of changes. Certainly, the I Ching teaches us profound insights which the West begins to appreciate. Behind its greatness some problems and issues are presented to us in our understanding of it.

6. Issues In The Study Of The I Ching.

To conclude and summarize our study of the I Ching it seems appropriate to present some of the issues and problems which we must bear in mind when we approach it. Most of the issues have already been dealt with in previous chapters but will remain to be the vital themes of discussion in the future investigations. There are at least four major areas with which the issues and problems in the study of the I Ching ought be concerned. One of them deals with the authenticity of its origin and formation. This question has been dealt with extensively in the second chapter of this book. The second issue has to do with the problem of interpretation, which is perhaps one of the most difficult ones which we have encountered. The third issue deals with the problem of divination, which brought misapprehension to the arrogant mind of the West. Finally, the problem which we need to struggle with is the problem in the way of thinking. The I Ching presents a category of "both/and" thinking, while we in the West are used to a category of "either/or" thinking. Let us summarize each separately.

First of all, the basic issue has to do with the authenticity of the origin of the I Ching. We have discussed extensively concerning the authorship of both the main texts and the appendixes of the I Ching in the second chapter of this book. However, the real issue which we have not discussed extensively is the origin of the Ho T'u or the River Map, which became a key not only to the formation of the eight trigrams but to the understanding of the divination method. In final analysis the authority of the I Ching lies in this map, which was traditionally accepted as the revelation of the divine.

The authority of the <u>I</u> <u>Ching</u> in a real sense cannot be questioned further than the existence of this map. Was this map really the revelation of the heaven? We cannot prove or disprove the origin of this map. If this map was received by Fu Hsi, the legendary king of China, and became the basis of Chinese civilization, we have no way to investigate historically the authenticity of this map. Thus, in last analysis the existence of this map is accepted by faith alone. The authority of the <u>I</u> <u>Ching</u> also lies in the centuries of experiments as well as our faith in this map.

The second issue, which deals with the problem of interpretation, is much more complex. We have already mentioned it in the fifth chapter of this book. However, the problem of interpretation is not something peculiar to the <u>I</u> <u>Ching</u>. Whether we study any classical literature or sacred book, we cannot avoid the problem of interpretation. This problem arises because of the symbolic nature of the book. Since symbols are not real in themselves, our interpretation of the symbols deals with that which they signify. Since the <u>I</u> <u>Ching</u> is the book of unusual symbols, the problem of interpretation becomes much more complex. Unlike many other books, the <u>I</u> <u>Ching</u> contains two distinctive forms of symbolism: the primary symbolism which is expressed in the most primitive form of lines in the hexagrams, and the secondary symbolism which expresses the primary symbols in words. The secondary symbols are the Judgments (<u>kua</u> <u>tz'u</u>) which are relative to the primary symbols or the hexagrams (<u>kua</u>). Because of this relative degree of authority in symbolization, the problem of interpretation becomes complex. Moreover, there are Lines or judgments on lines (<u>hsiao</u> <u>tz'u</u>) which are relative to the Judgments on the hexagrams as a whole. Thus in a strict sense there are the triple degrees of symbolization in the <u>I</u>

<u>Ching</u>: the hexagrams, the Judgments, and the lines. They are mutually in-
terdependent and inseparable. Because of the hierarchical symbolization in
the <u>I Ching</u>, we have to face more problems in interpretation. Another problem
has to do with some of the inconsistencies in the interpretation of the hexagrams. Sometimes the hexagrams are interpreted according to the shapes of
their structure, while some other times according to the attributes of the
constituent trigrams. Let us illustrate the interpretation of the hexagrams
according to the attributes of the constituent trigrams. Most of the hexagrams
are subject to this kind of interpretation. One of the good examples of this
is found in hexagram 11, <u>T'ai</u> or Peace, which consists of both the trigram
<u>Ch'ien</u> or Creativity below and the trigram <u>K'un</u> or Responsivity above.

The concept of peace in this hexagram is definitely derived from the attributes
of both trigrams which move towards the center in a peaceful harmony. However,
if we look at hexagram 20, <u>Kuan</u> or Contemplation (or Observation), we see its

interpretation is based on the shape of its structural appearance. As we
see the structure of the hexagram, it looks like the tower for a wide view of
the country. Thus it is <u>Kuan</u>, which literally means "view" or "to behold."
Another example of this type of interpretation is found in hexagram 27, <u>I</u>
or Jaws. The name of this hexagram certainly comes from the shape of its

structure. As we observe the structure of the hexagram, it resembles a picture of an open mouth. Some of these examples make clear that the interpretation of the hexagrams is based on either the attributes of the constituting trigrams or the shapes of its structural appearance. We have no guide line to follow as to how one form of interpretation is more appropriate in a certain situation than another. The difficulty of interpretation is clearly evidenced when we try to classify the hexagrams into a system.

In addition to these problems we need to consider symbolization in relation to its culture and civilization. Since the symbols are grown out of civilization in time, we cannot understand the symbols fully unless we know the civilization in which the symbols arose. If the Ta Chuan is right,[1] the hexagrams have become not only the foundations but the byproducts of early Chinese civilization. The intimate relationship between the hexagrams and the Chinese civilization is unquestionable. The secondary symbols which are the products of the early Chou dynasty, must be studied in relation to the civilization of that particular period. In our interpretation of the secondary symbols, we must consider also the problems with the Chinese language. The lack of grammatical precisions and the ample rooms for suggestiveness in Chinese make far more difficult for the Westerners to comprehend the original meaning of the I Ching. For those who have to rely on the translations, it is important for them to remind themselves that the translations are interpretations in

----

[1]See Ta Chuan, Sec. II, ch. 2.

a strict sense. Hence, the problems in the interpretation of the <u>I Ching</u>
are enormous.

Divination is another issue which is to be dealt with in our study
of the <u>I Ching</u>. Since we often practice the chance operations in one way or
another, the question is not as to whether we believe in divination or not.
The real question is the reliability of divination. In order to examine the
reliability of divination, we need to consider the relationship between freedom and fate, the material and spiritual, space and time, and the conscious
and unconscious. All these relationships are vital factors to support the
reliability of divination through the use of the <u>I Ching</u>. The first question
is whether we find freedom for decision in the <u>I Ching</u> for divination. As we
have already indicated, the <u>I Ching</u> provides freedom but a limited one.
Freedom is relative and limited, because man is relative to time and space.
Absolute freedom is an impossibility. Man's freedom is relative to the actualization of the potentially given situation. This kind of limited freedom is
not only realistic to our experience but relevant to the theory of relativity.
Because of man's dreedom to actualize the germinal situation in which he is,
the <u>I Ching</u> denies the power of fate to control his own life. The primary
purpose of divination through the use of the <u>I Ching</u> is not the acceptance of
our fate blindly, but the control of our destiny before too late. That is
why the <u>I Ching</u> is unique from other divination books which encourage us to
accept our fate rather than to overcome it. The <u>I Ching</u> points the future
for us so that we can actualize it by ourselves. The question is whether
our freedom is relative to the situation or is absolutely irrelative to the
situation. The West has claimed that man has the freedom to alter his destiny
according to his own will. In the <u>I Ching</u> man's freedom cannot transcend the

germinal situation where he is placed. Thus the issue is the degree of man's freedom to control his destiny.

Another problem is the correlation between the spiritual and the material or between the inner and outer phenomena of the world. The I Ching presupposes that the spiritual activities are correlated with the physical symbols. Without this presupposition the reliability of divination cannot be established. As we have already pointed out, there are many examples in which the physical activities are influenced by the spiritual powers. Such as the speaking in tongues, spiritual healings, and ecstatic prophecies are good examples. Also materials like the water and the fire have their inner meanings. The water has its inner meaning of washing and purifying. The fire has its inner meaning of clinging and dryness. The I Ching uses the external objects such as the mountain, the lake, the water, fire and so on to signify their inner meanings. The mountain signifies steadiness, the lake the joy, the fire the clinging together, and so on. The possibility of correlation between the spiritual and the material and between the inner meaning and outer appearance must be meaningful and coherent. The meaningful correlation between the intrinsic meaning and the external appearance is enormously difficult.

Divination deals with the concept of time. If the function of divination is to predict the future predicaments, it must stress the element of time as the decisive importance for its reliability. It can predict the future, because the future is understood only as the pointedness of the present experience. In the germinal situation, the hexagram, there is no distinction between the past, present and future. In this undifferentiated continuum of

time, the past is present, and the present is the future. According to
the linear movement of time, time moves from one point to another, so that
the distinction between the past and future is inevitable. Consequently, the
I Ching rejects the linear movement of time, which is deeply entered into the
mind of the West. The whole concept of history is at stake. The question
concerning the sequence of time will continue to be a vital issue between
the West and the East.

Finally, diviation is closely related to the psychic condition of
man. Divination is reliable because the correlation between the conscious
and unconscious is possible. If the coincidence of the conscious and the unconscious at the process of divination would occur by a mere chance, divination
is not more reliable than a mere chance operation. The reliability of divination is almost totally dependent on the idea of "synchronicity," which is
an acausal principle of coincidence between the conscious and the unconscious
strata. This acausal connecting principle is based on neither the laws of
causality nor the law of probablity. It is reliable but is not always exact.
Since synchronicity is an acausal principle, it is possible because of chance;
but it is impossible to investigate it, because it does come under the laws of
causality. Thus the problem may remain to be unanswered.

The fourth and the last issue which is related in the study of the I
Ching is the way of thinking. The principle of changes in the I Ching is
fundamentally the interplay of yin and yang forces. The characteristic emphasis of this interplay is not the conflict but the complement of the opposites. Everything in the universe is in the process of changes through the
eternal interplay of yin and yang forces. All things are described in terms

of this complementary relationship. Our way of thinking is no exception to this. The way of complementary thinking can be described in terms of the category of "both/and" thinking, which is the denial of not only the absolute but the onesideness. The category of both/and thinking is a counterpart of the category of "either/or" thinking in the West. The former deals with the most inclusive and integral reality of the whole existence, while the latter with the exclusive and analytical approaches to the reality of the world phenomena. It has been the either/or category of thinking which made the scientific and logical mentality of the West possible. On the other hand, the both/and category of thinking has provided the East the intuitive and aesthetic insights. However, the trend in the West seems to recognize the validity of "both/and" thinking. Many observe that the contemporary science is moving closer to this complementary thinking. It is true that they tend to move away from absolutism and to come to assert the complement of the opposites. For example, they do not accept either the wave theory or the quantum of light but accept both of them at the same time. Nels Ferré, a well-known theologian in America, recognizes the necessity of use of the category of "both/and" thinking, which he calls "contrapletal logic." He says, "There is here no place for paradox, excluded middle, totum simul or Alles auf einmal. What we need is a contrapletal ontology or theology expressible only in terms of contrapletal logic."[1] The prime example of use of this contrapletal logic, he admits, has been the Chinese use of yin and yang.[2]

---

[1]Nels F. S. Ferré, The Universal Word: A Theology for a Universal Faith (Philadelphia: The Westminster Press, 1969), p. 80.

[2]Ibid., p. 100.

Wilfred Smith also expressed his personal favor of using the "both/and"
category of thinking. He said, "What I myself see in the yang-yin symbol
with regards to this matter, if I may be allowed this personal note, is
not the first solution only, not merely an image that would reduce Christian Truth to a part of some larger Truth. Rather I find it a circle
embracing for Christian Truth itself... In this, the image says to me, as
in all ultimate matters, Truth lies not in an either/or, but in a both/and."[1]
The growing interest of the "both/and" category of thinking or contrapletal
logic is evident in the West. However, the question is whether it can
replace the "either/or" category of thinking, which is deeply accustomed to
the Western people. Even though the Einsteinian world of relativity could
replace the Newtonian world of the absolute time and space, it is questionable whether the category of "both/and" thinking will dominate the mental
activity of the West. Whatever the further way of thinking might be, the
I Ching has taught the West that at least there is a possibility of alter-
ing our way of thinking.